# William Evans

ERS ⟶

## REPORT FORM

If you have any comments on entries in this guide, please let us have them.

If you have a favourite shoot, or are the manager or agent of a shoot which you would like us to consider, please let us know about it too.

Report on Shoot: _____

Section: England / Scotland / Wales / Ireland    Page Reference _____

New Recommendation

Name of Shoot: _____

Address: _____

_____

_____

Tel no: _____

Address of agent or shoot manager: _____

My reasons for writing are:

Please give us your name and address if we may contact you.

*William Evans Limited*
*67a St. James Street, London SW1A 1PH*

*Tel: 020-7493 0415*          *Fax: 020-7499 1912*
*email: sales@williamevans.com*          *VAT Reg: 563 1428 51*

# The William Evans
# Good Shoot Guide

## Tony Jackson

### Editor

This PB edition first published in the UK in 2003
by Gibson Square Books Ltd
15 Gibson Square, London N1 0RD
Tel: +44 (0)20 7689 4790; Fax: +44 (0)20 7689 7395
publicity@gibsonsquare.com
www.gibsonsquare.com

UK & Ireland sales by Signature
34 High Petergate, York YO1 7EH
Tel 01904 631 320; Fax 01904 675 445
sales@signaturebooks.co.uk

UK & European distribution by Central Books Ltd
99 Wallis Road, UK London E9 5LN
Tel +44 (0)845 458 9911; Fax +44 (0)845 458 9912
info@centralbooks.com
www.centralbooks.com

Australian, New Zealand and South Africa, US sales, please contact
Gibson Square Books Ltd for contact details.

© 2003 by William Evans Ltd

ISBN 1-903933-33-1

Printed by WS Bookwell Ltd

# CONTENTS

# FOREWORD

## CLARISSA DICKSON WRIGHT

This is a most useful and useable book. How many of us, whether we be corporate brokers, hosts intent on giving one's friends a good day's shooting or just a group of friends who want to go and experience shooting in different terrains or disciplines, find ourselves at a loss where to start? No one wants to end up with a poor day or indifferent birds having spent a fair sum of money. Then there is the problem of where to stay or who to contact. This Guide solves all these problems.

*The William Evans Good Shoot Guide* is meticulous, precise and accurate, as all those of us who enjoy Tony Jackson's writing would expect. One gets a clear picture of the shoot in a few simple details. I wish all guides were so clear and good.

All types of shooting, whether for pheasants, partridges, pigeons or ptarmigan, are covered, as well as stalking and even the novel simulated game shooting days which are becoming so popular out of season. Everything is covered, from cartridge/bird ratios (not perhaps relevant in my case!) and costs to local accommodation favoured by

Guns — useful in these days when a wrong booking might find one enjoying an evening among a convention of antis! Details range from bag expectations, contact names and that vital, but often missing piece of information, how to get to the shoot.

The Guide is very enjoyable reading and I find myself thumbing through its pages day-dreaming of mature woodlands, stands of kale and friendly banter among friends. It is an enjoyable way to while away the out-of-season hours.

All who love shooting will enjoy this book and find it invaluable, well written and concise in its descriptions. It will certainly provide me with the answer to Christmas presents for years to come.

# INTRODUCTION

## TONY JACKSON

Over the past quarter of a century or more the shooting scene in Britain has altered almost beyond recognition. Thirty or 40 years ago driven shooting was dominated by the closed world of private estate shooting, supplemented by the organised syndicate shoot. Let days to private individuals and parties were few and a publication such as *The William Evans Good Shoot Guide* would have been of only limited value.

Fuelled perhaps by the Thatcherite revolution – not to mention large city bonuses – a third type of shooting began to emerge, the commercial shoot, modelled on private estate shoot lines. Anybody with money could book their party's day's shooting.

Today the boundaries are becoming increasingly blurred. Shooting, in all its aspects, is enjoying a resurgence of popularity right across the social board. Commercial shoots devoted solely to letting days are thriving throughout the country, while both private estates and syndicates increasingly find that they have the capacity —and perhaps need—to let one, two or more days.

Whereas even a few years ago it would have been considered slightly unusual for a private shoot to let the odd day, today it is becoming accepted as the norm.

In addition, a new phenomenon has arisen: the roaming syndicate. The conventional syndicate, based on one estate, has many advantages. It is enjoyed by those who prefer familiarity and the pleasures derived from understanding the idiosyncrasies of a known shoot. However, a steadily increasing number of shooting men and women now seek the challenge of shooting in a new and different terrain and prefer to visit hitherto unknown shoots to test themselves against the claims of 'the highest, the fastest and the best'.

Today let days come in a variety of shapes. Foremost is the driven bird shoot, though walked-up days for pheasants and a mixed bag are increasingly sought after, while grouse over dogs or walked-up over pointers successfully compete with driven days. There is also ready access to wildfowl, woodcock, snipe, pigeon, hares and rabbits in a variety of shooting situations. The sportsman can choose to flight geese inland or on the foreshore, try his or her hand at driven snipe or 'cock, or perhaps tackle pigeon over decoys on rape or laid corn. Stalking, whether for red deer in the Highlands or low ground roe, is a sport rapidly gaining in popularity and one which makes singular demands on the individual, experienced or novice.

Whether you require driven grouse, pheasants or partridges, decoyed pigeons or walked-up snipe, stalking, or simulated shooting, we have aimed to make the *William Evans Good Shoot Guide* a comprehensive reference guide in an easy-to-use format, providing the opportunity to explore a wealth of sporting opportunities throughout Britain. The Guide is the first of its kind and will be an essential accessory to both the visitor from overseas and private sportsman at home.

Certain aspects of the Guide must be made clear. No information provided by shoots and sporting agents has been paid for, and in every case has been accepted by the publishers in good faith. Furthermore, no attempt has been made to offer any judgement on entries or to provide a starring system. Nor have William Evans any financial interest in the entries or their promotion.

A brief word about William Evans. Established in 1883, the company is today London's only independent gunmaker, committed to the provision of selling good, affordable English guns and rifles. The addition of new premises has enabled the company to expand its retail operation and make the shop a 'one-stop destination', as part of its policy of adapting to the changing times of the 21$^{st}$ century.

William Evans is sponsoring this guide to give readers the widest choice of shoots possible and also to help give them value for money. In this respect *The William Evans Good Shoot Guide* flags up the Company's policy of combining traditional values with a modern approach to the world of gunmaking and shooting.

I hope you will enjoy and use the Guide, and that you will not hesitate to use the feedback forms at the back of the book to provide additional information that will help us keep the Guide comprehensive and up to date.

# GAME SHOOTING IN THE UK TODAY

## ROBERT GRAY

Over one million people participate in shooting sports throughout the UK. Take time to digest that statistic because it's pretty impressive. In other words, more members of the voting public shoot than play rugby, hockey or do athletics. Though shooting is sometimes a solitary occupation, the country sportsman is certainly not alone.

Currently shooting pumps more than £600 million into the rural economy and it is estimated that 40,000 jobs are dependent on the sport. An area the size of Scotland is managed by Britain's gamekeepers and should you be one of an estimated 250,000 driven game shooters, you will be familiar with their exceptional work. Pest and predator control is a year-round activity but on a single day an observant Gun will notice the numbers of skylarks, thrushes, lapwings and other non-quarry species which are allowed to thrive on shooting land. Eighty per cent of small woodlands in England are managed for shooting and flourishing within are four times as many butterflies and three times as many plants as in unmanaged areas. In a recent Game Conservancy Trust/British Trust for Ornithology survey on 30 sporting estates no fewer than 27 different songbirds were counted in game crops planted to hold pheasants. Findings such as these have led to Government grants under the Countryside Stewardship Scheme further enhancing the good things that game shooting brings to the British countryside.

Despite the catastrophic effects of the Foot-and-Mouth epidemic, 2002 was a remarkably good year for shooting, with the gun trade reporting excellent sales. As many celebrities and business luminaries elected to take up the sport, shooting was labelled 'the new golf' in a blaze of positive publicity. Shooting schools are currently reporting substantial numbers of newcomers booking shooting lessons while membership of fieldsports organisations is at record levels.

The largest growth area in driven shooting is in syndicates, according to the British Association for Shooting and Conservation. It predicts that there could be a significant amount of new land becoming available over the next few years as government schemes to encourage diversification in farming progress. Shooting, says BASC, will be attractive to both farmers and the authorities because of its business, conservation and pest control elements.

A not insignificant number of *Shooting Times* readers have shown a propensity towards smaller mixed days with the emphasis on good old-fashioned rough shooting. However, while in some parts of Britain, like South Wales, where the shooting man can still knock on the farmer's door, such opportunities have declined dramatically over the last 30 years. This is where a plethora of fine sporting hotels and reputable sporting agents (the best are featured in this book) can offer a range of mixed shooting, stalking and fishing.

It is obvious then that there is much to celebrate about shooting in the UK in 2003, but bad news inevitably follows good. Flicking through decades-old issues of *Shooting Times* I have found the occasional reference to anti-shooting zealots who have always been small in number but now attract the all-seeing eye of the media and the funds of organised activists masquerading as conservation bodies. Never have so few received so much attention. While it is tempting to be flippant, shooting must stand or fall by self-regulation.

Here's John Swift, chief executive of BASC: 'We have to be super-sensitive to other countryside users – and that means moderation and avoidance of excess. We must set high standards of proficiency in management, and competence from those who come to shoot with us. If there is one phrase above all others that will decide the political future it is "animal welfare". Shooting hundreds of cartridges at extreme range (with little visible result) and the nigh-on certainty of pricked birds will not be sustainable. It is also inescapable shot game must go for food. Shoots must have a good home for their shot birds. If we think we can survive as if in some afterglow of Edwardian golden age, or greed gets the better of sound judgement, some future government will run commercial shooting by quango – or simply ban it. I wouldn't give it ten years.'

The National Gamekeepers' Organisation agrees with BASC that self-regulation is the way forward. Policy advisor Charles Nodder said: 'Gamekeepers are adamant that the Code of Good Shooting Practice represents the best way of securing the sport long term'. A similar code for game rearing produced by the Game Farmers' Association has become widely accepted as the industry standard, and as Paul Jeavons, former GFA chairman, reflected: 'Unless we do the job well, in five years time we may not be doing it at all'.

The withdrawal of Emtryl to combat gamebird disease has been met with a mixed response. While many consider the move a disaster which will lead to an astronomical rise in the cost of driven shooting, several heavyweights in the shooting industry have suggested that a reduction in the number of reared birds is no bad thing and will lead to more responsible game management.

While the Government has pledged not to ban shooting, its politicians are certainly doing their best to cause death by a thousand cuts. There are regular attacks on issues as diverse as airguns, gamebird health, young shots, ammunition type and hygiene. As politicians realise that the big issues such as war, poverty and health cannot be solved they turn and leap on to smaller bandwagons. It is why so much parliamentary time is wasted on trivial issues. Thankfully the shooting organisations are in place to monitor these unpleasant developments and *Shooting Times* is there to report them. In the meantime, you can crack on and enjoy some terrific sport because, undertaken safely and responsibly, there is no argument that can bring down shooting. Be proud of what you do.

Robert Gray is the Editor of *Shooting Times and Countryside Magazine.*

# SCOTLAND FOR SHOOTING

## COLIN MCKELVIE

To cross the Border into Scotland, be it to the west at Gretna or the east at Berwick, is to enter a part of Britain where sporting shooting is part of the warp and weft of life. More than in any other part of the Kingdom, it looms large in the lives of a very high proportion of the country's small population of barely five million. Scottish sport has a long and continuing track record of attracting discerning sportsmen from across the world, because so much of the shooting it has to offer is, quite simply, unique.

Nowhere else in the world offers daylight, bare-ground stalking of a unique race of red deer that has adapted from the species' customary woodland habits to life on high, open hills. Three species of grouse become fair game in August, and there are hopes that the very recently-protected capercaillie may some day recover to a point where a measured sporting harvest may once again be sustainable. Meantime, the combination of ptarmigan, black grouse and the unique British Isles race of the red grouse makes up an enticing trio, unavailable anywhere else.

Red grouse are notoriously prone to cyclical ups and downs in numbers, with the added complications of diseases such as strongylosis and louping ill; but bumper years do still occur, when everything (most critically, the late spring weather) comes just right, and then driven bags of 200-plus brace may be achieved by a typical eight-Gun team. More typical, however, and infinitely more affordable, is a driven day of 40-50 brace, which still provides a lot of shooting at what is always an exceptionally difficult bird. Late August and September grouse are challenging enough, but the immensely vigorous, agile, fast-flying grouse of October and November are in a class of their own. Hurtling downwind on a stiff breeze, and able to jink instantly in any direction with a momentary wing-tilt, they come like animated bullets. There are probably fewer than two dozen Guns in the world who have the skill and practice to kill late-season grouse with real consistency.

For the duck enthusiast, with a choice of inland flighting, and driven birds, coastal flighting at dawn, dusk and with the tides, and punt-gunning on the massive fowl-attracting firths, and for the goose shooter, with flighting and decoying available from September 1 right through to February 20 on the foreshore, there are widespread and abundant opportunities. The vast westward-reaching gulf of the Solway Firth lies right on Scotland's south-western border, and northwards there are superb wildfowling haunts all the way to Caithness and north Sutherland and, far beyond, among the island groups of Orkney, Shetland and Outer Hebrides.

The folded, rolling hills of the southern Border country and the more rugged glens and straths of the Highlands provide swooping contours where driven pheasants can be shown magnificently; and although indigenous wild grey partridges have declined here, as throughout Britain, there is a large and rapidly growing selection of

Scottish shoots offering top-class driven redleg days. Often these are on lower ground adjacent to heather-dominated grouse moors, and although concerns are voiced about the risk of disease spreading from partridges and becoming endemic amongst grouse, these consistently productive shoots can provide the revenue that enables estate owners and shoot managers to maintain full-time grouse keepers in employment, attending to the all-important tasks of heather management, predator control, the provision of medicated grit, and the maintenance of butts and hill access roads that are all so vital for grouse and the many other species of flora and fauna that share this unique, sometimes sub-Alpine, habitat.

Close to the east and west coasts alike, snipe and woodcock hot-spots abound, and there is a choice of shooting over pointers, walking-up and driven days, according to taste and, inevitably, your budget. An October outing in the Hebrides at the height of the snipe migration, or a January session among Highland birch woods that harbour high densities of wintering woodcock, may be among the very reddest of red-letter shooting days.

A visitor's mental image of Scotland may be of a wild and sometimes semi-wilderness landscape, but there are large swathes of fertile arable land across much of eastern Scotland, from the Border as far north as eastern Ross-shire and into Caithness, where the pigeon shooter can enjoy himself all year round, with excellent spring to autumn decoying, and superb opportunities for roost shooting in late winter. On a windy evening the sport can be fast and furious, and if you get the chance to shoot roost-flighting or beechmast-feeding pigeons from a high tower, which increasing numbers of farms and estates are erecting, don't miss it.

Rabbits have rebounded to pre-myxomatosis levels across much of Scotland, and a day with ferrets or walking-up with spaniels may mean very heavy game-bags and hot barrels. Brown hares occur in shootable numbers in parts of south-east Scotland, and in the east and central Highlands the smaller, shorter-eared blue or mountain hare is ubiquitous and in some places abundant. Because of the grazing damage they do, and their ticks which carry the lethal-to-grouse louping-ill disease, grouse-moor keepers and hill farmers need to keep numbers in check, and many grouse estates organise driven hare shoots after the main grouse season is over. The hill hare in its startling all-white winter pelage is a handsome addition to Scotland's game, and driven hare shooting is especially popular with European visitors.

The sporting rifleman has virtually year-round scope for his skills and fieldcraft, with everything from rabbits and hares to the increasingly popular and conservation-valuable shooting of foxes and crows and, of course, Scotland's four resident species of deer—the native red and roe, the introduced and rapidly spreading Japanese sika, and the familiar fallow, which are locally abundant in some areas. The really dedicated stalker in Scotland need only be idle for four or five weeks of the year at most, with the various species of stags, bucks, hinds and does extending the stalking season to almost 11 months.

The classic Scottish stalking experience, exclusive to this country, is a day on the hill after red deer stags, beginning at around 9.30 am with the departure of the visiting Rifle with the tweed-suited professional stalker, perhaps a rifle-ghillie to carry the rifle, and one or two ponymen leading sure-footed, sturdily-boned Highland ponies (garrons) rigged with special deer saddles. 'The finest sight in Scotland' is how one enthusiast described the vision of the party returning from the dun-brown hills in late afternoon, with stalker and guest strolling contentedly in the wake of two stag-laden garrons, their well-oiled leather strappings creaking gently from their burdens. More prosaically, you may jolt and bounce your way back to the lodge in an all-terrain vehicle, but the use of deer ponies, once in eclipse, has expanded recently.

This is no trophy hunter's affair, because culling the poorer heads is always imperative, but a switch-headed stag can be every bit as testing to stalk as the biggest of 12-pointed Royals or 14-pointed Imperials, and when the rut begins in late September there is a particularly spell-binding atmosphere among the glens and corries for the last few weeks of the stag season, as the hills and crags echo to the roaring challenge of mature males vying for harems of hinds. Although the yield is nothing to hang your hat on, red deer hinds are just as challenging, come at a far lower cost, and provide the added frisson of tackling Highland hills in some of the most physically demanding weather of the northern year.

In what seems like a splendid Irish-ism, the typical Highland deer estate is known as a forest, even though it is totally devoid of trees. But Scotland is, in fact, very heavily forested in many areas, and those are the haunts not only of some of the very biggest and most handsome red deer, but also the exceptionally wary and tough to kill sika, the ubiquitous roe, the fallow and, increasingly, the sika-red hybrids that now threaten the genetic purity of both species in mainland Scotland. Some authorities now maintain that Scotland's only truly pure red deer stocks are to be found in the Outer Hebrides, beyond swimming range of even the most resolute mainland beast.

In January 2003 Scotland's new parliament enacted a Land Reform Act that could potentially wreak major, possibly revolutionary, upheavals in land ownership and management. Undoubtedly, the existing structures of land management and sporting arrangements will change, but it is still far too early to say how or to what extent. But change they clearly will—which makes it all the more urgent to place Scotland high on your shooting wish-list, make your inquiries, place your booking, and go! Few who do so fail to return, again and again. Scottish shooting ought to carry a warning—it is highly addictive!

# FIGHTING FOR OUR SPORT

## EDWARD DASHWOOD

The Countryside Alliance's Campaign for Shooting strategy to promote and protect our sport embraces many areas. Principally, we are a campaigning organisation and, as such, we will continue to emphasise the positive benefits of shooting through our members, the media and wherever required. We will challenge all misconceptions and misrepresentations wherever they occur and highlight the threats against shooting.

At the same time we will reinforce and maintain links with the Home Office, the Home Office Affairs Select Committee and the Firearms Consultative Committee as well as reinforcing the shooting case to individual Ministers.

Furthermore, strongly believing as we do in participation, anyone can try shooting for themselves and in order to encourage young people to learn to shoot we will promote education in rural and shooting issues, young shot initiatives, school visits, shows and information packs.

It is essential that the Campaign for Shooting continues to support and work together with the many other excellent shooting organisations who believe in the same cause and we are deeply involved with them in the promotion of the Code of Good Shooting Practice. The Code is continually leading the way forward as the self-regulatory model of game shooting and is fundamental in this respect. Openness and better advice for all game shooters is essential to deter criticism and further unnecessary government legislation.

In some cases we can help with funding and we intend to support and commission scientific research to strengthen the arguments for game management and shooting in general. The Campaign is, in fact, engaged with DEFRA in a three-year project to promote the consumption of game.

We need the support of all who shoot to raise funds to continue to fight, for this is the very nature of any campaigning organisation. It is as simple as that. We can only operate with the resources our members and supporters generate in the face of huge opposition. This means sustained help year after year. Remember the enjoyment you have had shooting and how future generations may not have the same opportunities. Please stand up for your sport, wear your badges, display your stickers, attend our marches and, above all, give generously and encourage others likewise.

Sir Edward Dashwood Bt is Chairman of the Countryside Alliance's Campaign for Shooting

# ENGLAND

# PHEASANTS

# ALMER SHOOT

*NR WIMBORNE, DORSET*

Empire Game Farm
Throop Road
Templecombe,
Somerset
BA8 0HR

Tel/Fax: 01963 370502          Mobile: 07970 187546

Driven pheasants and partridges on this private estate, which is mainly arable with numerous small, well laid out coverts. With the assistance of game crops the shoot produces some excellent and varied driven shooting. Although the terrain is fairly flat the birds are fast and climb quickly so expect the occasional challenge. There is easy access to most stands although some walking may be necessary. No ground game or woodcock are permitted.

*Shooting acreage:* 2,000
*Status:* Private with let days
*Shoot manager:* J. Bennett
*Contact:* J.Bennett
*Sporting agent:* N/a
*Headkeeper/staff:* Mrs Sue Wall
*Number of available days:* 5
*Number of drives:* 5 per shoot day out of approx 20
*Bag expectations* 100 to 150
*Average cartridge to kill ratio:* 3:1
*Lunch:* Usually shoot through with mid-morning refreshments provided and lunch at end of day served in the Shoot Room on the Estate
*Price structure:* £250 to £375 per gun
*Accommodation:* Various local hotels and pubs to suit all budgets. Plummer Manor in Sturminster Newton is a particular favourite of many of the Guns who shoot at Almer.
*Access:* By road: The estate is situated on A31 between Wimborne and Bere Regis. By rail: Templecombe station. By air: Bournemouth. Transport can be arranged
*Other comments:* Well-behaved dogs only. Almer is happy to cater for single Guns.

# BAYDON

*BAYDON HOUSE FARM, BAYDON, BERKSHIRE*

UK Shooting Services Ltd
Hatswell
Lower Washfield
Tiverton
Devon
EX16 9PE

Tel: 01488 639 026 Mobile: 07801 903287
frank@shootingservices.co.uk www.shootingservices.co.uk

Baydon is a shoot situated within easy striking distance of London. This estate has some steep contours that produce very challenging pheasants and partridges. The ground is either downland or arable with a system of woods throughout the valleys. The drives are mainly gamestrips that are sited to make best use of the topography. The partridges are driven over the banks and will starburst over the guns providing fantastic shooting. The pheasants are driven in similar fashion but using more of the woods. On a typical day you will meet at the main House and have coffee and sausages while the host gives the briefing. Guns will not return to the House until lunch but will have elevenses in the field. Lunch can be taken at the end of the day if requested and partners are catered for. Baydon is run by a family who wish to make you feel as relaxed as possible.

*Shooting acreage:* 1,200
*Status:* Syndicate with let days
*Owner:* UK Shooting Services Ltd
*Contact:* Frank Speir
*Sporting agent:* UK Shooting Services Ltd, as above
*Headkeeper/staff:* Andew Gray
*Number of available days:* 2–3 days
*Number of drives:* 15
*Bag expectations:* 200-400
*Average cartridge to kill ratio:* 3:1 plus
*Lunch:* In main House
*Price structure:* £28 per bird
*Accommodation:* Local pubs/hotels
*Access:* 7 minutes off Jct 14, M4

# BELVOIR CASTLE SHOOT

*BELVOIR, NR GRANTHAM, RUTLAND*

Estate Agent
Belvoir Castle
Nr Grantham
Leicestershire
NG32 1PD

Tel: 01476 870 262　　　　　　　　Fax: 01476 070 443

Set amidst outstandingly lovely English countryside, with rolling hills and valleys, the Belvoir Castle Shoot represents the archetypal English driven game shoot and the quality of the birds, both pheasants and partridges, and their presentation must please the connoisseur. This is classical driven game shooting.

*Shooting acreage:* 7,000 acres
*Status:* Private with let days
*Sporting agent:* N/A
*Headkeeper:* Malcolm Partridge
*Number of available days:* 30
*Number of drives:* 40
*Bag expectations:* 250-400
*Average cartridge to kill ratio:* 3:1
*Lunch:* Lunch taken in Belvoir Castle
*Price structure:* £27 per bird plus VAT
*Accommodation:* By special arrangement limited parties can be accommodated in Belvoir Castle, otherwise local hotels.
*Access:* By road: Five miles west of A1, near Grantham and off A72
*Other comments:* Well-behaved gundogs welcome

# BECKERINGS PARK SHOOT

*BECKERINGS PARK, NR WOBURN, BEDFORSHIRE*

Grindsbrook House
69 Oxford Road
Banbury
OX16 9AJ

Tel: 01295 277197          Fax: 01295 268651
james@ejchurchill.com

The Beckerings Park Shoot has justifiably acquired a reputation for showing good quality driven partridges and pheasants from carefully planted and sited game covers and woodland. The shoot is very well run and makes a virtue of its excellent hospitality. It also has the advantage for busy Guns of being relatively close to London.

*Shooting acreage:* 2,000
*Status:* Commercial
*Contact:* James Chapel
*Sporting agent:* E.J.Churchill Sporting, as above
*Headkeeper:* Two keepers
*Number of available days:* 12 to 16
*Number of drives:* 15
*Bag expectations:* 250 to 400
*Average cartridge to kill ratio:* 3:1. Recommend double-guns for the larger bag days
*Lunch:* Excellent hospitality provided in speciality converted traditional barn
*Price structure:* POA but very good value for shoot so close to London
*Accommodation:* Teams are usually accommodated at the excellent Flitwick Manor, Flitwick
*Access:* The shoot is only five minutes from Jct.13 of the M21
*Other comments:* Well-behaved gundogs welcome

# BRIMPSFIELD PARK ESTATE

## *BRIMPSFIELD PARK, GLOUCESTERSHIRE*

Brimpsfield Park
Gloucestershire
GL4 8LE

Tel: 01452 863163                    Fax: 01452 863135
rlarthe@brimpsfieldparkIT.com        www.brimpsfieldparkIT.com

Brimpsfield Park has been in the Larthe family for 43 years and is on the edge of the Cotswold Escarpment, nestling on the side of a gloriously deep valley. The house, which is of historical importance, features in the Domesday Book. Constructed of mellow Cotswold stone, it has a commanding view over the valley. The shooting has been developed over the past 43 years and now has a reputation for providing some of the most enjoyable shooting in the country. The season starts at the beginning of October with some outstandingly exciting partridge driving and then, as the season progresses, the pheasant drives in the main valley come into their own, the high trees and flushing points ensuring that the birds are exceptionally high before crossing the valley. The shoot is overseen and run by the Owners and attention to detail is exceptional. A great deal of effort is put into encouraging young shots and a full day's shooting is held every season for young shots. The shoot attempts to create a relaxed and enjoyable day's sport. There is no sense of being rushed, lunch is an integral part of the day and the visitor can be assured of outstanding sport and excellent hospitality.

*Shooting acreage:* 2,000
*Status:* Private with let days
*Owner:* Richard Larthe as above
*Headkeeper/staff:* Andrew Woods. Beat-keepers; James Osborne, Rebecca Woods
*Number of available days:* 3
*Number of drives:* 48
*Bag expectations:* 250 plus
*Average cartridge to kill ratio:* 4.5:1
*Lunch:* Lunch is taken in the Main House and the fare and wine are both excellent
*Price structure:* £26.50 per bird plus VAT
*Accommodation:* In the Main House or Cowley Manor, Cowley (2 miles), Painswick Hotel, Painswick (3 miles)
*Access:* By road: M5, Jct.11a four miles away. M4, Jct. 15 is 30 miles away. Helicopter pad in front of House.
*Other comments:* Well trained gundogs welcome

# BRICKHOUSE SHOOT

*EAST SUSSEX*

1 Hollingrove Cottage
Brightling
Robertsbridge
TN32 5HU

Tel: 01424 838303                    Fax: 01424 838303

The Brickhouse Shoot, which is 100 per cent family run, is set in a glorious part of East Sussex with the intention of providing quality shooting, rather than large bags. The shoot covers two large valleys and birds are driven from either 10 acres of mixed game crops in the earlier part of the season, or woodland later on. Some 4,000 pheasants are released. The majority of the drives show excellent birds, and though high most are shootable. There is a three-acre lake but no duck are, at present, shot. At the end of a day's shooting Guns are given a brace of oven-ready pheasants.

*Shooting acreage:* 850
*Status:* Commercial, syndicate
*Owner:* Richard Hoad and Alf Hoad
*Contact:* As above
*Sporting agent:* N/a
*Headkeeper/staff:* Richard Hoad
*Number of available days:* 12
*Number of drives:* 11
*Average cartridge to kill ratio:* 3:1
*Lunch:* Lunch, which is seasonal food, is taken in the Shoot Lodge and prepared and cooked on the day
*Price structure:* £24 per bird. No VAT
*Accommodation:* The Bear, at Burwash, three miles away, provides motel accommodation
*Access:* By road: Approximately four miles west of the A21 between Hastings and Tunbridge Wells, turning off at Robertsbridge, 12 miles north of Hastings. By rail: Robertsbridge.

# BUSCOT PARK SHOOT

*OXFORDSHIRE*

The Estate Office
Buscot Park
Faringdon
Oxfordshire
SN7 8BU

Tel: 01367 241794                    Fax: 01367 241794
estabuscot@aol.com

Buscot Park is a long-established family shoot with a few let days each year. The atmosphere is relaxed and informal, with the emphasis on providing a really enjoyable day for parties of up to eight Guns. The country covered is rolling West Oxfordshire land with a fascinating diversity of terrain, ranging over parkland, woodland and open fields, offering an excitingly wide variety of drives. The main quarry is pheasants, with some partridges and other wild species, including the occasional woodcock, while the several lakes on the Estate also hold duck. Transport between drives is provided in an estate vehicle, in which all the party travels together. The keeper, John Downes, has been with the Buscot Park Shoot for many years, and has a really enthusiastic beating team to ensure a well-organised day.

*Shooting acreage:* 3,000
*Status:* Private with let days
*Owner:* Buscot Park
*Contact:* as above
*Sporting agent:* N/a
*Headkeeper:* John Downes
*Number of available days:* 5
*Number of drives:* 8-10
*Bag expectations:* 200-300. Sometimes up to 400 by arrangement. Maximum 8 Guns.
*Average cartridge to kill ratio:* Varies greatly according to skill of Guns
*Lunch:* A three-course hearty lunch (all wine and drinks provided) is included in the price, as is afternoon tea at the end of the day
*Price structure:* £27.50 per bird. No VAT
*Accommodation:* Excellent hotels, such as the Bibury Court, or Sudbury House, Faringdon, can be arranged in the vicinity
*Access:* By road: On the A417, between Faringdon and Lechlade, nine miles from the M4, Jct. 15 at Swindon.
*Other comments:* Well trained gundogs welcome by arrangement

# CALTHORPE SHOOT

*CALTHORPE ST INGHAM, NORWICH, NORFOLK*

Broadland Game Supplies
Hydaway
The Game Farm
Calthorpe St Ingham
Norwich
Norfolk
NR12 9TF

Tel: 01692 581966              Mobile: 07787 534804
gjgrapes@supanet.com

The Calthorpe Shoot is a typical small driven pheasants, partridges and duck shoot over 400 acres. Its close proximity to the Broads ensures a good mixture of sport. The shoot consists of arable farmland, woods and marshes and the intention is to provide a relaxed atmosphere.

*Shooting acreage:* 400
*Status:* Private with let days
*Owner:* Broadland Game Supplies
*Contact:* G.J.Grapes
*Sporting agent:* N/a
*Number of available days:* 8-10
*Number of drives:* Total 17(6-8) per day
*Bag expectations:* 100-150
*Average cartridge to kill ratio:* 3:1 dependent upon ability!
*Lunch:* Shoot through with morning snack (not provided). Evening meal at Swan Inn, Ingham included.
*Price structure:* £18 per bird
*Accommodation:* Local B&Bs, pubs and hotels
*Access:* Just off B1151, 15 miles from Norwich. By rail: Norwich Station. By air: Norwich Airport. Transport available by arrangement.
*Other comments:* Well-behaved gundogs welcome

## CHECKLEY, NANTWICH, CHESHIRE

Bank Farm
Checkley Lane
Checkley
Nantwich
Cheshire
CW5 7QA

Tel: 01270 520315
javor@checkleywood.fsnet.co.uk

Checkley Wood Shoot is set within the beautiful South Cheshire/Shropshire countryside and is an ideal location for a great day's sport. The shoot, which includes driven pheasants and partridges, has a large range of diverse drives and no two days are ever the same. The quality of the birds is enviable and the highly trained keepers provide all Guns with high birds, making an excellent day out. One of the best drives features a well-placed cover crop over a steep drop leading the beaters to produce birds at great height over the Guns. The drives are well maintained and with the wealth of experience from our keepers we would like to provide all Guns with the chance not only to shoot to their best ability, but also enjoy a great day out. The reputation of the Cheshire countryside sells itself. The shoot prides itself on its welcoming atmosphere, with a relaxing pace and either a warming lunch or a hearty dinner.

*Shooting acreage:* 6,000
*Status:* Commercial, syndicates and private with let days
*Owner:* Ivor Beavis
*Contact:* As above
*Sporting agent:* N/A
*Headkeeper/staff:* Nicholas Beavis
*Number of available days:* 5
*Number of drives:* As many as required
*Bag expectations:* To suit – average 150. Duck also available
*Average cartridge to kill ratio:* 3 or 4:1
*Lunch:* Lunch is available in our own shoot lodge and later in the season roast dinners are served
*Price structure:* £22 per bird
*Accommodation:* Local hotels and country pubs available for recommendation
*Access:* By road: a short distance from Junction 16 of the M6. By rail: Crewe station. By air: 45 minutes from Manchester Airport.

# CHIDEOCK MANOR SHOOT

*DORSET*

Chideock Manor
Chideock
Bridport
Dorset
DT6 6LF

Tel: 0207 937 0842 or 0207 670 2500   Mobile: 07976 327 853
hbc@makinson-cowell.co.uk

Driven pheasants on an excellent private shoot amidst spectacular West Dorset country and close to the sea, between Bridport and Lyme Regis. High pheasants are driven over small steep valleys on the 1,000 acre arable, grass and well-wooded estate. This is a particularly friendly shoot which prides itself on producing a classical driven day.

*Shooting acreage:* 1,000
*Status:* Private with let days
*Owner:* Howard Coates
*Contact:* Howard Coates
*Sporting agent:* N/a
*Headkeeper:* Danny Joliffe
*Number of available days:* 7
*Number of drives:* 5 to 8 per day
*Bag expectations:* 200-250
*Average cartridge to kill ratio:* 4:1
*Lunch:* Served in the Manor
*Price structure:* POA
*Accommodation:* Excellent local hotel and pubs. There are also holiday cottages available on the estate although these need to be booked well in advance
*Access:* By road: A303/M27–A35. By rail: Axminster/Dorchester South stations. By air: Exeter. Transport by arrangement.
*Other comments:* Well-behaved dogs welcome

E * 10

# COMBE SYDENHAM SHOOT

*EXMOOR NATIONAL PARK, DEVON*

Loyton
Morebath
Tiverton
Devon
EX16 9AS

Tel: 01398 331051          Fax: 01398 331052
shooting@loyton.com          www.loyton.com

Combe Sydenham is a relatively newly established shoot with enormous potential. Over the last two seasons it has produced pheasants of exceptional quality. It is run as a commercial shoot, selling 20 days throughout the season, with the emphasis on sporting fun in an enjoyable environment. Located in the Exmoor National Park between the villages of Monksilver and Elworthy, the Combe Sydenham shoot covers approximately 2,000 acres of shooting rights. The glorious wooded valleys, typical of this part of the country, produce high bird pheasant shooting of great quality, with the birds usually driven from cover crops planted on the top of the hills. It is worth emphasising that the shoot is set in an area of immense beauty. The keepers, beaters and pickers-up are friendly and welcoming.

*Shooting acreage:* 2,000
*Status:* Commercial
*Contact:* Angus Barnes as above
*Sporting agent:* N/a
*Headkeeper/staff:* Headkeeper Peter Conachie. Under-keeper Edward Bradbury
*Number of available days:* 20
*Number of drives:* 20
*Bag expectations:* 100-300
*Average cartridge to kill ratio:* 5:1
*Lunch:* An excellent shoot lunch is taken in the shooting lodge
*Price structure:* £29 per bird plus VAT
*Accommodation:* A shooting lodge is currently under construction, which will have up to 14 bedrooms and facilities so that all Guns can stay there in comfort. This will be completed by the start of the 2003/4 season.
*Access:* By road: Jct. 25 of the M5, then A358, B3224. By rail: Taunton. By air: Exeter or Bristol
*Other comments:* Well trained gun dogs welcome, also non-shooting guests. There is, in addition, a clay shooting ground.

# CONISTON HALL ESTATE

*NORTH YORKSHIRE*

Coniston Cold
Skipton
North Yorkshire
BD23 4EB

Tel: 01756 749551            Fax: 01756 749551
conistonhall@clara.net       www.conistonhall.co.uk

Driven pheasants over the 1,200 acre estate owned by the Bannister family and centred around a 24 acre lake. Coniston Hall is situated just outside the village of Coniston Cold in the Yorkshire Dales. The general terrain is easy going and the shooting well organised and very friendly. In addition, the Craven Shooting Ground is located within the estate grounds and offers DTL, English and ISU Skeet and English and FITASC sporting layouts.

*Shooting acreage:* 1,200
*Status:* Private with a few let days
*Owner:* The Bannister Family
*Contact:* Michael Bannister
*Sporting agent:* N/a
*Headkeeper/staff:* C. Wild
*Number of available days:* 1 to 2
*Number of drives:* 6
*Bag expectations:* 150-200
*Average cartridge to kill ratio:* 3:1
*Lunch:* Family run at house
*Price structure:* £25 per bird
*Accommodation:* Available at the 40 bedroomed Coniston Hall Hotel, opened in 1998. The hotel has been awarded an AA Rosette for its cuisine
*Access:* By road: M1 and M6 both one hour away. By air: Both Leeds and Manchester airports are one hour away. Transport to and from Airports can be arranged.
*Other comments:* Gundogs/dogs not accommodated

# CORNBURY PARK SHOOT

## CORNBURY PARK, NR WOODSTOCK, OXFORDSHIRE

Grindsbrook House
69 Oxford Road
Banbury
Oxfordshire
OX16 9AJ

Tel: 01295 277197          Fax: 01295 268651
james@ejchurchill.com

This is a lovely private driven pheasant shoot showing good quality birds over mature, broad-leaved woodland with the Guns standing in sunken rides. The shooting mostly takes place in the beautiful Wychwood Forest, one of the largest forests in the country.

*Shooting acreage:* 6,000
*Status:* Private with let days
*Contact:* James Chapel
*Sporting agent:* E.J. Churchill Sporting
*Headkeeper:* Jeremy Harvey
*Number of available days:* 12
*Number of drives:* 8
*Bag expectations:* 150 to 250
*Average cartridge to kill ratio:* 3:1
*Lunch:* Lunch is taken in a fully furnished outbuilding with a professional chef in attendance
*Price structure:* POA
*Accommodation:* Guests always enjoy staying at The Feathers in Woodstock
*Access:* Less than one hour's drive on M40, A40, A44 from Heathrow to Woodstock. 20 minutes drive from Oxford
*Other comments:* Well-behaved gundogs welcome

# DELBURY SHOOT

*DUDLEBURY, NR LUDLOW, SHROPSHIRE*

St George's House
29 St George's Rd
Cheltenham
Gloucestershire
GL50 3DU

Tel: 01242 514478                    Fax: 01242 224697
info@coley.co.uk                     www.coley.co.uk

This is largely a driven pheasant shoot with a few partridges and is set in a lovely countryside of valleys and hills dotted with woodland and planted up with game crops. The result is very challenging shooting in a beautiful setting. The Delbury Shoot, apart from excellent sport shown, also has a reputation for being very friendly.

*Shooting acreage:* 1,500
*Status:* Commercial
*Sporting agent:* Ian Coley Sporting, as above
*Headkeeper:* Graham Jones
*Number of available days:* 25
*Number of drives:* 20 plus
*Bag expectations:* 300-400
*Average cartridge to kill ratio:* 4.5:1
*Lunch:* Lunch is taken in converted shooting lodge
*Price structure:* £27 per bird plus VAT
*Accommodation:* The Willow, Bettws Hall, nr Newton or local hotels
*Access:* By road: five miles north of Ludlow off the B4368.
*Other comments:* Well-controlled dogs welcome

*BIDEFORD, DEVON*

Bird Shooting Ltd
Worlington House
New Road
Instow
North Devon EX39 4LN

Tel: 01271 860202                    Mobile: 07810 006445
chris@birdshooting.co.uk

Bird Shooting Limited holds the sporting rights to some 6,000 acres of glorious countryside in North Devon and North Cornwall. The company specialises in providing Guns with an excellent day's sport with a modest bag. One hundred bird pheasant days are organised, also mixed 50 bird pheasant days with drives before lunch followed by driven snipe and woodcock in the afternoon, ending with a wild duck flight. Although bags are small, the shooting is outstanding. Pheasants fly high and fast, 'the woodcock are testing and the snipe impossible and to round the day off under a pack of teal or mallard makes a wonderful sporting day'.

*Shooting acreage*: 6,000
*Status:* Commercial.
*Owner:* Bird Shooting Limited
*Contact:* Christian Bird
*Sporting agent:* N/a
*Headkeeper/staff:* James Hancock
*Number of available days:* 40
*Number of drives*: Total 40 plus – 6 per day
*Bag expectations:* Pheasants 50-100, mixed day 50 head, pheasant, snipe, woodcock and duck.
*Gun/cartridge recommendations:* Only fibre wads permitted
*Average cartridge to kill ratio:* 4:1
*Lunch:* Provided in local pub inclusive
*Price structure:* £21+ VAT per bird for 100 bird pheasant days. £135 + VAT per Gun for 50 pheasants, snipe, woodcock and duck
*Accommodation:* Excellent local accommodation arranged to meet all tastes
*Access:* By road: 40 minutes from M5 Jct 27. By rail: Tiverton Parkway Station
*Other comments:* Well-behaved dogs welcome

# EDGCOTT

*EXFORD, DEVON*

Edgcott Farm
Exford
Devon
TA24 7QG

Tel: 01643 831 334　　　　　　　　Fax: 01643 831 631
Mobile: 0774 766 1166

Edgcott shoot, offering driven pheasants, is in the heart of Exmoor very close to Exford village. As a result of the terrain, the birds are high and will test even the most experienced Gun. The shoot is run as a family shoot. On arrival coffee will be provided in the specially converted shoot lodge where the briefing for the day will take place. Elevenses are sometimes taken in the field but more often Guns return to the lodge for soup, sausages and Champagne. Lunch is normally taken in the middle of the day but sometimes we shoot through according to guests' personal preference. The intention at Edgcott is to make a Gun feel a guest and not a client. Edgcott is still in its early years and there are always drives to be improved as well as created, however, we strive to produce first-class shooting at reasonable prices compared to most West Country shoots.

*Shooting acreage:* 1,200
*Status:* Private with let days
*Contact:* Linley Williams, as above
*Sporting agent:* UK Shooting Services Ltd (tel: 01884 254 056, Edward Watson)
*Headkeeper/staff:* Richard Tapp
*Number of available days:* 3 to 5
*Number of drives:* 10
*Bag expectations:* 200-400
*Average cartridge to kill ratio:* 5:1 plus
*Lunch:* In Lodge. Tea also served
*Price structure:* £29:00 per bird
*Accommodation:* Local pubs/hotels
*Access:* Tiverton Train Station 40 mins drive via Dulverton. By road: Jct 27 of M5 – A361 then A396. Air Exeter and Bristol

*THETFORD, NORFOLK*

Elveden Estate
Elveden
Thetford
Norfolk
IP24 3TQ

Tel: 01842 890223                    Fax: 01842 890070
jim.rudderham@elveden.com            www.elveden.com

This famous Estate of 23,000 acres offers plentiful opportunities for driven and walked-up shooting of wild birds. This is the Estate which was once owned by one of the most colourful characters to parade across the British shooting scene, the Maharajah Duleep Singh. Given a pension by the Government in the 1860s, he turned the Estate into one of the finest sporting shoots in England. On his death the estate was sold to the then Lord Iveagh. Today vast tracts of lowland heath and woodland provide an historic setting for driven wild pheasant shooting and walked-up sport over pointers on a shoot which is still family owned. While let days are available, they are in short supply due to Elveden's popularity.

*Shooting acreage:* 18,000
*Status:* Private with let days
*Owner:* The Elveden Estate
*Contact:* Jim Rudderham, as above
*Sporting agent:* N/a
*Headkeeper/staff:* Jim Rudderham, Headkeeper and manager plus seven beat keepers
*Number of available days:* very few but worth applying
*Number of drives:* Over 60
*Bag expectations:* Driven wild bird 100. Walked-up 30-40
*Average cartridge to kill ratio:* 3:1
*Lunch:* Driven local pub or bistro. Walked-up taken in the field
*Price structure:* POA
*Accommodation:* Well-appointed self-catering lodges available on the Estate
*Access:* By road: A11 between Cambridge and Norwich. By rail: Cambridge
*Other comments:* Well trained gundogs very welcome

# EXEBRIDGE SHOOT

*NEAR DULVERTON, EXMOOR*

33-34 Fore Street
Chudleigh
South Devon
TQ13 0HX

Tel: 01626 854793                    Fax: 01626 854779
Mobile: 07711 215542
richard@westcountry-sporting.co.uk   www.w-s-w.co.uk

This driven pheasant shoot offers some of the best value high bird shooting on Exmoor and is run by a renowned owner and keeper. Drives are largely from cover crops sited on steep hill summits or sides, ensuring high but shootable birds. This is glorious West Country countryside with some spectacular drives, some of which require limited walking although quad bikes are available if necessary.

*Shooting acreage:* 700
*Status:* Syndicate with let days
*Contact:* Richard Hutcheon
*Sporting agent:* Westcountry Sporting Worldwide
*Headkeeper:* Ian Parkhouse
*Number of available days:* 6
*Number of drives:* 12 in total with 4-6 per day
*Bag expectations:* 250-400
*Average cartridge to kill ratio:* 5:1
*Lunch:* Taken in the shoot owner's house
*Price structure:* £27.50 per bird inclusive
*Accommodation:* Ample local good hotels and inns. Royal Oak, Exford is highly recommended
*Access:* By road: 20 minutes from M5 Jct27 then A361 and A396 to Exebridge. By rail: Taunton Station. By air: Bristol and Exeter. Transport can be arranged.
*Other comments:* Well trained gundogs are welcome

*EXWICK BARTON, NR EXETER, DEVON*

Brindifield Farm
Black Dog
Crediton
Devon
EX17 4QU

Tel: 01884 841644 Mobile: 07967 806059

Driven and walked-up for pheasants, partridges and duck over 1,500 acres of outstanding Devon countryside. Four ponds, fed by a stream running through a steep valley serve this well-established shoot, offering the promise of high, fast birds. Access is easy to the woodland and game covered drives. Hospitality can be found at a range of local hostelries and accommodation to suit all budgets.

*Shooting acreage:* 1,500
*Status:* Commercial
*Contact:* Sandra Turner or John Leach
*Sporting agent:* N/a
*Headkeeper/staff:* John Leach
*Number of available days:* 40
*Number of drives:* 15 in total 4-5 per day
*Bag expectations:* 50-400
*Average cartridge to kill ratio:* 5:1
*Lunch:* Arranged in local country inn - inclusive
*Price structure:* From £25 per bird
*Accommodation:* Variety of local inns and hotels to suit all budgets
*Access:* By road: 15 mins off Jct 27 M5. By rail: St David's Station, Exeter. By air: Exeter Airport. Pick ups can be arranged.
*Other comments:* Well-behaved dogs are welcome

# EYNSHAM PARK SHOOT

*EYNSHAM, NR OXFORD*

St George's House
29 St George's Road
Cheltenham
Gloucestershire
GL50 3DU

Tel: 01242 514478          Fax: 01242 224697
info@coley.co.uk          www.coley.co.uk

The Eynsham Park Shoot provides excellent driven pheasants shooting, supplemented by some partridges. Drives are from mature woodlands, game crops and plantations in historic parkland and, although relatively level ground, good birds are shown by an enthusiastic team of beaters and staff.

*Shooting acreage:* 2,000
*Status:* Private with let days
*Sporting agent:* Ian Coley Sporting, as above
*Headkeeper/staff:* Not given
*Number of available days:* 20
*Number of drives:* 20
*Bag expectations:* 300
*Average cartridge to kill ratio:* 3:1
*Lunch:* Taken in owner's house at Eynsham Park
*Price structure:* On application
*Accommodation:* Local hotels and inns
*Access:* By road: Just off the A34, and 10 miles north-west of Oxford. By rail: Oxford Station; By air: Heathrow.
Comments: Well-controlled dogs welcome

E * 20

# FACCOMBE ESTATE

## *NORTH WESSEX DOWNS, HAMPSHIRE*

Faccombe Estates Ltd
The Estate Office
Faccombe
Andover
Hants
SP11 0DS

Tel: 01264 737247                    Fax: 01264 737367
dfh@faccombe.co.uk

Faccombe Estate has long been recognised as one of the premier shoots in Southern England. It is situated on the North Wessex Downs equidistant from Newbury, Andover and Hungerford. The land rises to over 900ft above sea-level. The undulating countryside provides first-class pheasant and partridge shooting amongst beautiful and well-maintained surroundings.

*Shooting acreage:* 4250 acres of which 1,200 acres are mixed woodland
*Status:* Private with let days
*Owner:* Faccombe Estates Ltd
*Contact:* D.F. Harbottle or J.A.F. Harbottle
*Sporting agent:* N/a
*Headkeeper/staff:* Headkeeper and two beatkeepers
*Number of available days:* Normally 20
*Number of drives:* 45
*Bag expectations:* 325 average (not more than 400)
*Average cartridge to kill ratio:* 3:1
*Lunch:* A mid-morning break with consomme etc is provided. Lunch is taken in a specially converted shoot room with modern amenities. Pre-lunch drinks, three-course lunch with wine is served followed by coffee and port. Tea and cake at the end of the day. Guns can shoot through if they wish
*Price structure:* £27.00 plus VAT per bird up to Christmas. £27.50 plus VAT after Christmas
*Accommodation:* Esseborne Manor Hotel on A343, adjacent to the Estate. Tel 01264 736444. The Vineyard, Stockcross, on A4 near Newbury. Tel: 01635 528770
*Access:* Within easy reach of both the M4 and M3. Situated 3 miles off the A343 north-west of Hurstbourne Tarrant
*Other comments:* Four-wheel drive vehicles can be made available if needed. Only fibre and biodegradable wadded cartridges are allowed. Loaders/stuffers can be provided at the Gun's expense. Well-trained, soft-mouthed gundogs are welcome.

# FIFIELD SHOOT

## *WILTSHIRE DOWNS, WILTSHIRE*

Manor Farm
Fifield Bavant
Broadchalke
Salisbury

Tel: 01722 780600        Fax: 01722 780600
reis@farmersweekly.net

The Fifield Shoot is situated in the beautiful South Wiltshire Downs between Salisbury and Shaftesbury in the centre of the Cranborne Chase area of outstanding natural beauty. The owners are fortunate enough to be able to take advantage of a diverse landscape, ranging from mature woodland to open grassland valleys, to show both pheasants and partridges to their full potential. Both birds often appear in the same drives, making for extremely exciting sport. The Fifield Shoot caters for full teams of eight to nine Guns, and non-shooting guests to a total of 15. The day will normally consist of six drives, with four in the morning and two after lunch, with Guns and guests driven to their pegs in the 'Gun bus', towed by a tractor. The aim is to provide a smooth running day with extremely testing and exciting shooting, all in a relaxed and jovial atmosphere.

*Shooting acreage:* 860
*Status:* Private with let days
*Owner:* Andrew Reis
*Contact:* Andrew Reis
*Sporting agent:* N/a
*Headkeeper:* Adrian Brine
*Number of available days:* 13
*Number of drives:* 6 per day
*Bag expectations:* 200
*Average cartridge to kill ratio:* 3.5:1
*Lunch:* A sit-down lunch and tea are provided in a well-converted granary by a highly respected local caterer, with wine chosen by the host. Menus are sent out to clients one/two weeks before the shoot
*Price structure:* 200 bird days are £23 per bird plus VAT within a 10 per cent margin
*Accommodation:* Howards House Teffont or Castleman at Chettle
*Access:* By road: situated eight miles west of Salisbury close to the A30 and A354. Some 40 minutes drive from Southampton. By rail: Salisbury
*Other comments:* Well trained gundogs welcome

# FRIESLAND SHOOT

Prospect Cottage
Chorley
Nr Bridgnorth
Shropshire
WV16 6PP

Tel/Fax: 01746 718536.

Friesland borders the beautiful Welsh Marches and is well known for its high birds driven off the Longmynd Hills over woodland-covered valleys. This shoot offers pheasants and has recently introduced partridges. There is little walking to be done here with easy access to all drives and pegs. Friesland has acquired a reputation for its friendly atmosphere.

*Shooting acreage:* 2,600
*Status:* Private syndicate shoot with let days
*Shoot manager:* Michael John Blick
*Contact:* Michael John Blick
*Sporting agent:* N/a
*Headkeeper/staff:* Julian Dickens
*Number of available days:* 4
*Number of drives:* 20 – usually 6 per day
*Bag expectations:* 150+
*Average cartridge to kill ratio:* 3:1
*Lunch:* Served in the gunroom
*Price structure:* £18 per bird
*Accommodation:* Several local hotels
*Access:* By road: 4 miles off A49. By rail: Craven Arms station. By air: Birmingham Airport
*Other comments:* Well-behaved gundogs welcome

# GREAT BARTON SHOOT

*BEAFORD, WINKLEIGH, DEVON*

Upcott Barton
Beaford
Winkleigh
Devon
EX19 8AQ

Tel: 01805 603207 (Michael Underhill)
Tel: 01805 603280 (John Heal)

Driven and walked-up pheasants over 2,000 acres covering five farms. Small, deep valleys and gulleys in conjunction with game crops on high ground ensure high but shootable birds. Average bag around 150 pheasants and emphasis is on a thoroughly enjoyable day, not a vast bag. There are, in addition, a small number of partridges and duck. Some walked-up days also available.

*Shooting acreage*: 2,000
*Status*: Commercial
*Owners*: Michael Underhill and John Heal
*Contact*: Michael Underhill
*Sporting agent*: N/a
*Headkeeper*: Mark Sutton
*Number of available days*: 28
*Number of drives*: 16 total – 5-6 per day
*Bag expectations*: 50-250
*Average cartridge to kill ratio*: 4.5:1
*Lunch*: Break for short lunch at farmhouse, and main meal taken in local pub after shooting and tea
*Price structure*: Price on application
*Accommodation*: Local pubs and hotels to suit all budgets
*Access*: By road: from Exeter or Taunton. By rail: Exeter Station. By air: Exeter. Transport by arrangement
*Other comments*: Well-behaved gundogs welcome, as are wives and children

# GURSTON DOWN

Gurston Farm
Broadchalke
Salisbury
Wiltshire
SP5 5HR

Tel: 01722 780888                      Fax: 01722 780398
rjhitch@gurston.fsbusiness.co.uk      www.gurstondownshoot.co.uk

Gurston Down, situated in the glorious Chalke Valley, near Salisbury, might have been created for the showing of quality driven pheasants and partridges. Renowned for its high flying birds, the shoot was created over 35 years ago by David Hitchings, a pioneer of 'high' pheasants and to this day Gurston Down remains one of the finest and most sporting shoots in the country. Today, although his father still keeps a friendly eye on proceedings, the shoot is run by Robert Hitchings and continues to provide superb quality shooting amid splendid scenery. Exciting, challenging birds, a relaxed atmosphere and delicious lunch make a day's shooting at Gurston Down a memorable experience.

*Shooting acreage*: 3,000
*Status*: Commercial
*Owner*: Robert Hitchings
*Contact*: Robert Hitchings, as above
*Headkeeper*: Ray Rabbetts
*Number of available days*: 32
*Number of drives*: 20
*Bag expectations*: In the region of 300
*Average cartridge to kill ratio*: 4:1
*Lunch*: a traditional three-course lunch is taken in the shooting lodge
*Price structure*: £32 plus VAT as a guide. No excess charged
*Accommodation*: A selection of three superb hotels within a radius of three miles
*Access*: By road: A303 to Salisbury, the A354 with Broadchalke 14 miles south-west of Salisbury. By rail: Salisbury Station. By air: Southampton
*Other comments*: Well-trained gundogs are welcome

# HEYDON HALL ESTATE

*HEYDON, NORWICH, NORFOLK*

Broadland Game Supplies
Hydaway
The Game Farm
Calthorpe
St Ingham
Norwich
Norfolk
NR12 9TF

Tel: 01692 581966                    Mobile: 07787 534804
gjgrapes@supanet.com

Driven pheasants, partridges and duck over 2,800 acres situated near a picturesque North Norfolk village. Heydon Hall itself is a large 16th Century house set in parkland with 500 acres of woodland and a six acre lake which provide the backdrop to this shoot. The Estate is fully keepered to provide quality sport with days available throughout the season for single, team or syndicate Guns.

*Shooting acreage*: 2,800
*Status*: Commercial, syndicate with let days
*Owner*: Broadland Game Supplies
*Contact*: G.J.Grapes
*Sporting agent*: N/a
*Headkeeper/staff*: Ben Driver and Andrew Lincoln
*Number of available days*: 24
*Number of drives*: Over 40 – 6-8 per day
*Bag expectations*: 200-400
*Average cartridge to kill ratio*: 3:1 dependent upon ability
*Lunch*: Two-course lunch with wine at Earle Inn, Heydon, included
*Price structure*: £21 per bird plus VAT
*Accommodation*: Aylsham Lodge Hotel plus other local pubs and hotels.
*Access*: By road: A140 8 miles from Norwich. By rail: Norwich Station. By air: Norwich Airport. Transport can be arranged.
*Other comments*: Well-behaved gundogs welcome

*WELLS-NEXT-THE-SEA, NORFOLK*

Holkham Estate Office
Wells-next-the-Sea
Norfolk NR23 1AB

Tel: 01328 713104       Fax: 01328 711707
s.lester@holkham.co.uk     www.holkham.co.uk

Holkham, the Earl of Leicester's north Norfolk Estate, is arguably the most famous wild bird shoot in the country. Reputed to be the birthplace of driven shooting, the Estate is perhaps best known for drives such as Scarborough Clump and Joe's Stop. Although the family take the majority of the main days, a small number of rough shoot days are available. The rough shoot days are designed for six Guns and aim to give guests a taste of the huge variety of shooting to be enjoyed on this historic estate. The mini-driven days, run by the headkeeper and his team of seven beatkeepers, are tailored to a team's requirements. At the end of the day the shoot card is likely to feature wild pheasants, French partridges, woodcock, geese, wild duck, pigeons, rabbits and hares. The atmosphere is informal, with no beaters, just the keepers and their dogs. Lunch is taken on the hoof and the day rounded off with a drink at The Victoria at Holkham, the Estate's own hotel. Some teams also take the opportunity to enjoy an evening duck flight on one of the Estate's many flight ponds. These flights can also be booked separately.

*Shooting acreage*: 25,000, with approximately 16,000 acres shot over
*Status*: private with let days of rough shooting and evening duck flights
*Owner*: The Earl of Leicester
*Contact*: Please write (don't phone) to Simon Lester, Headkeeper, as above
*Headkeeper/staff*: Simon Lester and seven beatkeepers
*Number of available days*: limited, with an extremely high demand for them
*Number of drives*: Each day is planned for team's individual requirements
*Bag expectations*: Rough days 40-60 head
*Lunch*: Usually taken in the field. Packed lunches available from The Victoria Hotel, Holkham
*Price structure*: Rough days: £1,500 inc VAT per day. Duck flights: £100 inc VAT per Gun
*Accommodation*: Special rates for shooting parties at The Victoria Hotel at Holkham, Park Road, Holkham, Norfolk NR23 1RG. Tel: 01328 711008. victoria@holkham.co.uk
*Access*: By road: Holkham is two miles west of Wells-next-the-Sea on the main A149, within easy reach of Norwich on the A1067, King's Lynn on the A148 and London and Cambridge on the M11 and the A10.
*Other comments*: Guests must have their own insurance. Well-trained gundogs welcome.

# KEMPTON SHOOT

*NR CRAVEN ARMS, SHROPSHIRE*

St George's House
29 St George's Road
Cheltenham
Gloucestershire
GL50 3DU

Tel: 01242 514478                    Fax: 01242 224697
info@coley.co.uk                     www.coley.co.uk

The Kempton Shoot is renowned for its driven partridges and pheasants. This is rolling countryside, with the Welsh hills on the distant western horizon, while its valleys and banks, topped with game crops, lend themselves ideally to showing good birds. On several drives Guns need to be on their toes if they are to deal with the coveys of redlegs streaming over. A welcoming atmosphere and efficiently run by Headkeeper Tony Pearce.

*Shooting acreage*: 5,000
*Status*: Commercial
*Sporting agent*: Ian Coley Sporting, as above
*Headkeeper*: Tony Pearce
*Number of available days*: 35
*Number of drives*: 40 plus
*Bag expectations*: 300-400
*Average cartridge to kill ratio*: 4:1
*Lunch*: Taken in converted barn set on a hill
*Price structure*: £27 per bird plus VAT
*Accommodation*: The Willows, Bettws Hall, nr Newton or local hotels
*Access*: By road: four miles north-west of Craven Arms off A49; By rail: Shrewsbury
*Comments*: Well-controlled dogs welcome

# LINKENHOLT MANOR ESTATE

Linkenholt
Andover
Hampshire

Tel: 01264 737646　　　　　　Fax: 01264 737728 or
　　　　　　　　　　　　　　Fax: 01728 688950

Linkenholt Estate is situated on the North Hampshire Downs and enjoys totally unspoilt countryside, yet it is within easy reach of London. There are 14 days partridge and 16 days pheasant shooting split between a syndicate and let days on a commercial basis. The emphasis is on good quality, sporting birds in a private atmosphere amidst superb surroundings, emphasised by excellent food and wine. All the commercial days are let for the 2003/4 season, but a few single Guns remain in the syndicate.

*Shooting acreage*: 2,500
*Status*: Syndicate and commercial
*Owner*: Trustees of the Herbert and Peter Blagrave Charitable Trust
*Contact*: C.H. Bunbury
*Sporting agent*: N/a
*Headkeeper/staff*: Paul Ashton
*Number of available days*: 15
*Number of drives*: 22
*Bag expectations*: 300
*Average cartridge to kill ratio*: 3.5:1
*Lunch*: Taken at Christopher and Amanda Bunbury's house on the Estate
*Price structure*: £27.00 plus VAT per bird
*Accommodation*: Good local hotels
*Access*: M3, A303 from London, around 2 hours from central London. From Heathrow 1¼ hours.

# LOYTON SHOOT

*LOYTON, MOREBATH, TIVERTON, SOUTH DEVON*

Loyton
Morebath
Tiverton
Devon
EX16 9AS

Tel: 01398 331051          Fax: 01398 331052
shooting@loyton.com          www.loyton.com

The Loyton Shoot has been running in its current format for three years, although it had previously been organised as a private driven pheasant shoot for some 30 years. Nowadays it runs as part private, with a syndicate and lets some days. The atmosphere is still very much that of a private shoot. Located on the southern fringes of Exmoor, the Loyton Shoot takes in approximately 1,500 acres of shooting rights. The classical deep wooded valleys provide high bird shooting of great quality, with birds frequently driven from cover crops sited on the summit of hills. Branching off the principal valleys are several gullies which are used to offer very challenging partridge drives to maintain variety. In all there are some 20 drives to keep the Guns on their toes. Particularly enjoyable are the driven and walked-up black powder days, using vintage hammer and muzzle-loading guns. Bags vary significantly in size but keep the older shooting traditions alive. The keepers, beaters and pickers-up are all ready to assist the Guns.

*Shooting acreage*: 1,500
*Status*: Private, syndicate with let days
*Contact*: Angus Barnes, as above
Keeper/staff: Headkeeper Michael Conachie. Under-keeper Martin Ebworthy
*Number of available days*: 14, including black powder days. Walked-up and rough days also available
*Number of drives*: 20
*Bag expectations*: Driven 100-300
*Average cartridge to kill ratio*: 4:1
*Lunch*: An excellent lunch is taken in the shooting lodge
*Price structure*: £27 per bird plus VAT for driven. Walked-up, rough by arrangement
*Accommodation*: A shooting lodge is currently under construction, which will have up to 14 bedrooms and facilities, so that all Guns can stay there in comfort. This will be in operation by the start of the 2003/4 season.
*Access*: By road: Jct. 27 off M5, then A361 and A396, B3190 to Morebath. By rail: Taunton. By air: Exeter or Bristol.
*Other comments*: Well trained gundogs welcome, also non-shooting guests. There is also a clay shooting ground.

E * 30

## LYNEHAM, SOUTH DEVON

Estate Office
Lyneham
South Devon

Tel: 01752 882253          Fax: 01752 882232

Lyneham is set amidst the most stunning of locations in South Devon. It offers driven pheasant shooting of the very highest quality in an atmosphere that would be difficult to surpass. The owners make every effort to ensure that visiting Guns feel they are taking part in a private family day. The attention to detail from the moment of arrival at the 18th century house is outstanding. Transport is by a 12-seater gun-bus with the host, Damon Harvey, present on all shoot days to make sure that everything runs smoothly with plenty of banter after breathtaking drives such as Brushes Hill, Middle Drive and Balls Wood. If required, the Lyneham loaders are very skilled, patient and helpful. The beating team, led by Headkeeper Dale Hunt, are masters at producing high, challenging pheasants, with a minimum of noise, across the whole line. There is also a very large picking-up team.

*Shooting acreage*: 3,000
*Status*: private with let days
*Owner*: Damon Harvey
*Sporting agent*: N/a
*Headkeeper*: Dale Hunt
*Number of available days*: 7
*Number of drives*: Varies
*Average cartridge to kill ratio*: 4:1
*Lunch*: Taken at Lyneham House at the end of the day in the oak-panelled dining room
*Price structure*: POA
*Accommodation*: Kitley Hotel, Lyneham
*Access*: By road: A38 to Plymouth. By air: Plymouth Airport 15 minutes. Exeter Airport 30 minutes. By rail: Plymouth or Exeter

# MANOR FARM SHOOT

*NORFOLK*

Manor Farm
Common Lane
North Runcton
King's Lynn
Norfolk
PE33 0RF

Tel: 01553 842308                    Fax: 01553 840131

Driven red-legged partridges over hedges from mid-October, moving into pheasants in November. Also woodcock and snipe, but no ground game. This is a small and friendly shoot over some 3,000 acres offering varied shooting and some very sporting birds. There is easy access to most pegs and quad bikes are available for less fit Guns.

*Shooting acreage*: 3,000
*Status*: Syndicate and private shoot with let days.
*Owner*: Mark Fuller
*Contact*: Mark Fuller as above
*Sporting agent*: N/a
*Headkeeper/staff*: Nick Yarham
*Number of available days*: 14
*Number of drives*: 16 in total with 7 or 8 per shoot day
*Bag expectations*: 150-200
*Average cartridge to kill ratio*: 4:1
*Lunch*: Snack provided during day with evening meal in local pub.
*Price structure*: Mixed days £20 per bird. Pheasants £18 per bird.
*Accommodation*: At local hotel, the Arundel Lodge recommended. Tel 01553 810256. Other local accommodation also available.
*Access*: By road: ½ mile from A10. By rail: King's Lynn Station 2 miles. By air: Norwich Airport 45 miles. Transport by arrangement.
*Other comments*: Well-behaved dogs welcome

# MELCOMBE SHOOT

Melcombe
Exford
Somerset, TA24 7LU

Tel: 01643 831439          Fax: 0163 831139
chris@melcombe.com

Founded five years ago, this private-family style shoot is based in the heart of Exmoor. The combes and woods of this region create an opportunity to show constantly challenging birds. This is a traditional country-house shoot and the day is spent in the field with as little use of four-wheel drive vehicles as possible. Good shots, with a strong sense of humour, who enjoy high birds, stunning surroundings and a relaxed ambience will enjoy this day. The beating team does its very best to provide a steady stream of birds in different types of environment to test the technique of the Guns. This is a traditional shoot with an emphasis on enjoyment of the sport. Melcombe puts down pheasants and duck and regularly shoots a numbers of partridges, woodcock and the occasional snipe. Guinea-fowl are also reared to keep the Guns awake.

*Shooting acreage*: 600
*Status*: Private with let days
*Owner*: Melcombe Partners
*Contact*: Chris Kirby, as above
*Headkeeper*: Chris Hayes
*Number of available days*: 16 driven, six walked-up
*Number of drives*: 12
*Bag expectations*: 150-200 birds
*Average cartridge to kill ratio*: 4:1
*Lunch*: Hospitality is offered in the Georgian Rectory main house in front of log fires. Coffee served on arrival with a light hot field lunch mid-day with an opportunity to talk to the keeper and his team. There is a traditional full shoot dinner at the end of the day, using produce grown on the farm – this is usually roast beef and all the trimmings. An extensive drinks cabinet is included in the price.
*Price structure*: £30 per bird inclusive. Walked-up by arrangement.
*Accommodation*: There is a special arrangement with Simonsbath House Hotel to devote the entire hotel to the Guns and friends for any team of six Guns or more. There is a gunroom and drying room, and dogs are welcome plus transport to the shoot to avoid driving.
*Access*: By road: M5 Jct. 25 40 minutes drive. By rail: Taunton Station. By air: Bristol and Exeter Airports
*Other comments*: Fibre wad cartridges preferred. Dogs very welcome. Young Guns also welcome and extra party members included for the day if required. Partners included if trained to the whistle.

# MELLS PARK

Mells Park
Mells
Nr Frome
Somerset
BA11 3QB

Tel: 01373 812412/0208 663 4209
Mobile: 07831 696570          Fax: 0208 663 4307
msamuel@dylon.co.uk

Driven pheasants and partridges over steep valleys with some of the oldest woodland in the country. Mells Park is steeped in history. Once the site of a monastery, there now stands a beautiful Lutyens house, which for 500 years was home to the Horner family, of 'Little Jack' fame. The beautiful park and farmland has a river and ponds for duck flighting and there is easy access to all drives for the pheasant and partridge shooting. With accommodation available in the main house, shooting at Mells Park is an all-round, very enjoyable and interesting experience.

*Shooting acreage*: 1,200
*Status*: Private with a few let days
*Owner*: Trustees of the Mells Park Trust
*Contact*: Michael Samuel
*Sporting agent*: N/a
*Headkeeper/staff*: Chris Mitchell
*Number of available days*: 4
*Number of drives*: Total 20 – 5-6 per day
*Bag expectations*: 250 including partridges and duck
*Average cartridge to kill ratio*: 3:1
*Lunch*: Usually a shoot through day with mid-morning refreshments and lunch served in the Mells Park House dining room at the end of the day.
*Price structure*: Pheasants and partridges: £23 per bird plus VAT; duck £18 per bird plus VAT
*Accommodation*: Dinner, bed and breakfast is available at Mells Park for £110 per night. This does not include alcohol.
*Access*: By road: M3/A303 or M4 - through Frome following signs to Radstock, then turn left for Mells. After 1½ miles turn right sign-posted Mells and Vobster. In two miles Mells Park is on left hand side. By rail: Westbury or Bath Stations. By air: Bristol Airport.
*Other comments*: Although welcome on the shoot, there are no kennelling facilities and dogs are not permitted in the house

# NEW HAINTON SHOOT

## *HAINTON IN THE WOLD, LINCOLNSHIRE*

3 Scarlet Lane
Eagle
Lincoln
LN6 9EJ

Tel: 01522 868930                    Fax: 01522 868930
Mobile: 07887 67650
bwalker65@aol.com

The shoot consists of undulating land set in the Lincolnshire Wolds
and provides quite superb mixed driven shooting for both partridges
and pheasants. There are 25 game cover drives and, in January, a
dozen drives from woodland. Rolling, high banks and carefully sited
game crops ensure that Guns are tested to the utmost. Some 25 years
ago New Hainton was a prestigious shoot, and is now coming back
into its own.

*Shooting acreage*: 5,500
*Status*: Private syndicates with occasional let days
*Owner*: Brian Walker (sporting rights)
*Contact*: Brian Walker
*Sporting agent*: N/a
*Headkeeper/staff*: Headkeeper and beat keepers
*Number of available days*: Only a few days
*Number of drives*: 30 from cover crops, 15 from woodland
*Bag expectations*: 150 –300
*Average cartridge to kill ratio*: 5:1
*Lunch*: 'Elevenses' are taken mid-morning and the Guns shoot through,
with lunch at the end of the day
*Price structure*: £22.50 plus VAT per bird
*Accommodation*: The White Hart at Scarle can accommodate teams
*Access*: By road: A153 Wragby to Louth road

# OAKFORD SHOOT

*NR TIVERTON, DEVON*

Unit 1B
North Mills Trading Estate
Bridport
Dorset DT6 3BE

Tel: 01308 427757         Fax: 01308 427711
brabazonsporting@aol.com

A typical 'high bird' Devon shoot, Oakford consists of a mixture of deep wooded valleys and open country with game crops. Largely driven pheasant shoot, with a few walked-up days, the testing birds across the valleys offer exciting and challenging shooting, and it is fair to say this is not a shoot for novice Guns. Very secluded and tucked away, this is a private shoot which offers superb sport to the experienced Gun. Four-wheel drives are used for shoot access and Guns with a mobility problem can be driven to their pegs. There are also available, in addition to the driven days, small walked-up days for 50-60 head.

*Shooting acreage*: 3,000
*Status*: Private with let days
*Contact*: Steve Thomas
*Sporting agent*: N/a
*Headkeeper/staff*: Alan Hetherington and two beat keepers
*Number of available days*: 20 plus
*Number of drives*: 16
*Bag expectations*: Driven 250-400. Walked-up 50-60 head
*Average cartridge to kill ratio*: 4 to 4.5:1
*Lunch*: Guns can either choose to shoot through or take lunch mid-day in private house. Traditional shoot lunch with emphasis on fine wines
*Price structure*: POA to Steve Thomas
*Accommodation*: Bindon House Hotel at Langford Budville or The Royal Oak, Withypool
*Access*: 20 minutes drive from M5, 45 minutes from Exeter Airport and 25 minutes from Exeter Main Station
*Other comments*: Well-behaved gundogs welcome

---

## NEAR BEAMINSTER, WEST DORSET

33-34 Fore Street
Chudleigh
South Devon
TQ13 0HX

Tel: 01626 854793                    Fax: 01626 854779
Mobile: 07711 215542
richard@westcountry-sporting.co.uk  www.w-s-w.co.uk

The 1,000 acre plus Parnham Shoot, run by the hospitable Bowditch family, is one of Dorset's most renowned shoots, and offers excellent and reasonable pheasant and partridge shooting, in a glorious setting of rolling hills and moderate valleys, dotted with woodland and spinneys. On a clear day there are wonderful views to the coast and Lyme Regis. 4x4 transport is on hand to take the guns to their pegs where necessary.

*Shooting acreage*: 1,000 plus
*Status*: Commercial
*Contact*: Richard Hutcheon
*Sporting agent*: Westcountry Sporting Worldwide
*Headkeeper*: New keeper being appointed
*Number of available days*: 10
*Number of drives*: 20. 4-6 per day
*Bag expectations*: 150-300
*Average cartridge to kill ratio*: 4:1
*Lunch*: Taken in farmhouse, either in the middle of the day, or at the end if Guns prefer. Fare is traditional farmhouse cooking, usually a roast
*Price structure*: £26.50 per bird inclusive
*Accommodation*: Local hotels and inns. The Bridge House Hotel in Beaminster is recommended.
*Access*: By road: 30 minutes from A303, 10 minutes from Dorchester. By rail: Dorchester Station. By air: Bristol or Heathrow. Transport by arrangement.
*Other comments*: Well trained gundogs welcome

# PLUM PARK SHOOT

---

*MAER HALL, MAER, STAFFORDSHIRE*

39 Emery Avenue
Westlands
Newcastle
Staffordshire
ST5 2JG

Tel: 01782 868643                    Fax: 01782 866280
Mobile: 07740 511676

The Shoot is based on and around the picturesque North Staffordshire village of Maer and Maer hall, a Grade II listed building. The Hall and village were visited several times in the 19th century by Charles Darwin who makes mention of the 'autumnal shooting'. The shooting extends to 4,500 acres of rolling countryside, and which includes 500 acres of mature woodland. The Shoot has two syndicates and, in addition, lets a further 35 days. All pheasants are reared on the Estate's own game farm. Currently 25,000 pheasants are released and some 11,000 partridges. Shooting starts at the beginning of September with the partridges through to the end of October. The pheasant shooting then commences and on some drives there is a mixture of pheasants and partridges. All Guns are transported round the shoot in a purpose-built trailer accommodating 15 people.

*Shooting acreage*: 4,500
*Status*: Syndicate with let days
*Shoot managers*: John Bailey and Robert Latham.
*Headkeeper/staff*: Richard Thompson. Underkeepers, L.Huggins, N.Pearcy
*Number of available days*: 35
*Number of drives*: 28
*Bag expectations*: 150 to 500 for 10 Guns mid-season
*Average cartridge to kill ratio*: 4:1
*Lunch*: Coffee/tea is provided when Guns meet with a breakfast roll/bap. It is normal to break for hot soup, coffee and soft drinks with a cold lunch. An evening meal can be provided for an additional £15 per Gun. Non-shooting guests are welcome provided they are booked in and pay a charge of £5 for the lunch and breakfast.
*Price structure*: £24.50 per bird incl. VAT
*Accommodation*: Local award-winning B&Bs or Slaters Country Hotel on the edge of the Shoot. Tel 01782 680052
*Access*: By road: 10 minutes from Jct 16 of M6, and by the A51. By rail: Stoke-on-Trent, Crew or Stafford. By air: East Midlands Airport

---

## POWDERHAM CASTLE, EXETER

Estate Office
Powderham Castle
EX6 8JQ

Tel: 01626 890252       Fax: 01626 890729
castle@powderham.co.uk

Powderham Castle and its surrounding estate have been in the hands of the Courtenay family, Earls of Devon, for over 600 years, and there has been an actively managed shoot for most of the past 100 years or more. Until the 1950s this was purely a private shoot, but was then syndicated and in the past 20 years a few days have been let, mostly in November and December. The land rises from sea-level to 300 feet and the main woods produce high, fast pheasants, the majority from mature woodland. Unlike most West Country shoots, the birds are mostly within range of a normal game gun. Powderham is in the rain shadow of Dartmoor and enjoys an annual rainfall of about 30 inches. Prevailing winds are from the west which benefits many of the drives. Lord Devon normally hosts all let days, and thoroughly enjoys doing so.

*Shooting acreage*: Approximately 4,000
*Status*: Private with syndicate and let days
*Owner*: The Earl of Devon
*Contact*: The Earl of Devon as above or Headkeeper Graham Dunant
*Headkeeper/staff*: Graham Dunant. Two under-keepers
*Number of available days*: 6
*Number of drives*: Three beats with 6-8 drives in each
*Bag expectations*: 250-350
*Average cartridge to kill ratio*: Anything from 3 to 12:1
*Lunch*: Lunch is provided in the Castle
*Price structure*: £7,500 to £12,500 includes lunch. The Estate charges by the day and not on the actual bag. Team of Guns should be eight.
*Accommodation*: Excellent hotel accommodation available locally, but may also be available soon in the Castle
*Access*: By road: M5, Jct 30 six miles away: By rail: Exeter St David's Station eight miles. By air: Exeter Airport eight miles
*Other comments*: 12-bore cartridges in 28 or 39 gms can be supplied. Plastic wads not permitted. Guns can bring own dogs if well trained and allowance will be made for Guns to work their dogs in conjunction with pickers-up. Note that any Gun shooting at Powderham must be a member of the Countryside Alliance and covered by third party insurance. Single guns only are used. There is also a 50p per bird on the estimated bag for the Campaign for Shooting.

# RACECOURSE SHOOT GOODWOOD

## *SINGLETON, CHICHESTER, WEST SUSSEX*

Manor Farm
Singleton
Chichester
West Sussex

Tel 01243 811228                    Fax: 01243 811812

For 100 years Alex Brown's family have lived in the listed flint Jacobean farmhouse, rebuilt in the 1760s. Some 35 years ago, a small syndicate enjoyed quality partridge and pheasants shooting and this has now developed into a thriving commercial shoot, with visitors travelling to enjoy the superb sport, year after year, and many from all over the world. Alex and his team have gained a reputation for being amongst the most professional and well-organised shoots in West Sussex. Notable are drives such as 'Granny's Plantation' and 'Accident Corner Rew' where a jockey was killed during a race in the 18th century. The shoot is spread along the north face of the South Downs, in front of the Racecourse at Goodwood and incorporates four valleys with cover crops on top of the hills. The birds, partridges and pheasants, are to say the least challenging and extremely exciting!

*Shooting acreage*: 1,000
*Status*: Commercial
*Contact*: Alex Brown as above
*Sporting agent*: N/a
*Headkeeper*: Trevor Williams
*Number of available days*: 15 partridges, 15 pheasants
*Number of drives*: Per day pheasants 5/6, partridges 6/7
*Bag expectations*: 300-400
*Average cartridge to kill ratio*: 3:1 to 4:1
*Lunch*: Elevenses are taken in the field and lunch is served at the Farmhouse. Tea for the Guns at the end of shooting.
*Price structure*: £27 per bird plus VAT.
*Accommodation*: The Spread Eagle at Midhurst
*Access*: By road: The farmhouse is on the A286, 6 miles from Midhurst or 7 miles from Chichester. By rail: Chichester. By air: Goodwood Airport 3 miles.

# RAVENSWICK SHOOT

Ravenswick
Kirkbymoorside
York
YO62 7LR

Tel: 01751 432100          Fax: 01751 432215
sportselect@ravenswick.com

The Ravenswick driven pheasant shoot is situated in the picturesque North Yorkshire Moors National Park. The main drives use the 200 feet deep wooded valley with the guns placed beside the meandering River Dove. This 2,000 plus acre shoot provides up to five different days shooting per week. The shoot lunch, which is usually a generous sized roast, is provided in a purpose-built shoot cabin. Although it is a commercial shoot the general atmosphere is more like a syndicate and days can be tailored to guests' requirements. Walking can be reduced if necessary.

*Shooting acreage*: 2,000 plus
*Status*: Commercial
*Owner*: James Holt
*Sporting agent*: Julian Boddy, Sportselect Ltd
*Headkeeper/staff*: Stephen Todd + 3 underkeepers
*Number of available days*: On application
*Number of drives*: 33
*Bag expectations*: 200-500
*Average cartridge to kill ratio*: 4.5-5
*Lunch*: Two-course lunch and drinks provided in purpose-built shoot room.
*Price structure*: POA per bird shot
*Accommodation*: By arrangement at 'Ravenswick' or in various hotels and B&Bs
*Access*: By road: via A170. By rail: York Station. By air: Leeds, Tees-side or Newcastle Airports.

# SANDON SHOOT

*STAFFORDSHIRE*

Moat House
Church Lane
Sandon
Staffordshire
ST18 0DB

Tel: 01889 508417                    Fax: 01889 508417
kc.butler@virgin.net

This extensive driven pheasant shoot comprises largely arable, sheep and dairy country. The land tends to be undulating and birds are shot from mature woodland and game crops of maize and kale. Guns eat at the Headkeeper's house. The Sandon Shoot aims to make Guns feel that they are very welcome. Every effort is made to create a syndicate or private day approach to the sport. Gundogs can also be brought, but they are expected to be well-behaved. While the majority of the days are driven, walked-up shooting is also in popular demand.

*Shooting acreage*: Approximately 5,000
*Status*: Commercial with all let days
*Owner*: Sandon Pheasants Ltd. Address as above
*Contact*: Ken Butler, as above
*Headkeeper/staff*: Headkeeper and three underkeepers
*Number of available days*: 60 assorted days
*Number of drives*: 6 to 7 per day
*Bag expectations*: 50 – 300
*Gun/cartridge recommendations*: Standard game loads. Minimum 20-bore
*Average cartridge to kill ratio*: 4:1
*Lunch*: Lunch and drinks provided, but only for days above 150 birds
*Price structure*: Partridges £25 plus VAT. Pheasants £25 plus VAT
*Accommodation*: Local hotels can be arranged. Guns frequently use the Crown Hotel, Stone, Stafford, near Jct. 14 of the M6
*Access*: By road: 2 miles from M6 Jct.14; By rail: Stafford Station three miles. By air: Midway between Manchester and Birmingham Airports
*Other comments*: Well-behaved gundogs welcome

# SCHOLTZ & CO LIMITED

*STOUR VALLEY, SUFFOLK*

70 Little Yeldham Rd
Little Yeldham
Halstead
Essex
CO9 4LN

Tel: 01787 238482          Fax: 01787 237068
Mobile: 07771 703858
info@scholtzandco.co.uk          www.scholtzandco.co.uk

Scholtz & Co is a sporting agent for traditional driven partridge and pheasant shooting over four to six estates in the heart of Constable country (Stour Valley). The company organises corporate days, syndicate shooting, and private with let days and will also arrange accommodation in country-style hotels. Shooting starts in September with partridges, followed by mixed bag days. Partridges are mainly driven off rolling hills, and pheasants over woodland and hedgerows. There is easy access to all drives with little walking involved. Some of the estates also feature duck flighting over lakes and the Company can also offer stalking for roe, fallow and muntjac for those interested. Partners who do not wish to shoot can wander the streets of picturesque Long Melford, Clare and Lavenham, browsing the abundant antique shops.

*Shooting acreage*: Over 4 to 6 estates in Suffolk
*Status*: Corporate, syndicate and private with let days
*Owner*: Scholtz & Co Limited
*Contact*: Jan Scholtz
*Sporting agent*: N/a
*Number of available days*: 20 to 40
*Number of drives*: 5-6 per day
*Bag expectations*: 200 – 250 birds
*Average cartridge to kill ratio*: Varies considerably by location and ability
*Lunch*: Morning coffee, lunch, wine and beverages included
*Price structure*: Average £22.50 per bird
*Accommodation*: A variety of country hotels and local pubs available in the area. Particular recommendation is The Swan at Lavenham
*Access*: By road: Full directions can be obtained from Jan Scholtz depending upon the venue. By rail: Stow Market or Ipswich Stations. By air: Stansted Airport. Courtesy transport available from rail and airports
*Other comments*: Gundogs welcome

# SHERBORNE CASTLE HOME SHOOT

*NORTH DORSET*

Digby Estate Office
9 Cheap Street
Sherborne
Dorset
DT9 3PY

Tel: 01935 813182
william@sherbornecastle.com

Fax: 01935 816727
www.sherbornecastle.com

There are two shoots at Sherborne Castle, the Home Shoot and the Honeycombe Shoot. The Home Shoot is situated to the south of the attractive and historic small town of Sherborne in North Dorset. The Estate has been in the Ownership of the Digby family for some 400 years. This Shoot is based in, and around, the superb park at Sherborne Castle with views of the Castle, the Lake and the Deer Park. Guns meet in front of the lovely 18th century stables. It is driven pheasant shooting only at the present time, quite a bit of it in woodland, over undulating countryside between the 60 metre and 130 metre contours.

*Shooting acreage*: Covers approximately 7,000 acres of the Estate for both shoots
*Status*: Private with let days
*Owner*: Mr J.K. Wingfield Digby trading as Sherborne Castle Estates
*Contact*: Mr William Beveridge as above
*Headkeeper/staff*: Ken Day.
*Number of available days*: 10 let days
*Bag expectations*: 150 – 250
*Average cartridge to kill ratio*: 4:1
*Lunch*: Either in the middle of the day, or if Guns shoot through, at the end of the day in a small lodge in the Deer Park. Drinks provided and tea at the end of the day.
*Price structure*: £24 plus VAT per bird (lunch included)
*Accommodation*: Plumber Manor, Sturminster Newton. Tel: 01258 472507
*Access*: Approximately nine miles south-west off the A303 at Wincanton, Somerset. Rail to Sherborne (Waterloo/Exeter line). Air: Bournemouth, Exeter, Bristol. All around one hour
*Other comments*: Well trained gundogs welcome and Guns welcome to bring their own transport

# SHERBORNE CASTLE HONEYCOMBE SHOOT

Digby Estate Office
9 Cheap Street
Sherborne
Dorset
DT9 3PY

Tel: 01935 813182                     Fax: 01935 816727
william@sherbornecastle.com           www.sherbornecastle.com

There are two shoots at Sherborne Castle, the Honeycombe Shoot and
the Home Shoot. The Honeycombe Shoot is to the west of the Castle,
and to the south of the attractive and historic small town of Sherborne
in North Dorset. The Estate has been in the Ownership of the Digby
family for some 400 years. This shoot is set along a wooded
escarpment with magnificent views over the Yeo Valley. There is a fair
amount of woodland shooting, and although the sport mainly centres
on driven pheasants, there are also partridges and duck. Many of the
let days are to repeat clients, some of whom have been shooting at
Sherborne for many years.

*Shooting acreage*: Approximately 7,000
*Status*: Syndicate with let days
*Owner*: Mr J.K.Wingfield Digby trading as Sherborne Castle Estates
*Contact*: Mr William Beveridge as above
*Headkeeper/staff*: Mike Appleby
*Number of available days*: 8
*Number of drives*: 12
*Bag expectations*: 150 –250
*Average cartridge to kill ratio*: 4:1
*Lunch*: Either in the middle of the day or, if Guns shoot through, at the end
of the day in a small lodge in the Deer Park
*Price structure*: £24 plus VAT per bird
*Accommodation*: Plumber Manor, Sturminster Newton. Tel: 01258 472507
*Access*: Sherborne Castle is approximately 9 miles south-west off A303 at
Wincanton, Somerset. Main station at Sherborne (Waterloo/Exeter line) and
air at Bournemouth, Exeter, Bristol, all around one hour's drive
*Other comments*: Well trained gundogs welcome. Transport provided for
Guns

# SOUTHILL ESTATE

## BIGGLESWADE, BEDFORDSHIRE

The Estate Office
Southill Park
Southill
Biggleswade
Bedfordshire
SG18 9LJ

Tel: 01462 813209           Fax: 01462 812235
enquiries@southillestate.co.uk

This is a private, family-run shoot offering both driven pheasants and partridges within easy access of London. The shooting is over game covers and woodland drives which provide a varied combination of sport, and the dedicated Southill Park team work hard to ensure an enjoyable day for all. A 4x4 shoot vehicle is provided to transport the Guns, although limited walking over relatively easy terrain is required on some drives. Southill House is Edwardian and sits in 800 acres of parkland, which together with the 30 acre lake provides the perfect setting for this well-run shoot.

*Shooting acreage*: 3,500
*Status*: Private with let days
*Owner*: The Southill Estate
*Contact*: The Estate Office as above
*Sporting agent*: N/a
*Headkeeper/staff*: 1 Headkeeper and 2 underkeepers
*Number of available days*: 4
*Number of drives*: 25 in total (6 per day)
*Bag expectations*: Between 200-300 (by request)
*Average cartridge to kill ratio*: not known
*Lunch*: Lunch is provided in the dedicated shoot room adjoining Southill House. A typical shooting lunch is provided with alcohol included. Tea is also provided at the end of the day. Lunch can be served at the end of the day if a 'shoot through' is requested. If more than 10 people require lunch there is an additional charge of £20 per person
*Price structure*: £21.00 per bird plus VAT
*Accommodation*: There are local pubs and hotels in the area and recommendations can be given on request
*Access*: By road: A1 10 mins or M1 20 mins. By rail: Biggleswade Station. By air: Luton Airport
*Other comments*: Partners and gundogs are very welcome

St George's House
29 St George's Road
Cheltenham
Gloucestershire
GL50 3DU

Tel: 01242 514478                    Fax: 01242 224697
info@coley.co.uk                     www.coley.co.uk

The rolling, undulating Warwickshire countryside and the high hedges on the Spernal Park Shoot lend themselves to traditional partridge shooting. In addition, there is also excellent driven pheasant shooting, making use of woodland coverts and game crops. This is a shoot with a deserved reputation for thoroughly sporting birds presented by a team who know their business. The shoot adheres to the amiable traditions of the classic game shoot.

*Shooting acreage*: 5,000 plus
*Status*: Commercial
*Sporting agent*: Ian Coley Sporting, as above
*Headkeeper*: Peter Chattaway
*Number of available days*: 35
*Number of drives*: 30 plus
*Bag expectations*: 300-400
*Average cartridge to kill ratio*: 3:1
*Lunch*: Lunch is taken in Spernal House
*Price structure*: £27 per bird plus VAT
*Accommodation*: Exclusive accommodation in Spernal House
*Access*: By road: Just off the A435 near Studley; By rail: Stratford-upon-Avon Station
*Other comments*: Well-behaved dogs welcome

# STANWAY SHOOT

## *GLOUCESTERSHIRE*

St George's House
29 St George's Road
Cheltenham
Gloucestershire
GL50 3DU

Tel: 01242 514478               Fax: 01242 224697
info@coley.co.uk                www.coley.co.uk

Those Guns who know their shooting and have been there, generally agree that the Stanway Shoot can be counted as one of Gloucestershire's finest driven pheasant shoots. Set on the edge of the Cotswold escarpment, the steep sides and deep valleys lend themselves ideally to showing high, classical driven birds. There is a small number of partridges, but the pheasants can be guaranteed to test the skills of the most accomplished shots. A friendly shoot which captures the atmosphere of a private day.

*Shooting acreage*: 2,000
*Status*: Commercial
*Sporting agent*: Ian Coley Sporting, as above
*Headkeeper*: Philip Smith
*Number of available days*: 15
*Number of drives*: 20 plus
*Bag expectations*: 300-400
*Average cartridge to kill ratio*: 4:1
*Lunch*: The shoot has a reputation for an excellent luncheon taken in a recently converted stable. Lunches and puddings 'like mother used to make'.
*Price structure*: £27 per bird plus VAT
*Accommodation*: Many of the classic Cotswold Country House hotels are within a 10 mile radius
*Access*: By road: M5, Jct. 10; By rail: Cheltenham Station; By air: Gloucester Airport
*Comments*: Well-controlled dogs welcome

# STOCKS DOWN FARM SHOOT

*BETWEEN PETERSFIELD AND WINCHESTER, HANTS.*

St George's House
29 St George's Road
Cheltenham
Gloucestershire
GL50 3DU

Tel: 01242 514478                    Fax: 01242 224697
info@coley.co.uk                     www.coley.co.uk

Stocks Down Farm Shoot represents a classic Hampshire driven pheasant shoot with wooded slopes, valleys and although a relatively new shoot is already showing considerable promise. Very good quality birds are shown by keeper Rodney Rowell and his team. This shoot is run by Bruce Faulds, father of Richard Faulds, the Olympic Gold Medallist.

*Shooting acreage*: 750
*Status*: Private with let days
*Sporting agent*: Ian Coley Sporting, as above
*Headkeeper*: Rodney Rowell
*Number of available days*: 10
*Number of drives*: 12
*Bag expectations*: 150-200
*Average cartridge to kill ratio*: 3:1
*Lunch*: Lunch taken in local hotel
*Price structure*: £25 per bird plus VAT
*Accommodation*: Local hotels
*Access*: By road: M3, Jct. 9 and then off A272. By rail: Winchester Station. By air: Southampton
*Comments*: Well-controlled dogs welcome

# STOKE EDITH SHOOT

*NR HEREFORD*

St George's House
29 St George's Road
Cheltenham
Gloucestershire
GL50 3DU

Tel: 01242 514478                    Fax: 01242 224697
info@coley.co.uk                     www.coley.co.uk

The well-known Stoke Edith Shoot is largely a driven pheasant shoot supplemented by some partridges. This is a countryside of rolling hills clad with woodland, copses and valleys. This ideal shooting terrain, assisted by well-sited game crops, ensures that teams of Guns enjoy some really challenging sport over an extensive acreage.

*Shooting acreage*: 5,000
*Status*: Commercial
*Sporting agent*: Ian Coley Sporting, as above
*Headkeeper*: Chris Walker
*Number of available days*: 30
*Number of drives*: 40 plus
*Bag expectations*: 300
*Average cartridge to kill ratio*: 3.5:1
*Lunch*: Taken in Stoke Edith House
*Price structure*: £25 plus VAT
*Accommodation*: Local hotels
*Access*: By road: Off the A438 between Ledbury and Hereford. By rail: Hereford and Ledbury Stations.
*Comments*: Well-controlled dogs welcome

*HAWKENDON, NR BURY ST EDMONDS, SUFFOLK*

Rectory Bungalow
Depden
Bury St Edmunds
Suffolk
IP29 4BU

Tel: 01284 850512                    Mobile: 07876 203997

Driven pheasants over 4,000 acres of undulating countryside with mature woodland. Swan's Hall dates back to the 14th century and is surrounded by farmland with a lake in its centre. This is a friendly, informal sporting shoot with an excellent reputation, offering value for money with good quality birds, including some partridges, duck and woodcock. The shoot also offers walk-up days, beat and shoot for 18 guns as well as its standard driven days, which now includes one Ladies day during the season. No ground game permitted.

*Shooting acreage*: 4,000
*Status*: Commercial.
*Owner*: Suffolk Sporting Ltd.
*Contact*: Mrs Sue Mabbett
*Sporting agent*: N/a
*Headkeeper*: Mrs Sue Mabbett
*Number of available days*: 6 driven, 14 walk-and-stand
*Number of drives*: 10 on any day out of total 25
*Bag expectations*: 100 bird driven days. Walk-and-stand average 60 birds.
*Average cartridge to kill ratio*: 4:1
*Lunch*: Hot meal provided on site. Breakfast on arrival if requested.
*Price structure*: Driven day for 9 Guns £235 per Gun. Walk-and-stand £95 per Gun.
*Accommodation*: Local B&B or 4 star Bell Hotel in Claire
*Access*: By road: Off A143. By rail: 12 miles from Bury St Edmunds station. By air: one hour from Stansted Airport. Pick up available from airport or station.
*Other comments*: Well-behaved dogs welcome.

# THE ARUNDELL ARMS HOTEL

*NR LIFTON, DEVON*

Lifton
Devon
PL16 0AA

Tel: 01566 784666
reservations@arundellarms.com

Fax: 01566 784494
www.arundellarms.com

A variety of driven pheasant days on neighbouring well-known estates ranging from 125 to 300 bird days. Birds are exceptionally high due to steep wooded valleys. Complete parties of six to eight Guns preferred, but smaller parties can sometimes be accommodated. Walked-up, small driven days and duck flighting are offered from late October to January 31 for parties of six to eight Guns. These consist of a mixture of pheasant, duck, pigeon, woodcock and snipe. An evening's duck flighting is an optional extra.

*Status*: Sporting Hotel
*Owner*: The Arundell Arms Hotel
*Contact*: Anne Voss-Bark
*Sporting agent*: N/a
*Number of available days*: Throughout the relevant season
*Bag expectations*: Varies enormously according to experience of the Guns
*Lunch*: Informally in hotel bar, at conveniently sited inn or on the Shoot premises
*Price structure*: Driven pheasants: £25 to £35 per bird shot, including lunch and VAT (where applicable). Walk-up days and duck flighting: £150 per Gun per day, including light lunch and evening's duck flighting if required.
*Accommodation*: The Arundell Arms Hotel, a former coaching inn, is on the Cornwall/Devon border. It has a three AA-rosetted restaurant with three Master Chefs. All rooms have private bathrooms or showers, colour TV and direct dial phones.
*Access*: By road: half a mile off the A30, midway between Dartmoor and Bodmin. By rail: Exeter Station. By air: Exeter or Newquay. Transport by arrangement.
*Other comments*: Shooting clients must have third part-indemnity to £1 million. Written assurance is required before joining a shoot. Also, automatic shotguns are not allowed. Well-behaved dogs are welcome in the hotel and on most of the shoots.

# THE BURGATE SHOOT

## BURGATE AND REDGRAVE, SUFFOLK

Waveney Water Gardens
Park Road
Diss
Norfolk IP22 3AS

Tel: 01379 642697

Situated on the Norfolk/Suffolk border, the Burgate Shoot is close to Diss in Norfolk. The shoot provides some excellent driven partridge shooting over undulating farmland and in January good pheasants over woodland rides and cover strips of maize and millet. Little walking is required on this exceptionally friendly shoot, which offers sporting birds. Shoot days begin at the Park Hotel, Diss, with all transport provided for the Guns.

*Shooting acreage*: 2,500
*Status*: Commercial
*Shoot manager*: David Laughlin
*Contact*: David Laughlin
*Sporting agent*: N/a
*Headkeeper/staff*: D.I.Borley
*Number of available days*: 20
*Number of drives*: 18 total – 7 per day
*Bag expectations*: 150 to 200
*Average cartridge to kill ratio*: 3:1
*Lunch*: Lunch is served on the farm in the shoot lodge
*Price structure*: £18 per bird
*Accommodation*: The Park Hotel, Diss, offer special rates for Guns
*Access*: By road: All and A14. By rail: Diss station. By air: Norwich Airport. Transport available on request.
*Other comments*: Well-behaved dogs welcome

# THE FARLEY HALL SHOOT

*BERKSHIRE*

Estate Office
Farley Hall
Castle Road
Farley Hill
Reading
RG7 1UL

Tel: 01189 730047        Fax: 01189 730385
markr@farleyfarms.co.uk

The Estate is centred round Farley Hall, a Grade 1 listed house dating from 1729. It is surrounded by 1,800 acres of mixed farmland, bordered on three sides by tributaries of the Thames (Whitewater, Blackwater and Loddon). The Estate has hills in the centre with more open areas containing ancient woodlands nearer the rivers. The shoot comprises 25 drives of well-presented pheasants, and is professionally run to offer reasonable birds on exciting drives. Though the shoot would not be able to match the high birds of Devon, the location of Farley Hall makes it very attractive, being only 45 miles from London

*Shooting acreage*: 1,750
*Status*: Private with let days
*Owner*: Rt Hon Viscount Bearsted t/a Farley Estate
*Contact*: Mark Robins, Estate Manager as above
*Sporting agent*: N/a
*Headkeeper*: John Gamblen (Headkeeper) Keith West (Under-keeper)
*Number of available days*: 16
*Number of drives*: 25
*Bag expectations*: 120-250
*Average cartridge to kill ratio*: 3.5:1
*Lunch*: Taken in shoot dining room at Farley Hall. Tea, coffee, biscuits on arrival, followed by mid-morning break for soup and sausages. There is then a break for lunch with departure after tea and cake.
*Price structure*: £2- £25 plus VAT per bird
*Accommodation*: Available at Farley Hall. All rooms have their own bathrooms, the majority en-suite. Price in the region of £200 - £250 per head and £75 for partners for bed, breakfast and evening meal. All prices exclusive of VAT
*Access*: M4, Junct.11, then A33, or M3, Junct. 6, A33. Reading Station 6 miles. London Heathrow 40 minutes via M4
*Other comments*: Well trained gundogs welcome

# THE FAWLEY COURT SHOOT

Fawley Court Farm
Henley-on-Thames
Oxfordshire
RG9 3AH

Tel: 01494 715540                     Fax: 01494 715403
Mobile: 07770 868448
phil@tudorcourtgundogs.co.uk

The 1,000 acre Fawley Court Shoot is small and informal with the aim of organising relaxed days. Up to 10 species can be shot on any given day and the shoot is situated beside the Thames with some 30 pools and ponds dotted throughout lovely wooded valleys. Bag includes pheasants, red and grey partridges, snipe, woodcock, duck and geese.

*Shooting acreage*: 1,000
*Status*: Commercial, syndicate with private let days
*Owner*: Philip Hopper
*Contact*: Philip Hopper
*Sporting agent*: N/a
*Number of available days*: 20
*Number of drives*: Total 20 – 5-6 per day
*Bag expectations*: Anything up to 300 bird days
*Average cartridge to kill ratio*: Not known
*Lunch*: Local pub on driven days
*Price structure*: With such a variety of species price depends on the requirements of the client.
*Accommodation*: Variety of local B&Bs, pubs and hotels to suit requirements.
*Access*: Very easy to find on the A4155. One mile from Henley town centre
*Other comments*: Well-behaved dogs welcome

# THE GLEMHAM HALL ESTATE SHOOT

*LITTLE GLEMHAM, WOODBRIDGE, EAST SUFFOLK*

Glemham Hall
Little Glemham
Woodbridge
Suffolk IP13 0BT

Tel: 01728 746219          Fax: 01728 746704
hopecobbold@btinternet.co.uk

This is a typical undulating attractive rural East Suffolk landscape, close to the Heritage coast. The shooting is from woodland, coverts, game cover, hedgerows, fields and the Alde River valley, and game will include pheasants, partridges, woodcock and duck. Guns should be experienced, observing the recognised etiquette, sportsmanship and safety in the shooting field, and be a member of one of the major organisations representing field sports and conservation. Collections/sweeps are held for the organisations. The estate abides by 'The Code of Good Shooting Practice' and aims to produce challenging shooting. All Guns travel in the well-fitted gamecart, and any camp followers may need to share their own 4wd transport, depending on numbers. Guns must possess valid Shotgun Certificates, Game Licences and Liability Insurance cover. Overseas visitors must be in possession of visitors' certificates.

*Shooting acreage*: 2,800
*Status*: Private with let days
*Owner*: Major Philip Hope-Cobbold
*Contact*: As above
*Headkeeper/staff*: Andrew Bayfield. Under-keeper Pat Gilbert
*Number of available days*: 16
*Number of drives*: 5 or 6 per day
*Bag expectations*: 180 but can be tailored
*Average cartridge to kill ratio*: 3:1
*Lunch*: Lunch normally taken at 1pm in the magnificent dining room in the Hall inclusive of drinks. Shooting through for late lunch available.
*Price structure*: £4,100 plus VAT for team of 8-10 Guns. Excess game over 185 by arrangement at £22.50 plus VAT per head. Any extra guests for lunch at £16 plus VAT.
*Accommodation*: Seckford Hall Hotel, Woodbridge (8 miles) tel: 01394 385678. Brudenell Hotel, Aldeburgh (10 miles), tel. 01728 452071. Crown Hotel, Framlingham (6 miles), tel. 01728 723521.
*Access*: The Hall is an imposing red-brick mansion in parkland, clearly visible from directional signs off the A12 between Woodbridge and Saxmundham. By road: London 3 hours, Cambridge 1½ hours. By rail: London Liverpool Street Station – Ipswich (1 hour) plus taxi ½ hour. By air: Stansted plus taxi (2 hours). Ferry: Harwich (1½ hours), follow A120/A12 (n)
*Other comments*: Well-behaved gundogs welcome, as are well trained partners of Guns! Ladies, mixed or young shots, more than welcome.

# THE HOAR EDGE SHOOT

Teal Sports UK
53 Hermitage Road
Saughall
Chester
CH1 6AQ

Tel: 01244 880553                    Mobile: 07971 445329

Walked-up and part driven over 1,000 acres. The Hoar Edge Shoot comprises a steep, wild marshy valley with good holding and is excellent for both woodcock, snipe and pheasants. Guns should be able to walk reasonable distances, approx 4 to 5 miles per day, to enjoy good rough shooting. Ideal for parties who like to work their own dogs.

*Shooting acreage*: 1,000
*Status*: Private with let days
*Contact*: Geoff Hewitt,
*Sporting agent*: N/a
*Number of available days*: 5-10
*Number of drives*: 4 -5 walk-ups
*Bag expectations*: 30-40 mixed bag consisting of woodcock, pheasants, snipe and duck..
*Average cartridge to kill ratio*: 4:1 dependent upon Gun's ability
*Lunch*: Served either in the farmhouse or in good weather a picnic can be arranged
*Price structure*: From £100 per Gun per day. Single Guns accepted, though prefer small parties of six Guns.
*Accommodation*: Local hotels or B&Bs
*Access*: By road: M54/M6 approx 30 minutes. By rail: Shrewsbury Station
*Other comments*: Well-behaved dogs are very welcome

# THE RIPLEY CASTLE SHOOT

*RIPLEY, NR HARROGATE, NORTH YORKSHIRE*

The Old Hall
Burton Leonard
Nr Harrogate,
North Yorkshire HG3 3SE

Tel: 01423 322370 (day)            Fax: 01423 324334 (day)
Tel: 01765 677343 (evening)        Fax: 01765 677861 (evening)
info@ripleycastleshoot.co.uk

The Ripley Castle driven pheasant shoot covers the Ripley Castle Estate, the Hob Green Estate, the Nidd Beat of the Nidd Estate and other areas leased from neighbouring farmers. The main drives are all classic as, historically, the estates were landscaped and woodlands planted to produce good quality birds. The mature woodlands and lakes make excellent use of the many natural contours which are an attractive part of the Estate. The birds are well presented and are generally of a good to a very good standard, with a number of drives being noted for producing very testing birds. Although the actual shooting is important to the Guns, as today there is more than enough pressure and stress, the main priority on the day is for Guns to enjoy themselves. So far there have been no complaints!

*Shooting acreage*: 7,000
*Status*: Private offering shooting for individual Guns, small parties and full Corporate days
*Owner*: Frank Boddy (leaseholder)
*Contact*: Frank Boddy
*Headkeeper*: Stephen Jackson assisted by three beat-keepers and two part-time keepers
*Number of available days*: 52
*Number of drives*: 60
*Bag expectations*: 125, 200 and 300 bird days. The shoot normally averages 10 per cent over the bag each day
*Average cartridge to kill ratio*: 2.9:1
*Lunch*: Taken in The Boar's Head Hotel or The Hob Green Hotel, stopping for lunch early season and shooting through from early November onwards
*Price structure*: POA
*Accommodation*: The Boar's Head, Ripley. Tel: 01423 771888 and The Hob Green Hotel, Markington. Tel: 01423 770031. Both hotels are award-winning and on the shoot. Special rates have been arranged for shoot guests.
*Access*: Ripley Village is on the edge of the Dales, 10 mins drive from Harrogate, 40 mins from York and 30 mins from Leeds/Bradford Airport
*Other comments*: Well trained gundogs very welcome. Guns can bring loaders or one can be arranged. All guns cleaned at end of the day and a brace of dressed game is available to each Gun.

# THE STEVENTON ESTATE

Litchfield Grange
South Litchfield
Overton
Hampshire
RG25 3BN

Tel: 01256 771740            Fax: 01256 770657

The Steventon Estate is within one hour of Central London in a convenient area of rolling Hampshire farmland. The Estate provides 15 days shooting most of which are filled by repeat bookings. However, from time to time a vacancy arises. It is recognised by local syndicates and agents as providing a welcoming atmosphere in an attractive area of countryside. The emphasis is on surprisingly high-flying sporting pheasants and a few partridges in a relaxed and informal environment. This is typified by lunch in the family house, with log fires etc, and transport for the shoot is usually in a tractor and trailer.

*Shooting acreage*: 1,250
*Status*: Syndicate and let days
*Owner*: Peter Harrison
*Contact*: Peter Harrison as above
*Sporting agent*: N/a
*Headkeeper/staff*: Keith Roe
*Number of available days*: two or three
*Number of drives*: 12
*Bag expectations*: November/December 200-250; January 150
*Average cartridge to kill ratio*: 3.5 : 1
*Lunch*: Taken at home in Litchfield Grange
*Price structure*: £24.50 +VAT per bird, to include coffee, elevenses, lunch and tea
*Accommodation*: Various local hotels
*Access*: By road: Just off A303 by Popham Aerodrome – maps available on request. By rail: Micheldever Station
*Other comments*: Well trained gundogs welcome

# THE TARRANT SHOOT

*BLANDFORD FORUM, DORSET*

33-34 Fore Street
Chudleigh
South Devon
TQ13 0HX

Tel: 01626 854793         Fax: 01626 854779
Mobile: 07711 215542
richard@westcountry-sporting.co.uk    www.w-s-w.co.uk

The Tarrant Shoot is a well-known quality driven partridge and pheasant shoot set amidst typical central Dorset undulating countryside. The September downland red-legged partridge shooting comes highly recommended and invariably provides top quality sport. The pheasant shooting begins in mid-October, with birds driven from woodland and game cover.

*Shooting acreage*: 1,000 plus
*Status*: Syndicate with let days
*Sporting agent*: Westcountry Sporting Worldwide
*Contact*: Richard Hutcheon
*Number of available days*: 8
*Number of drives*: 20. 4-6 per day
*Bag expectations*: 200-400
*Average cartridge to kill ratio*: 3.5:1
*Lunch*: Lunch is served in the shooting lodge on the estates, either in the middle of the day or, if Guns prefer, at the end of the day's sport
*Price structure*: £26 per bird inclusive
*Accommodation*: Good hotels and inns locally available. The Anvil at Purton is recommended.
*Access*: By road: A303 to Blandford Forum. By rail: Blandford Forum Station. By air: Bournemouth. Transport by arrangement
*Other comments*: Well trained gundogs are welcome

## CHUDLEIGH, SOUTH DEVON

Ugbrooke Park
Chudleigh
South Devon
TQ13 0AD

Tel: 01626 852179          Fax: 01626 853322
ugbrooke@ugbrooke.fq.co.uk

Ugbrooke Park was landscaped by 'Capability' Brown during the period 1760 to 1780, while at the same time Robert Adams built the mock mediaeval castle. Delightful, deep valleys lie alongside the glorious naturally undulating countryside, typical of the West Country. Three lakes totalling 12.5 acres and five other ponds within the estate provide ideal settings for mallard, and the sight of high pheasants mingling with challenging duck offers shooting of a very high and testing character.

*Shooting acreage*: 1,500
*Status*: Private with let days and let shooting week-ends
*Owner*: Ugbrooke Enterprises
*Contact*: Lord Clifford, as above
*Sporting agent*: N/a
*Headkeeper/staff*: Alan Easterbrook
*Number of available days*: 15
*Number of drives*: 15 - 6 per day
*Bag expectations*: As requested. Recommend 250-350 birds
*Average cartridge to kill ratio*: 3:1
*Lunch*: Taken in the main dining room in Ugbrooke House
*Price structure*: Long week-end shoot, including black tie dinner Friday and Saturday and two 350 bird days, from Thursday night dinner to Sunday breakfast is £3,722 per Gun or £4,551 per Gun and wife. Short week-end shoot with one day's 350 bird shoot £2,003 per Gun or £2542 per Gun and wife. Single day shoot for team of eight Guns £32 per bird plus £35 per person for shooting lunch. Birds shot in excess of reserved bag charged at £32 per bird. Loaders are provided and do not expect tips. Hot soup and sloe gin after second drive.
*Accommodation*: 14 en-suite bedroom/bathrooms
*Access*: Exeter Airport 20 minutes drive. Exeter Abbot Station 15 minutes drive. Three minutes from A380 dual carriageway.
*Other comments*: No let days in January. Nine Guns maximum, seven minimum

# WASING PARK SHOOT

*NR READING, BERKSHIRE*

Estate Office, Wasing Park
Aldermaston
Nr Reading
Berkshire
RG7 4NG

Tel: 0118 9714140          Fax: 0118 9713251
ptodd@simmonsandsons.com

The shooting, both driven and walked-up, takes place over the extensive Wasing Estate, which includes 1,000 acres of woodland, eight miles of river, 80 acres of lakes as well as a great deal of low-lying wet and marshy areas. The topography, as far as shooting is concerned, is some of the best in Berkshire and ensures a day that will be mainly based on pheasants with some partridges and duck, with the chance of woodcock, snipe and geese. Variety and top quality sport are the watchwords. Apart from the driven and walked-up shooting, there is an opportunity for evening duck flighting for teams of up to six Guns on selected lakes and ponds. No bag guarantees but variety is a speciality. Separate all duck days, with a mixture of reared and wild, can also be organised. In addition, Wasing is offering 'Wasing Wild Days' for a minimum of eight Guns. This is old-fashioned rough shooting with a variety of game.

*Shooting acreage*: 3,000
*Status*: Commercial
*Owner*: T.J.S.Dugdale
*Contact*: Patrick Todd as above
*Headkeeper*: One Headkeeper, one under-keeper
*Number of available days*: 10 let days, 30-40 walked-up days
*Number of drives*: Numerous
*Bag expectations*: Up to 300 for let days, minimum 200. Walked-up 50
*Average cartridge to kill ratio*: 3:1
*Lunch*: Taken in the house for let days. Lunch not included for walked-up days, but taken in The Hind's Head, the best local pub in the area
*Price structure*: £26.50 plus VAT per bird for let days. Walked-up £140 plus VAT per person. Evening duck flighting £50 per person for up to six Guns. All duck days £20 per bird for 50 birds
*Accommodation*: Can be arranged locally if required. Good selection of hotels.
*Access*: Close to the M4. London 50 miles away. Mainline station at Reading. Airport: Heathrow/Gatwick
*Other comments*: Well trained dogs welcome

# WATERCOMBE SHOOT

*NR CORNWOOD, SOUTH DEVON*

Westcountry Sporting Worldwide
33-34 Fore Street
Chudleigh
South Devon
TQ13 0HX

Tel: 01626 854793                    Fax: 01626 854779
Mobile: 07711 215542
richard@westcountry-sporting.co.uk  www.w-s-w.co.uk

This is a quality high bird driven pheasant shoot over 1,000 plus acres of delightful Devon countryside and, in conjunction with a most generous host, offers excellent value for money. The steep, wooded banks and deep valleys create shooting very similar to that found on the Exmoor shoots. Owned by one of the leading game shots in the Country, the Watercombe Shoot and its sport reflect his ability. Not perhaps an ideal shoot for beginners or the less experienced.

*Shooting acreage*: 1000 plus
*Status*: Private with let days
*Sporting agent*: Richard Hutcheon
*Headkeeper*: Ian Conachie
*Number of available days*: 10
*Number of drives*: 20. 3-6 per day
*Bag expectations*: 150-400
*Average cartridge to kill ratio*: 4.5:1
*Lunch*: Taken in the shoot lodge. Guns can shoot through or choose to have lunch in the middle of the day.
*Price structure*: £26.50 per bird inclusive
*Accommodation*: Excellent local hotels and pubs available
*Access*: 30 minutes from Exeter, south on A38. By rail: Exeter or Plymouth Station. By air: Exeter and Plymouth. Transport by arrangement.
*Other comments*: Well trained gundogs welcome

# WESTON PARK – THE BRADFORD ESTATES

*SHIFNAL, SHROPSHIRE*

The Bradford Estates Office
Weston-under-Lizard
Shifnal
Shropshire TF11 8JU

Tel: 01952 852000        Fax: 01952 852004
ghooker@weston-estate.demon.co.uk bradford@porters.uk.com
www.weston.uk.com

What could be more wonderful than shooting in a Capability Brown landscape surrounding one of England's top Stately Homes, built in the 1670s? Weston Park became famous recently when it hosted the G8 Summit Retreat in 1998 and the Northern Ireland Peace Talks. The rolling parkland is perfect for pheasant shooting, and the top drives – the Rock, the Gorse and the Newport – are well known to produce testing birds for even the best shots. Allied to that is traditional driven partridge shooting outside the Park, where the hedges have been grown to ensure quality birds, with a mixture of English and French. There is also an extensive programme of rough shooting with a minimum of 50 birds per day.

*Shooting acreage:*
*Status:* Private with a considerable number of let days
*Owner:* The Earl of Bradford, Bradford Rural Estates Ltd
*Contact:* The Earl of Bradford or Ms Gill Hooker
*Headkeeper:* Gary Freegard
*Number of available days:* 15 to 20
*Number of drives:* Normally five or six per day, from a total of about 16
*Bag expectations:* 200-300 birds per day
*Average cartridge to kill ratio:* 4.5:1
*Lunch:* In the Old Stables at Weston Park, sympathetically converted for commercial use and looking out over the front of Weston Park
*Price structure:* £22.50 plus VAT for pheasants, charged on the actual bag shot on the day. £21.50 plus VAT for partridges
*Accommodation:* Luxury accommodation is available for parties at Weston Park
*Access:* By road: M54 (Jct 3) – 3 miles or M6 (Jct 12) – 7 miles. By rail: Stafford and Wolverhampton Stations. By air: Birmingham Airport. See website for full details
*Other comments:* Well-behaved gundogs welcome

# WITHINGTON MANOR SHOOT

## NR. COLESBOURNE, CHELTENHAM, GLOUCESTERSHIRE

Whitworth Rd
Cirencester
Gloucestershire

Tel: 01285 657527.          Fax: 01285 652535
contactus@cotswoldshooting.co.uk          www.cotswoldshooting.co.uk

This is predominantly a driven pheasant shoot with the attraction of a small number of partridges to add variety to the day. The Withington Manor Shoot easily rivals the West Country high bird shoots and is set in a stunning location, consisting of deep valleys and rolling hills in the Cotswolds. Drives tend to be long and birds are driven over tree belts. Guests are advised not to attempt to take out-of-range birds. The shoot's staff aim to be highly attentive to the needs of its guests.

*Shooting acreage*: 2,000
*Status*: The shoot caters for two syndicates and provides 10 commercial let days
*Contact/agent*: The Cotswold Shooting Co Ltd, as above
*Headkeeper/staff*: Headkeeper is Shaun Gage
*Number of available days*: 10
*Number of drives*: 47
*Bag expectations*: In the region of 200
*Average cartridge to kill ratio*: 4-1
*Lunch*: Taken in the Manor House after shooting through
*Price structure*: £29.50 per bird including VAT
*Accommodation*: Ample excellent accommodation locally in pubs, B&Bs and guest houses
*Access*: By road: Vary accessible as just off the M5, Jct. 10. By rail: Cheltenham on main line rail from London
*Other comments*: Well-behaved dogs welcome

# PARTRIDGES

# BOREHAM HALL SHOOT

## BOREHAM, NR CHELMSFORD, ESSEX

Tel: 01621 744075                    Mobile: 07767 898771

This is a high quality partridge and duck shoot with moderate pheasants later in the season. Boreham Hall is a large Palladian mansion set in 2,300 acres of farmland with the River Chelmer running through it. With small woods and gullies, the terrain is easy and the shoot prides itself on its traditional atmosphere and hospitality.

*Shooting acreage*: 2,300
*Status*: Syndicate with let days
*Shoot manager*: Paul Bibby
*Contact*: Paul Bibby
*Sporting agent*: N/a
*Headkeeper/staff*: Michael Hall
*Number of available days*: 25
*Number of drives*: 27 in total – 5-6 per day
*Bag expectations*: up to 300
*Gun/cartridge recommendations*: Non-toxic shot for duck drives
*Average cartridge to kill ratio*: 3.5:1
*Lunch*: Guns should bring light snack as meal included after day's shooting in a private room at the local pub
*Price structure*: £19 per bird
*Accommodation*: Can be arranged at three locations according to budget and requirements
*Access*: By road: minutes from A12. By rail: Chelmsford station. By air: Stansted Airport is 12 miles away. Pick up can be arranged
*Other comments*: Dogs are welcome and kennelling can be provided if required

# CHIPPENHAM PARK ESTATE

*ELY, CAMBRIDGESHIRE*

Chippenham Park
Ely
Cambridgeshire
CB7 5PT

Tel: 01638 720221                    Fax: 01638 721991

The Chippenham Park Estate was laid out more than 100 years ago for partridge shooting, at a time when the Prince of Wales, later King Edward VII, was a frequent guest. Partridge shooting was revived when Eustace Crawley, husband of the owner Anne Crawley, took over the shooting in 1990. He aims to average 250 bird partridge days. His keeper, Jim Irons and who has been headkeeper since he was appointed at the age of 22, is greatly concerned with the quality of the birds presented. The light land on which cereals, sugar-beet and vegetables are grown is, although fairly flat, excellent partridge country and the quality of the shooting provided is consistently high.

*Shooting acreage*: 3,000
*Status*: Private with paying guests on let days
*Owner*: Mrs Anne Crawley
*Contact*: As above
*Sporting agent*: N/a
*Headkeeper/staff*: Jim Irons
*Number of available days*: 3 or 4 and one or two Guns available of paying guest days
*Number of drives*: five per day
*Bag expectations*: 250
*Average cartridge to kill ratio*: N/a
*Lunch*: lunch, in the middle of the day, is taken in the dining room of a delightful house full of treasures collected over 200 years by Mrs Crawley's ancestors
*Price structure*: £25 per bird
*Accommodation*: Excellent local hotels can be arranged
*Access*: By road: One mile off the A11 and five miles north-east of Newmarket. By rail: Cambridge and Ely Stations
*Other comments*: Shooting on Thursdays and Saturdays

# EAGLE HALL SHOOT

## *LINCOLNSHIRE/NOTTINGHAMSHIRE BORDERS*

3 Scarlet Lane
Eagle
Lincoln
LN6 9EJ

Tel: 01522 868930                    Fax: 01522 868930
Mobile: 07887 676501
Bwalker65@aol.com

The Eagle Hall Shoot is sited on the Nottinghamshire/ Lincolnshire border and comprises largely arable land for root crops, such as sugarbeet, carrot and kale. Although the land is relatively flat, tall hedges ensure some outstanding driven partridge shooting in the traditional style.

*Shooting acreage*: 4,000
*Status*: Private with some let days
*Owner*: Brian Walker (sporting rights)
*Contact*: As above
*Sporting agent*: N/a
*Headkeeper*: Full-time keeper
*Number of available days*: 10
*Number of drives*: 16
*Bag expectations*: 100-150
*Average cartridge to kill ratio*: 3:1
*Lunch*: The practice is to shoot through, followed by lunch in a local pub
*Price structure*: Driven £17.50 per bird. Walked-up £12.50 per bird
*Accommodation*: Local Travel Lodge or The White Hart at Scarle
*Access*: By road: Situated off the A46 Newark to Lincoln road. By rail: Newark Northgate Station 15 minutes away.

# HUNTSTON SHOOT

## BURY ST EDMUNDS, SUFFOLK

Field and Marsh
Garden Cottage
The Street
Stowlangtoft
Bury St Edmunds
Suffolk
IP31 3JX

Tel: 01359 235062
fieldandmarsh@myopal.net

The 3,000 acre Huntston Shoot is primarily driven partridges with some pheasant shooting and, it is claimed, the partridges shown here are comparable to the best such shoots in the country. The rolling Suffolk hills and some 60 acres of strategically sited mixed game cover ensure excellent sport and some very sharp shooting. The pheasants, on a windy day, can also prove exciting, but Guns coming to Hunston are largely concerned with the red-legs.

*Shooting acreage*: 3,000
*Status*: Commercial and syndicate
*Owner*: Field and Marsh, see above
*Contact*: Mr S.J.Marsh, address as above
*Sporting agent*: N/a
*Headkeeper*: Stephen Marsh
*Number of available days*: 20
*Number of drives*: 30
*Bag expectations*: 200-400
*Average cartridge to kill ratio*: 3:1
*Lunch*: Guns normally enjoy a snack lunch and then dine at the end of the day at Garden Cottage
*Price structure*: £21 plus VAT per bird
*Accommodation*: The Grange Hotel at Thurston
*Access*: Five minutes from the A14 between Bury St Edmunds and Stowmarket. Rail to Bury St Edmunds
*Other comments*: Well trained gundogs welcome

# LONGWITTON SHOOT

Font House
Netherwitton
Morpeth
Northumberland
NE61 4NK

Tel: 01670 772249          Fax: 01670 772510
john@netherwitton.com

This is an historic family estate with shooting records going back to the 1880s. The estate is located 20 miles north-west of Newcastle-upon-Tyne in the beautiful Northumberland countryside. The Longwitton shoot covers 2,200 acres featuring small blocks of woodland, together with maize and kale game crops on undulating ground providing exciting shooting amidst the most glorious countryside. Over the last five years the partridge side of the shoot has been developed to make best use of the landscape. Single or double days can be offered with bags of between 150 to 250 per day of partridges and pheasants for teams of eight Guns. This is a thoroughly relaxed and friendly shoot.

*Shooting acreage*: 2,200
*Status*: Private with let days
*Owner*: John H.T. Trevelyan
*Contact*: As above
*Sporting agent*: N/a
*Headkeeper*: Dennis Stephenson
*Number of available days*: 7
*Number of drives*: 20
*Bag expectations*: 150 – 250
*Average cartridge to kill ratio*: 3:1
*Lunch*: A sit-down lunch is taken in Font House, a local pub—or teams can bring their own lunch
*Price structure*: £25 per bird inc. VAT but excluding lunch. £26 inc VAT and lunch
*Accommodation*: Excellent local hotels and can recommend the Otterburn Towers Hotel, 20 minutes away
*Access*: By road, seven miles off the A1. Rail to Newcastle-upon-Tyne or air to Newcastle International
*Other comments*: Well trained gundogs very welcome

# NORTH ORMSBY AND ACTHORPE

*LOUTH, LINCOLNSHIRE*

Acthorpe House
South Elkington
Louth
Lincolnshire
LN11 0SO

Tel: 01472 840536  Fax: 01472 840766
ont@ukhunting.com  www.ukhunting.com

Here we have traditional partridge shooting, in September and October, on rolling Lincolnshire wolds rising to 500 ft. Both English and French partridges are released. In addition, in November, December and January the emphasis switches to pheasants. There are a number of good valleys over which curling and difficult but shootable pheasants are driven. Shoot transport is provided or Guns are welcome to use their own vehicles. Double guns are accepted. The aim is to produce a good all-round day, one in which the Guns are made to feel like guests on a private shoot.

*Shooting acreage*: 7,000
*Status*: Syndicate and private with let days
*Owner*: David Nickerson
*Contact*: David Nickerson
*Sporting agent*: N/a
*Headkeeper/staff*: Headkeeper and three beat keepers
*Number of available days*: 50
*Number of drives*: 40 plus, depending on cropping
*Bag expectations*: 250 – 750
*Average cartridge to kill ratio*: 3 or 4:1
*Lunch*: Guns meet at David Nickerson's house where lunch is taken mid-day or at the end of the day, according to Guns' wishes. Always rib of beef on the bone or haunch, supplemented by plenty of good wine. There is a sloe-gin break mid-morning and afternoon tea if Guns take lunch mid-day
*Price structure*: £22 plus VAT per bird. Minimum £5,500 plus VAT per day
*Accommodation*: Brackenborough Arms or Kenwich Hotel, both within four miles of shoot
*Access*: By road: 50 minutes from A1 at Newark. By rail: 15 miles from Market Rasen Station. By air: 15 miles from Humberside Airport
*Other comments*: Good, well-trained dogs are welcome and pickers-up keep well back

# PAWTON MANOR

## NR WADEBRIDGE, CORNWALL

Westcountry Sporting Worldwide
33-34 Fore Street
Chudleigh
South Devon
TQ13 0HX

Tel: 01626 854793                    Fax: 01626 854779
Mobile: 07711 215542
richard@westcountry-sporting.co.uk   www.w-s-w.co.uk

The Pawton Manor Shoot has been created by the Wills family to
provide quite outstanding driven red-legged partridge shooting over
approximately 1,000 acres of attractive Cornish countryside. Birds are
driven from high belts and rolling stretches of open countryside to
offer excellent and testing sport. The shooting is very well organised,
and the hosts and beating team do their utmost to ensure a thoroughly
hospitable day for visiting Guns.

*Shooting acreage*: 1,000
*Status*: Commercial and family run
*Sporting agent*: Richard Hutcheon
*Headkeeper*: Matthew Wills
*Number of available days*: 12
*Number of drives*: 25. 4-6 per day
*Bag expectations*: 150-300
*Average cartridge to kill ratio*: 4:1
*Lunch*: Taken in the Pawton Manor farmhouse and is a thoroughly
hospitable and jovial occasion
*Price structure*: £23 per bird inclusive
*Accommodation*: Local hotels, pubs and B&Bs. Tredathy Manor, Tredathy,
is recommended
*Access*: By road: One hour's drive on A30 from Exeter. By rail: Wadebridge.
By air: Exeter and Plymouth
*Other comments*: Well trained gundogs welcome

# SALPERTON PARK ESTATE

## NR CHELTENHAM, GLOUCESTERSHIRE

St George's House
29 St George's Road
Cheltenham
Gloucestershire
GL50 3DU

Tel: 01242 514478          Fax: 01242 224697
info@coley.co.uk           www.coley.co.uk

At Salperton teams of Guns have the opportunity to participate in a classic Cotswold driven partridge shoot with the birds driven over deep valleys to offer exciting and testing shooting. Some drives offer exceptionally high but still shootable birds. There is also a number of pheasants, but partridges predominate. This is challenging shooting in a countryside with breath-taking views.

*Shooting acreage*: 2,500
*Status*: Commercial
*Sporting agent*: Ian Coley Sporting, as above
*Headkeeper*: Shane Cooper
*Number of available days*: 25
*Number of drives*: 20 plus
*Bag expectations*: 300-400
*Average cartridge to kill ratio*: 3.5:1
*Lunch*: Lunch taken in converted Cotswold barn
*Price structure*: £26 per bird plus VAT
*Accommodation*: Salperton Park House is available for the exclusive use of shooting parties
*Access*: By road: M5 Jct. 11a, then A40, six miles south of Cheltenham. By rail: Cheltenham or Gloucester Stations. By air: Gloucester
*Comments*: Well-controlled dogs welcome

# SUMMERDOWN FARM SHOOT

*WILTSHIRE DOWNS, WILTSHIRE*

Summerdown Farm
Everleigh
Marlborough
Wiltshire SN8 3EX

Tel: 01264 850505                    Fax: 01264 852728
summerdown@talk21.com

Summerdown Farm has been owned by the May family for more than 60 years, and the shoot has been run on the farm for that entire period. It is very much a family affair, with a relaxed atmosphere. Fast, exciting shooting is provided in beautiful surroundings. The shoot is situated on the Wiltshire Downs, a wild and unique environment with its open spaces, valleys and banks. This is one of the most natural partridge habitats in Britain and the terrain has been harnessed to show French partridges in a way similar to the English partridge shooting of earlier days. Partridge days are available from mid-September through October and November and mixed pheasant and partridge days from mid-November through to January and can be tailored to suit requirements. Days for six to ten Guns are offered, but inquiries from smaller parties or single Guns are very welcome. Loaders for double gun days can be arranged. There is also a fourteen-seat gun bus to transport teams round the shoot.

*Shooting acreage*: 1,200
*Status*: Commercial plus private days
Company: R.G.May & Sons
*Contact*: Christopher May, details as above
*Headkeeper*: Kenneth May
*Number of available days*: 20-25
*Number of drives*: 17
*Bag expectations*: 150 to 400
*Average cartridge to kill ratio*: between 3 and 4:1
*Lunch*: Lunch is taken at The Old Schoolhouse restaurant at Collingbourne Kingston, which is fully licensed and provides excellent cuisine and wines. There is a pause for drinks, coffee, soup and snacks mid to late morning, depending on whether Guns prefer to lunch mid-day or shoot through.
*Price structure*: £22 per bird for a 200 bird day with a sliding scale to £20 per bird for a 400 bird day. All prices include lunch but exclude VAT
*Accommodation*: The Ivy House Hotel in Marlborough, The Bear Hotel at Hungerford, Essebourne Manor Hotel near Andover. Also The Old Schoolhouse and Manor House Farm at Collingbourne Kingston both have B&B
*Access*: Summerdown Farm is well located between Marlborough and Andover on the edge of Salisbury Plain in Wiltshire. Easy access from M4 Junctions 14 and 15, Swindon and Hungerford or from M3 leading to the A303 Andover and Tidworth. Coloured maps provided for all Guns.

# TEFFONT MAGNA SHOOT

*WILTSHIRE*

Manor Farm
Teffont Magna
Salisbury
Wiltshire
SP3 5RD

Tel: 01722 716498     Fax: 01722 716078
Mobile: 07768 014277

Driven red-legged partridges and pheasants over 2,600 acres of prime Wiltshire partridge country. Teffont Magna is a classic thatched Wiltshire village some 16 miles from Stonehenge and Manor Farm itself sits in rolling secluded countryside with purpose-planted game coverts and numerous banks providing excellent partridge shooting. Although principally a partridge shoot, there are also some excellent pheasant drives and in addition to the French partridges, some 1,000 grey partridges are also put down. Quad bikes are available for the less fit although all drives and pegs are easily accessible. This is very much a family-run shoot, offering a friendly relaxed atmosphere in one of the most beautiful unspoiled parts of the country.

*Shooting acreage*: 2,600
*Status*: Commercial and syndicate
*Owner*: Edward Waddington
*Contact*: Edward Waddington
*Headkeeper/staff*: There are two keepers, Oliver James and Nigel Strong
*Number of available days*: 30 plus
*Number of drives*: 24 with 5-6 per day
*Bag expectations*: Between 150 and 600
*Average cartridge to kill ratio*: 3.5:1
*Lunch*: Early in the season the Guns stop for lunch, which is served in a wonderful old converted barn, and tea at the end of the day. Later on in the Season lunch is served at the end of the day with soup and sausages offered mid-morning. All meals and alcohol are included
*Price structure*: £24 plus VAT per bird. Price per day is also available on application
*Accommodation*: There are several good local hotels and pubs within a five mile radius. Two recommendations are The Lamb at Hindon and Howard's House in Teffont Magna
*Access*: By road: M3/A303 – 10 minutes from A303. By rail: Tisbury or Salisbury Stations. By air: London Gatwick or Heathrow, Bristol and Southampton Airports. Transport available by arrangement
*Other comments*: Dogs welcome

# THE DALTON ESTATE

*EAST YORKSHIRE WOLDS, YORKSHIRE*

The Estate Office
South Dalton
Beverley
East Riding
Yorkshire
HU17 7PN

Tel: 01430 810225                    Fax: 01430810746
office@daltonestate.co.uk

Owned by Lord Hotham, the Dalton Estate is approximately 11,000 acres and offers an opportunity for private individuals to book driven partridge shooting on this privately owned estate in the undulating East Yorkshire Wolds. A driven partridge shoot is available with an opportunity for Guns to shoot up to 200 brace of partridge a day. A number of days are available from September to January.

*Shooting acreage*: 11,000
*Status*: Private
*Owner*: The Dalton Estate
*Contact*: The Estate Office as above
*Sporting agent*: N/a
*Headkeeper/staff*: Paul Hammond
*Number of available days*: 15
*Number of drives*: Total 16 – 5-6 per day
*Bag expectations*: 75 to 200 brace
*Average cartridge to kill ratio*: 4:1
*Lunch*: lunch and refreshments are served in the Shoot Room on the Estate and are included in price
*Price structure*: £18 plus VAT per bird
*Accommodation*: A variety of accommodation, pubs and hotels are available locally to suit all requirements
*Access*: By road: 15 miles off M62. By rail: Beverley Station. By air: Tyneside Airport. Transport is available on arrangement

# WIDDINGTON FARM SHOOT

## *WILTSHIRE DOWNS, WILTSHIRE*

Widdington Farm
Upavon
Pewsey
Wiltshire
SN9 6EE

Tel: 01980 630011                   Fax: 01980 630990
Mobile: 07779 235195
jeremy@widdingtonfarm.fsnet.co.uk

This is a family-run driven partridge shoot over 1,000 acres of
Wiltshire Downs, and all drives take place over one long, deep valley.
The birds are high and fast and ideal for those expecting a challenge.
Good quality partridges are assured at a reasonable price. The three-
hundred-year-old farmhouse is in the centre of the valley and
although most drives are within easy walking distance from the house,
quad bikes are available should they be required.

*Shooting acreage*: 1,000
*Status*: Private with let days
*Owner*: Jeremy Horton
*Contact*: Jeremy Horton
*Sporting agent*: N/a
*Headkeeper*: Jeremy Horton
*Number of available days*: 25
*Number of drives*: 14 in total: 5-6 per day
*Bag expectations*: 150-500
*Average cartridge to kill ratio*: 5:1
*Lunch*: Flexible, either stop for lunch or shoot through. This is a traditional
shooting lunch served in Widdington Farmhouse. Refreshments are also
served during the day and alcohol is included.
*Price structure*: £23.50 per bird. Day rates also available on application
*Accommodation*: Local pubs and inns as well as several good hotels in
Marlborough. Accommodation can be booked by Mr Horton on request.
*Access*: By road: Either M4 or M3 via A345 or A303. By rail: Pewsey
Station. By air: Heathrow Airport. Transport available on request. Landing
access on farm for helicopters.
*Other comments*: Gundogs welcome

# WOODCOCK/SNIPE

# THE ARUNDELL ARMS HOTEL

Lifton
Devon
PL16 0AA

Tel: 01566 784666          Fax: 01566 784494
reservations@arundellarms.com     www.arundellarms.com

Driven snipe shoots have been organised by The Arundell Arms for
many years and have acquired a unique reputation in the shooting
world. They are one or two day shoots, run every week from the end
of November to January 31, excluding Christmas. A minimum of five
and maximum of eight Guns are required for each shoot, and there is
an average of eight to 10 drives per day. The shoots take place within
a 15 mile radius of the hotel over a mixture of plough, grass and
marshland.

*Status*: Sporting Hotel
*Owner*: The Arundell Arms Hotel
*Contact*: Anne Voss-Bark
*Sporting agent*: N/a
*Number of available days*: Throughout the relevant season
*Bag expectations*: Varies enormously according to experience of the Guns
and number of snipe present.
*Average cartridge to kill ratio*: 7:1 to 10:1
*Lunch*: Informally in hotel bar, at conveniently sited inn or on the Shoot
premises
*Price structure*: Driven snipe: £170 per Gun per day, including lunch and
transport to drives and VAT. If all party provide their own transport to the
shoot, the cost is reduced to £150 per Gun.
*Accommodation*: The Arundell Arms Hotel, a former coaching inn, is on
the Cornwall/Devon border. It has a three AA-rosette restaurant with three
Master Chefs. All rooms have private bathrooms or showers, colour TV and
direct dial phones.
*Access*: By road: half a mile off the A30, midway between Dartmoor and
Bodmin. By rail: Exeter Station. By air: Exeter or Newquay. Transport by
arrangement.
*Other comments*: Shooting clients must have third part-indemnity to £1
million. Written assurance is required before joining a shoot. Also, automatic
shotguns are not allowed. Well-behaved dogs are welcome in the hotel and
on most of the shoots.

# GROUSE

# HARDCASTLE MOOR

*RIPLEY, NORTH YORKSHIRE*

C/o The Old Hall
Burton Leonard
Nr Harrogate, HG3 3SE

Tel: 01423 322370 (day)          Fax: 01423 324334 (day)
Tel: 01765 677343 (evening)      Fax: 01765 677861 (evening)
Mobile: 07774 271781
info@ripleycastleshoot.co.uk

This grouse moor, which covers 2,250 acres, is made up of undulating moorland with good areas of heather and some bent grass with a number of exciting gills. The grazing rights are in hand and are restricted in order not to be detrimental to the grouse. The High Moor will stand nine or ten Guns and has four lines of stone butts in excellent condition and also a line of hurdles, giving an option of five main drives together with a gill which provides two drives. There are also a number of gills which will be considered for further drives. The Low Moor, which will stand six Guns, has two lines of stone butts with four lines of pegs in small gills, giving an option of six drives. The shooting on the moor, which is owned by Lord Mountgarret, has recently been acquired on a long lease by Frank Boddy, and it is anticipated that with careful management, burning and vermin control, this moor should show some excellent sport. Like most moors in Nidderdale, returns in recent seasons have been variable and the intention is to build up the moor carefully by only shooting excess stock.

*Shooting acreage*: 2,250
*Status*: Private with let days
*Contact*: Frank Boddy (leaseholder)
*Sporting agent*: N/a
*Headkeeper*: George Reap, assisted by John Clayton
*Number of available days*: 8
*Number of drives*: 4/6
*Bag expectations*: 25-45 brace
*Average cartridge to kill ratio*: Depends on Guns' skill
*Lunch*: Taken in well-equipped shoot box purpose built in the 1880s
*Price structure*: POA
*Accommodation*: The Boar's Head, Ripley. Tel: 01423 771888. Hob Green Hotel, Markington. Tel: 01423 770031. The Sportsman's Arms, Wath, nr Pateley Bridge. Tel: 01423 711303
*Access*: By road: Ripley is 10 minutes from Harrogate and 40 minutes from York. By air: Ripley is 30 minutes from Leeds/Bradford Airport. The High Moor borders the B6265
*Other comments*: Guns are in very limited supply

# HEATHFIELD MOOR

## *NEAR RIPLEY, NORTH YORKSHIRE*

The Old Hall
Burton Leonard
Nr Harrogate
HG3 3SE

Tel: 01423 322370 (day)           Fax: 01423 324334 (day)
Tel: 01765 677343 (evening)        Fax: 01765 677861 (evening)
info@ripleycastle.co.uk

The Heathfield grouse moor covers approximately 2,250 acres, and is
almost entirely clad in heather, with only a small amount of bent
grass. It has been farmed and burned with due consideration to the
quality of the heather in order to achieve good breeding conditions for
the grouse. There are seven lines of butts which will stand up to
eleven Guns, giving a variety of eight drives, though nine Guns will
normally be fielded. This has been a very productive moor in the past
with some excellent returns. However, like most grouse moors in
Nidderdale, Heathfield has suffered from variable returns in recent
seasons and the stock of birds will be built up by only shooting excess
numbers.

*Shooting acreage*: 2,250
*Status*: Private with let days
*Contact*: Frank Boddy
*Sporting agent*: N/a
*Headkeeper*: George Reap assisted by John Clayton
*Number of available days*: 7
*Number of drives*: 8
*Bag expectations*: 25 – 45 brace
Average cartridge to kill ratio: Depends on Guns
*Lunch*: Lunch taken in well-appointed shooting box on the moor
*Price structure*: POA
*Accommodation*: The Boar's Head, Ripley. Tel: 01423 771888. Hob Green
Hotel, Markington. Tel: 01423 770031. The Sportsman's Arms, Wath,
Pateley Bridge. Tel: 01423 711303
*Access*: By road: Ripley is 10 minutes from Harrogate, 40 minutes from
York. By air: 30 minutes from Leeds/Bradford Airport
*Other comments*: Guns are in extremely short supply

# ROSEDALE MOOR

The Estate Office
Faccombe
Andover
Hants
SP1 0DS

Tel: 01264 73247           Fax: 01264 737367
dfh@faccombe.co.uk

This moor (see also the Westerdale Moor entry) includes Hartoff Moor and Harmer moor. The moors are consistent, lying mainly between 975ft and 1,300ft above sea level with good heather cover. Bracken has been controlled and both heather and bilberry growth is vigorous. The grouse stocks are likewise in good health. These two moors lie adjacent to each other with a short common boundary. Access to both moors is good from public roads and internal Estate tracks. The butts on both moors are well made and in an excellent state of repair.

*Shooting acreage*: Rosedale Moor 4,130 acres
*Status*: Private with let days
*Owner*: Faccombe Estates Ltd
*Contact*: D.F.Habottle
*Sporting agent*: N/a
*Headkeeper/staff*: Headkeeper, 1 beatkeeper and 2 under-keepers
*Number of available days*: Normally 8 to 10 let per season
Number of butts: 34, some of which involve return drives
*Bag expectations*: up to 100 brace
*Lunch*: Use of two lunch huts. Pre-lunch drinks, three course lunch with wine, followed by coffee
*Price structure*: £110 per brace plus VAT for first week of season. £100 per brace plus VAT thereafter
*Accommodation*: Milburn Arms, Rosedale, N.Yorks. Tel: 01751 417312. Star Inn, Harome, N.Yorks. Tel: 01439 770397. Black Swan, Helmsley, N.Yorks. Tel: 0845 7585593. Feversham Arms, Helmsley, N.Yorks. Tel: 01439 770766. Grinkle Park Hotel, N.Yorks. Tel: 01287 640515
*Access*: York – 37 miles. Helmsley – 15 miles. Middlesbrough – 31 miles. Tees-side Airport – 31 miles
*Other comments*: Only fibre and biodegradable wadded cartridges allowed. Loaders/stuffers can be provided at Guns' expense. Well trained soft mouthed gundogs welcome

# SNILESWORTH SHOOT

## NR HELMSLEY, NORTH YORKSHIRE

Grindsbrook House
69 Oxford Road
Banbury
Oxfordshire
OX16 9AJ

Tel: 01295 27197          Fax: 01295 268651
james@ejchurchill.com

Snilesworth offers a delightful mixed sporting estate set in the heart of the North Yorks Moors and although primarily a three-day driven grouse moor, a very testing partridge and pheasant shoot has now been developed in the gills and gullies on the moorland edge. Although this low-ground shooting is largely driven, there is also the capacity for some walked-up sport.

*Shooting acreage*: 8,000
*Status*: Private with let days
*Contact*: James Chapel
*Sporting agent*: E.J.Churchill Sporting, as above
*Headkeeper/staff*: Headkeeper and two beat keepers
*Number of available days*: On application
*Number of drives*: Grouse 16, partridges 12, pheasants 8
*Bag expectations*: Grouse 50 to 100 brace, partridges and pheasants 100 to 300 birds
*Average cartridge to kill ratio*: Between 2.8 and 4:1
*Lunch*: A fully catered lunch is provided
*Price structure*: POA
*Accommodation*: Teams typically enjoy staying at the Feversham Arms at Helmsley or the Hawnby Hotel at Hawnby
*Access*: 30 minutes drive from the A1. One hour from York Station and 40 minutes from Tees-side Airport
*Other comments*: Well trained gundogs welcome

E * 86

# WESTERDALE MOOR

The Estate Office
Faccombe
Andover
Hants
SP1 0DS

Tel: 01264 73247          Fax: 01264 737367
dfh@faccombe.co.uk

Rising from 700ft to 1,400ft Westerdale Moor comprises part of Farndale Moor and High Blakey Moor, and surrounds the village and valley of Westerdale. Westerdale is probably one of the most improved moors in the North Yorks Moors, having been subject to an intensive bracken control programme. There is now a vigorous regeneration of bilberry and heather and, as a result, the grouse stock is in good health.

*Shooting acreage*: 5,777 acres
*Status*: Private with let days
*Owner*: Faccombe Estates Ltd
*Contact*: D.F.Habottle
*Sporting agent*: N/a
*Headkeeper/staff*: Headkeeper, 1 beatkeeper and 2 under-keepers
*Number of available days*: Normally 8 to 10 let per season
Number of butts: 34, some of which involve return drives
*Bag expectations*: up to 100 brace
*Lunch*: Use of two lunch huts. Pre-lunch drinks, three-course lunch with wine, followed by coffee
*Price structure*: £110 per brace plus VAT for first week of season. £100 per brace plus VAT thereafter
*Accommodation*: Milburn Arms, Rosedale, N.Yorks. Tel: 01751 417312. Star Inn, Harome, N.Yorks. Tel: 01439 770397. Black Swan, Helmsley, N.Yorks. Tel: 0845 7585593. Feversham Arms, Helmsley, N.Yorks. Tel: 01439 770766. Grinkle Park Hotel, N.Yorks. Tel: 01287 640515
*Access*: Tees-side Airport – 25 miles. Darlington – 30 miles. Tees-side – 18 miles. Whitby – 15 miles.
*Other comments*: Only fibre and biodegradable wadded cartridges allowed. Loaders/stuffers can be provided at Guns' expense. Well trained soft mouthed gundogs welcome

# WILDFOWLING

# CHESIL BANK DUCK SHOOT

Rodden Farm
Rodden
Weymouth
Dorset

Tel: 01258 454327                    Mobile: 07960 235311

The Chesil Bank Duck Shoot is sited some five miles from Weymouth in West Dorset, amidst some of England's most beautiful countryside, with panoramic views of Portland, Weymouth and the Heritage Coast. The shooting is for driven duck only, but these are in a class of their own. Ponds are strategically sited on the summit of hills and downland, ensuring that these birds are high, wild and testing and have nothing in common with standard driven duck. Parties of six to seven Guns are ideal, but individual Guns can be catered for and, if required, tuition is available. When the day is over Guns are each presented with an oven-ready duck or ducks in the feather. This is a thoroughly sporting shoot, providing exceptional and exciting shooting.

*Shooting acreage*: 425
*Status*: Commercial
*Owners*: Paul Swaffield and William Poole
*Contact*: William Poole on 07960 235311
*Sporting agent*: N/a
*Headkeeper/staff*: Keepered by owners
*Number of available days*: 8. Tuesdays and Fridays
*Number of drives*: 11 in total, usually 6 or 7 per day
*Bag expectations*: 150 – 300
*Average cartridge to kill ratio*: 4:1. Only non-toxic shot
*Lunch*: When Guns arrive at the shoot they are greeted with coffee, sausages and sloe gin, taken in traditional Dorset farmhouse. A three-course roast lunch is taken around 1pm, followed by a further two to four drives. The bag is then counted and tea, sandwiches and cake are offered.
*Price structure*: £19 per bird inclusive of all refreshments. No VAT
*Accommodation*: Guns usually stay at the Ilchester Arms, Abbotsbury.
*Access*: By road: A35 to Dorchester. Roddon is just off B3157 to the south-west of Dorchester, or A354 to Weymouth and B3157 to Roddon. By rail: Dorchester or Weymouth
*Other comments*: Well-trained gundogs are very welcome

# GRANGE FARM

## NOTTINGHAMSHIRE

Grange Farm
Gainsborough Road
Girton
Newark
Nottinghamshire

Tel: 07951 682166

Goose and duck shooting on inland lakes and rivers, also rough and pigeon shooting over some 4,000 acres. This is private shooting with let days. Package includes morning and evening flights interspersed with rough shooting. Bag should include snipe, various species of duck, geese, pheasants and partridges. Something for everyone over easy terrain.

*Shooting acreage*: 4,000
*Status*: Private with let days
*Owner*: Grange Farm Leisure
*Contact*: A.Chamberlain as above
*Sporting agent*: N/a
*Headkeeper/staff*: A Chamberlain
*Number of available days*: Throughout relevant seasons
*Number of drives*: Average 8-9
*Bag expectations*: 50-100 on mixed bag days. 150+ driven pheasants and partridges
*Average cartridge to kill ratio*: Approx 3:1
*Lunch*: Guns are required to bring their own packed lunch
*Price structure*: POA
*Accommodation*: Farmhouse offers B&B with en-suite facilities and Sky TV. Local pub for evening meals.
*Access*: By road: 10 mins from A1 or can arrange pick-up from airports
*Other comments*: Gundogs are welcome and kennelling is available. Shooting can be arranged to suit clients' wishes.

*WELLS-NEXT-THE-SEA, NORFOLK*

Holkham Estate Office
Wells-next-the-Sea
Norfolk
NR23 1AB

Tel: 01328 713104
s.lester@holkham.co.uk

Fax: 01328 711707
www.holkham.co.uk

This historic estate, the Earl of Leicester's north Norfolk Estate (see complete entry under pheasants), offers evening duck flights on one of the Estate's many flight ponds. These flights can also be booked separately.

*Shooting acreage*: 25,000, with approximately 16,000 acres shot over
*Status*: private with a small number of rough shoot days and evening duck flights to let
*Owner*: The Earl of Leicester
*Contact*: Please write (don't phone) to the headkeeper, Simon Lester, at the Holkham Estate Office (address above) or email him at s.lester@holkham.co.uk.
*Sporting agent*: N/a
*Headkeeper/staff*: Simon Lester and seven beatkeepers
*Number of available days*: Available on application
*Number of drives*: Each day is planned for team's individual requirements
*Bag expectations*: Rough days 40-60 head
*Lunch*: Usually taken in the field. Packed lunches available from The Victoria Hotel, Holkham
*Price structure*: Rough days: £1,500 inc VAT per day. Duck flights: £100 inc VAT per Gun
*Accommodation*: Special rates for shooting parties at The Victoria Hotel at Holkham, Park Road, Holkham, Norfolk NR23 1RG. Tel: 01328 711008. victoria@holkham.co.uk
*Access*: By road: Holkham is two miles west of Wells-next-the-Sea on the main A149, within easy reach of Norwich on the A1067, King's Lynn on the A148 and London and Cambridge on the M11 and the A10
*Other comments*: Guests must have their own insurance. Well trained gundogs welcome. The demand for rough shoot days and evening duck flights is extremely high and only a limited number are available.

# PRO SPORTS

## LANCASHIRE AND CHESHIRE

Tel: 01942 734845
Mobile: 07970 265038 / 07979 533491
mail@prosports.fsnet.co.uk          www.decoying.co.uk

Pro Sports offers shooting over several estates and farms throughout Lancashire and Cheshire. Flighted grey geese, mainly pinkfeet, over decoys and decoyed pigeon in the spring and summer months over 5,000 acres. Also wild duck flighting over ponds. All the land is arable farmland and therefore the terrain is all easy going and suitable for all types.

*Shooting acreage*: 5000
*Status*: Commercial
*Owner*: Pro Sports/Decoying.Co.Uk
*Contact*: Mark Taylor, as above
*Sporting agent*: Pro Sports
*Number of available days*: Throughout relevant seasons
*Bag expectations*: There is no bag limit on pigeons or duck, but a limit of three geese per Gun per flight is imposed
*Gun/cartridge recommendations*: 12 or 10-bores for geese with 1¼oz No 3 shot. Bismuth preferred
*Average cartridge to kill ratio*: varies
*Lunch*: Provided on some packages. By arrangement in local pub
*Price structure*: £60 per flight for geese, £50 a flight for duck and £60 a day for woodpigeons
*Accommodation*: Luxury barn conversion with all meals by arrangement
*Access*: By road: Very accessible via major motorways. 20 minutes off the M6. Maps provided. By rail: Southport station. By air: Manchester or Liverpool airports. Pick-ups can be arranged
*Other comments*: Well-behaved dogs are welcome

# PIGEON

# PHILIP BEASLEY SPORTING AGENCY

## OXFORDSHIRE, BUCKINGHAMSHIRE, BERKSHIRE AND HAMPSHIRE

Box Farm
Castle Street
Marsh Gibbon
Bicester
Oxfordshire
OX27 OHJ

Tel: 01869 277534
PABSPAG@aol.com                    www.ukhunting.co.uk

Decoyed pigeon shooting takes place over 200,000 acres of prime farmland in Oxfordshire, Buckinghamshire, Berkshire and Hampshire. The Philip Beasley Sporting Agency, armed with over 30 years practical field experience, is well furnished with the best decoying equipment available, Landrover 4x4s and quad bikes to take Guns to the hides. During peak shooting periods there is a maximum of six Guns per day. Although pigeon shooting is available throughout the year, best times are normally from the end of March/beginning of April through to September/October.

*Shooting acreage*: 200,000
*Status*: Commercial
*Owner*: Philip Beasley Sporting Agency
*Contact*: Philip or Will Beasley
*Sporting agent*: N/a
*Number of available days*: Throughout the year
*Bag expectations*: As required
*Average cartridge to kill ratio*: 3:1
*Lunch*: A packed lunch is provided
*Price structure*: From £40 to £250 per day, depending on the level of service required
*Accommodation*: Bed and breakfast type accommodation ranging from £25 to £30 per night, and supplemented by excellent pubs and restaurants
*Access*: Box Farm is located conveniently next to the M40 at Bicester, near Oxford and is one hour's drive from London or Birmingham. By rail: Bicester Station. By air: Heathrow. Transport can be arranged.
*Other comments*: Well-behaved dogs welcome

# PIGEON SHOOTING

*LINCOLNSHIRE*

3 Scarlet Lane
Eagle
Lincoln
LN6 9EJ

Tel: 01522 868930                    Fax: 01522 868930
Mobile: 07887 676501
bwalker65@aol.com

Lincolnshire is renowned for its pigeon shooting and substantial bags can be made over decoys. Brian Walker, employing a professional guide, can arrange decoyed days over peas, beans, oil-seed rape and other crops according to the season. All hides, decoys are supplied and sport is usually excellent, though the point is made that one is dealing with a wild bird. The shooting acreage is extensive and allows a reasonable choice of venue

*Shooting acreage*: 20,000
*Status*: Commercial
*Contact*: Brian Walker as above
*Sporting agent*: N/a
*Number of available days*: Throughout year
*Bag expectations*: One to several hundred!
*Average cartridge to kill ratio*: Varies enormously according to skill
*Lunch*: Taken in the field
*Price structure*: Relates to the bag outcome. Usually £50 to £100 per person per day
*Accommodation*: White Hart Hotel at Scarle, also local B&B
*Access*: Via Brian Walker

E * 96

# STALKING

# DEER MANAGEMENT

The Old Bunching Shed
Watery Lane
Tincleton
Puddletown
Dorchester
Dorset
DT2 8QP

Tel: 01305 848952                    Fax: 01305 848952

Tincleton is a quiet rural village set in farmland five miles from the historic market town of Dorchester and 11 miles from the seaside town of Weymouth. For the non-stalking guest the local area offers a wide range of activities easily accessible by car. As members of the Association of Professional Deer Managers, Paul and Bryony run a hunting business in a secluded part of Dorset and offer a professional stalking service balanced with a warm and relaxing atmosphere. All stalking is accompanied one to one with guides holding a minimum of DMQ1 certification. The varied terrain consists of chalk downland, field margins and mixed woodland and stalking is either on foot or from high seats. Animals are carefully selected and, due to year-round observations, the average mature trophy buck can be calculated at approximately 350 grams with 25 per cent reaching CIC medal class.

*Stalking acreage*: 20,000
*Status*: Commercial
*Company*: Deer Management
*Contact*: Paul and Bryony Taylor as above
*Staff*: Two resident stalkers and four part-time
*Available stalking*: Roe bucks, roe does and some sika
*Rifle recommendations*: .243 or above up to .30 calibre
*Price structure*: Roe £100 to £1,000 plus. Sika £100 to £1,000 plus
*Accommodation*: Self-contained four bedroom cottage separate from main house with comfortable living area, kitchen, bathroom and drying facilities. Meals taken in main house, catered to client's needs with an emphasis on fresh local produce and game. Mealtimes flexible to suit hunting times and include full English breakfast and evening meal with glass of wine.
*Access*: By road: A35 to Dorchester, then 5 miles south-east country lane to Tincleton. By rail: Dorchester or Weymouth. By air: All major airports in southern England. Full travel details from Paul Taylor
*Other comments*: A specialist accredited taxidermist is on hand for trophy preparation, including full head/body mounts if required

# DEVON GAME SERVICES

*DEVON AND SOMERSET*

Blue Ball Lodge
Millhayes
Stockland
Honiton
Devon
EX14 9DB

Tel: 01404 881599　　　　　　Fax: 01404 881729
devongame@stockland.ex　　　www.devongame.com

Devon Game Services can offer can offer an extensive acreage of outstanding roe stalking in Devon and Somerset, including red deer stags. The roebuck stalking season, from April 1 to October 31, has produced, over the years, some good trophies and a high success rate for clients. A skilled stalker accompanies each Rifle, cross-country vehicles are used and selection of trophies is by agreement with the stalker. Every paying guest who wishes to stalk must be in possession of a current Firearms Certificate. Permits and Certificates are arranged for overseas visitors. The country incorporates rolling hills, valleys, woodland and copses. The red deer stags have, on the whole, excellent heads and good body weights.

*Stalking acreage*: Approximately 30,000 acres
*Status*: Commercial
*Owner*: Devon Game Services
*Contact*: Brian Turner as above
*Sporting agent*: N/a
*Staff*: Brian Turner and three experienced stalkers
*Available stalking*: Throughout season
*Rifle recommendations*: .243 or similar for roe and .270, .308 or similar for red deer
*Price structure*: £55 per outing. Rifle hire £20 per day. Firearm permit £40. Non- hunter accompanying hunter £30 per day. Roe buck trophy fees from £100 to £600 for 500 gram head. Over 500 grams £8 per gram. Cull bucks £100 each
*Accommodation*: Local hotels, B&B and also newly opened shooting lodge at Millhayes
*Access*: A303 or M5, Jct. 25 and 26 to Stockland. Nearest airport Exeter. Rail Waterloo to Axminster. Clients can be collected
*Other comments*: N/a

# EGDON STALKING

*CENTRAL AND SOUTH DORSET*

Upwater Barn
Sutton Road
Sutton Poyntz
Weymouth
Dorset
DT3 6LW

Tel: 01305 835710                    Fax: 10305 835710
fenn@upwater.fsnet.co.uk

Egdon Stalking, owned and run by Charles Fenn, enjoys access to extensive grounds in Central and South Dorset, the country varying from open downland to mixed woodlands and offering outstanding roe and sika stalking. This is, without question, some of the finest stalking available in England and is easily accessible for clients both from this country and overseas. Excellent high seats are available and all clients are individually guided. The area is renowned for the quality of both its roe and sika heads. Novice stalkers are particularly welcome and tuition can be arranged. All permits and licences are organised for overseas visitors. Stalking is available throughout the year. Charles Fenn is a qualified stalker with over 30 years experience. He is also a BASC Accredited Witness and an official measurer for the CIC UK Permanent National Trophy Commission.

*Stalking acreage*: Over 2,000
*Status*: Commercial
*Owner*: Charles Fenn
*Contact*: Charles Fenn, as above
*Sporting agent*: N/a
Staff: Charles Fenn is Headstalker
*Available stalking*: Throughout season
*Rifle recommendations*: .243 or similar for roe and .270, .308 or similar for sika.
*Price structure*: £50 per outing. Trophy prices: Roebucks from £100 to £600. Sika stags from £100 to £800. Further details on request.
*Accommodation*: Excellent B&B accommodation plus evening meal is provided at Upwater Barn, Sutton Poyntz.
*Access*: Very accessible by road, rail and air. Dorchester five miles away, Weymouth four miles, both with main line stations. Clients can be collected from stations or Bournemouth or Exeter airports.

# ELVEDEN

## THETFORD, NORFOLK

The Estate Office
Elveden
Thetford
Norfolk
IP24 3TQ

Tel: 01842 890223          Fax: 01842 890070
jim.rudderhan@elveden.com          www.elveden.com

This historic Estate (see Elveden under pheasant shooting) offers 23,000 acres of woodland and heathland stalking for four species of deer – red, roe, fallow and muntjac – all of which are present in abundance. However, while a small amount of days are available, much of the stalking is already committed. There is a cull of 500 beasts across all four species.

*Stalking acreage*: 23,000
*Status*: Private with let days
*Owner*: The Elveden Estate
*Contact*: Jim Rudderham as above
*Staff*: Two stalkers
*Available stalking*: A few days may be available
*Rifle recommendations*: .243 to .308
*Price structure*: POA
*Accommodation*: Well appointed self-catering lodges are available on the Estate
*Access*: By road A11 between Cambridge and Norwich. By rail: Cambridge

# GREENLEE HOUSE

## HEXHAM, NORTHUMBERLAND

Greenlee House
Bardon Mill
Hexham
Northumberland
NE47 7AS

Tel: 01434 344067                    Fax: 01434 344067
Greenleehouse@aol.com

Roe stalking over 6,000 acres of mixed farmland and woodland, much of which is close to the house. The owner, Jon Snowdon, always accompanies stalking outings and he will take a maximum of two Rifles. The terrain varies greatly so outings can be organised for all fitness levels and ages. There are normally two outings a day, dawn and dusk, and there is no charge for trophy fees. For those seeking to achieve a DMQ Level 2, Jon Snowdon is a DMQ Accredited Witness and can offer instruction on any aspect of deer stalking. Greenlee House, an isolated 18th-century farmhouse, is situated in the heart of the Northumberland National Park with stunning views. Guests are welcomed into the Snowdon's home and should expect a relaxed family atmosphere.

*Stalking acreage*: 6,000
*Status*: Private farmhouse
*Owner*: Jon Snowdon
*Contact*: Jon Snowdon
*Sporting agent*: N/a
Staff: Jon Snowdon himself takes guests on all stalking outings
*Available stalking*: Throughout relevant season
*Rifle recommendations*: .243-.308 calibre rifles recommended. Estate rifles are available as required
*Price structure*: £140 per day per Rifle roe buck stalking
*Accommodation*: Greenlee House. Bed, breakfast and evening meal available at cost of £40. All meals organised around the sporting day. The aim is to provide a friendly atmosphere and guests are expected to treat the house as their home.
*Access*: By road: M6 20 minutes away or A1 45 minutes away. By rail: Bardon Mill Station. By air: Newcastle Airport. Transport is available by arrangement.
*Other comments*: Dogs are welcome.

# NORTH WILTSHIRE DEER SERVICES

*WILTSHIRE AND GLOUCESTERSHIRE*

106 Pavenhill
Purton
Swindon
Wiltshire
SN5 4DB

Tel: 01793 770807                     Fax: 01793 771807
Mobile: 07950 918969
pete@northwiltsdeerservices.com
www.northwiltsdeerservices.com

Roe deer stalking over approximately 20,000 acres of woods and farmland on the borders of Wiltshire and Gloucestershire. The type of ground and stalking varies considerably with both Cotswold stone walls and Wiltshire hedges. High seats are available if required and all individual needs catered for.

*Stalking acreage*: 20,000
*Status*: Commercial
Stalking *Owner*: North Wilts Deer Services
*Contact*: Peter Griffin
*Sporting agent*: N/a
*Staff*: Two guides for stalking
*Available stalking*: Throughout season
*Rifle recommendations*: None given
*Price structure*: On application
*Accommodation*: Local accommodation can be arranged to suit any requirements in the stalking areas
*Access*: By road: M4/M5. By rail: Swindon Station. By air: Heathrow, Bristol or Birmingham. Transport is available on request

# THE FIELDCRAFT COUNTRY MANAGEMENT

Fieldcraft Country Management
56 Erle Havard Rd
West Bergholt
Colchester
CO6 3LH

Tel: 07743 517838
steve@fieldcraft.fsnet.co.uk          Website: www.fieldcraft.net

Fieldcraft Country Management can provide muntjac, roe and fallow stalking on ground in South Suffolk. Stalks are conducted on a personal level and can be in the morning or evening. During the roe and fallow ruts Rifles can sit up all day if they wish. The ground varies from open country with intermittent blocks of woodland which is where the fallow are found, to secluded fields enclosed by hedgerows, the haunt of roe. When not stalking Rifles can tour and enjoy some of the local and historical villages and their pubs and restaurants or even visit some of Constable's famous painting locations.

*Stalking acreage*: 2,000
*Status*: Commercial
*Sporting agent*: N/a
*Available stalking*: Muntjac, roe and fallow in season
*Rifle recommendations*: .243 or similar for roe and muntjac. .243 or .270 or similar for fallow.
*Price structure*: £80 per morning or evening stalk
*Accommodation*: Local hotels and B&Bs
*Access*: A12, Colchester North Station or Stansted Airport

# THE ULTIMATE HIGHSEAT COMPANY

## SUFFOLK/ESSEX BORDER

5 The Brickfields
Stowmarket
Suffolk
IP14 1RZ

Tel: 01449 675903        Fax: 01787 211188
highseats@tiscali.co.uk      www.highseats.co.uk

The stalking offered covers 3,000 acres on the Suffolk/Essex border and includes 100 acres of open grazed woodland and about 50 acres of coppiced woodland. Deer available are roe, fallow, muntjac and a very few red deer. High seats are available, or clients can choose to stalk. There are three experienced guides available on a one-to-one basis. Heads can be measured and arrangements made to have trophies prepared.

*Stalking acreage*: 3,000
*Status*: Commercial
*Contact*: David Morgan on mobile: 07814 313534 or Stephen Horton on mobile: 07966 515582
*Staff*: Three experienced stalkers
*Available stalking*: According to seasons
*Rifle recommendations*: .243 or similar for roe and muntjac. .270 or .308 for fallow and red
*Price structure*: £90 per stalk. No trophy charges
*Accommodation*: Local B&Bs or The Mill Hotel, Sudbury, Suffolk
*Access*: Contact David Morgan or Stephen Horton for directions

# THE VISCOUNT COWDRAY'S ESTATE

Cowdray Estate Office
Cowdray Park
Midhurst
West Sussex GU29 0AQ

Tel: 01730 812423
stalking@cowdray.co.uk

Fax: 01730 815608
www.deerstalking.co.uk

The Viscount Cowdray's Estate in West Sussex, which encompasses some of the most beautiful land in England, has Midhurst at its centre. The commercial woodland consists of 60 percent conifers and 40 per cent broadleaved trees. Roe deer are abundant throughout the entire Estate, while fallow are few in number and confine themselves to the southern boundary along the line of the South Downs. After 20 years co-ordinated deer management, the annual cull of roe and fallow has settled down to figures which appear suitable for central Southern England. Abundant food is available for wildlife throughout the year as a result of a relatively mild climate. Some 160 High Seats are available, but ground butts have also been constructed and employed in order that, even in the event of unfavourable stalking weather, individuals can be positioned with some prospect of success.

*Stalking acreage*: 16,500 acres, of which 6,500 acres is commercial woodland
*Status*: Private with let stalking
*Owner*: Viscount Cowdray – Cowdray Estate
*Contact*: As above
*Staff*: One full-time deer manager plus one assistant
*Available stalking*: Throughout season
*Rifle recommendations*: Deer legal calibres - .243 or similar for roe. Estate rifle available. Estate ammunition £1 per round.
*Price structure*: Charges from April 2003 – February 2004 (including VAT):
Weekly standing charge of eight outings, 3 hours each: £500 per person
A day's charge of two outings, 3 hours each: £125 per person
One outing of 3 hours: £65 per person
Success charges: Roe yearlings £30. Mature or old roe bucks up to 300 gram £125. Over 300 gram £2.50 per gram (e.g. 310 grams equals £300 plus £25. Total £150). Mature or old fallow £200. Pricket £50. Mature muntjac bucks £150. Young £30.
*Accommodation*: Own Estate holiday cottages, or local hotels, B&Bs. Cowdray Estate Green Book provides full information
*Access*: By road: A272/A286 Midhurst. By rail: Haslemere or Chichester Stations. By air: Heathrow or Gatwick Airports
*Other comments*: All stalkers are provided with Cowdray Estate Green Book of information and guidelines. Training and assessment for DMQ Level 2 at no extra charge.

# SIMULATED GAME SHOOTING

# BBSH LIMITED

Carpenters Cottage
Burkham
Nr Alton
Hants
GU34 5RR

Tel: 01256 381259          Fax: 01256 381259

Simulated game shooting is virtually identical to a 1000 bird game shooting day, the only difference being that one shoots at flushes of clay pigeons rather than pheasants launched from 10 traps at up to 120 ft above the guns. Two teams of eight shoot 5 drives each and each gun can fire 300-600 cartridges at any time of the year at a fraction of the cost of the real thing. We have two venues and prices start at £145 per gun when customers take an entire day or £160 per Gun when 15 or less are booked. The price includes lunch, drinks, etc but not cartridges which can be supplied on the day and must be fibre-wad. The days are for Shot-gun Certificate holders who are familiar with driven game shooting. We recommend that Guns use over-and-unders rather than relatively light side-by-sides as they soak up recoil better and are much more robust. Some died-in-the-wool game shooters are hesitant about coming first time but once they have been come back frequently when they see how closely the day resembles a real game shoot. The two main locations are over classic Wiltshire farmland offering varied terrain. BBSH also have locations in Hampshire, details can be obtained on application.

*Owner*: BBSH Limited
*Contact*: Warwick Hawes
*Sporting agent*: N/a
*Gun hire*: O/U 12 bores @ £25 per gun
*Lunch*: Elevenses, lunch and drinks are included in price. Served either in a farmhouse, log cabin or local pub.
*Price structure*: £145-£160 per gun depending on whether single guns or whole day for 16 guns is taken
*Accommodation*: Local hotels, pubs and B&Bs all available
*Access*: Both locations are accessible from M3, one off the A303 and the other off the A30. By rail: Salisbury
*Other comments*: No dogs allowed

# IAN COLEY SPORTING

## *GLOUCESTERSHIRE*

St George's House
29 St George's Road
Cheltenham
Gloucestershire
GL50 3DU

Tel: 01242 514478                    Fax: 01242 224697
info@coley.co.uk                     www.coley.co.uk

This day, as the name suggests, is run in exactly the same way as a live day's driven game shooting, with the clays acting as birds. An excellent introduction to live shooting for the beginner, a day's simulated game shooting also helps the experienced shot keep his eye in during the off-season, or acts as a reminder just before the season gets under way. It also provides the opportunity for unusual corporate days. Guns can wear their normal game shooting clothing or, if they wish, choose a more casual approach. As they days mostly take place from April to July the weather often dictates the day's fashion. Loaders and instructors can be arranged if required. Days are organised for eight, 12 and 16 Guns.

*Venues*: Ian Coley Sporting simulated game shooting days normally take place at Chatcombe Estate, near Cheltenham, or at another classic Cotswold estate in the area
*Contact*: Ian Coley Sporting, as above
*Sporting agent*: N/a
*Gun hire*: Can be arranged
*Price structure*: From £200 per head, depending on venue and numbers
*Accommodation*: Local hotels
*Access*: M5, Jct. 11a or 11. Gloucestershire Airport or rail to Gloucester.

# THE KENNETT SHOOT

East Kennett Manor
Marlborough
Wiltshire
SN8 4EY

Tel: 01672 861607      Fax: 01672 861036
james.cameron@kennettshoot.com    www.kennettshoot.com

This 700 acre estate, enjoying glorious views and steep valleys, lends itself perfectly to simulated game shooting, while the Georgian Manor is the ideal setting for Guns to have coffee, lunch and tea. Days are run in exactly the same fashion as driven game days. There is a mixture of drives, including high pheasants, grouse over butts, partridges and hares, while all traps are, of course, concealed. All standards of shooting are catered for and there are unlimited clays. There are two types of day: 'The Kennett Day' which is designed for corporate entertainment with all the frills. Instructors, loaders, guns, cartridges and 4x4s are all supplied, and a delicious lunch is laid on. On a 'Crackshots and Syndicates Day' there are unlimited clays, and a picnic or pub lunch. There is a minimum of eight Guns. Shoot Director is Bruce Gauntlett.

*Shooting acreage*: 700
*Status*: Commercial
*Owner*: James Cameron
*Contact*: James Cameron, as above
*Sporting agent*: N/a
*Gun hire*: Yes
*Lunch*: Lunch with wine and coffee at East Kennett Manor, or picnic on the estate or local pub or restaurant
*Price structure*: Kennett Day: £4,800 (ex VAT) for up to 16 Guns, and totally inclusive. Crackshots and Syndicates Day: £200 per person for 16 Guns including lunch on the estate or £320 per person for 8 Guns (prices exclude cartridges, gun hire, transport on the estate)
*Accommodation*: Ivy House Hotel, Marlborough (4 miles), The Inn, Hungerford, or The Vine Yard near Newbury
*Access*: By road: 80 miles from London (M4), 40 miles from Bristol. By air: Heathrow and Bristol Airports. By rail: One hour from Paddington to Pewsey Station. Helicopter landing facilities
*Other comments*: Bookings taken all through the year on this private estate, normally for 8 or 16 Guns. Charity days are held at the Kennett Shoot and large numbers of Guns can be accommodated

# PLUMMER DIXON ASSOCIATES

*BERKS., BUCKS., DERBYSHIRE, GLOS., HANTS., SURREY*

Candlemas House
Sherborne
nr Cheltenham
Gloucestershire, GL54 3DR

Tel: 01451 844714           Fax: 01451 844814
Mob. Tel: 07860 873719
pda@shootandfish.co.uk      www.shootandfish.co.uk

Our simulated game shooting is almost indistinguishable from a traditional driven day's live shooting. Guns meet at a private house at 9.30am for coffee when the day's format is explained, with emphasis on safety. Guns are then introduced to loaders who look after them throughout the day. Each drive ends and starts with a whistle and clays are sent at random from concealed traps. There is a further drive and a small competition before lunch, followed by two further drives. Guns return to the house for tea at 4.30pm. Days can be booked for private groups, corporate entertaining, syndicates, groups of friends, or individuals can join on an open day. Non-shooting guests are also welcome. Days are normally organised for 10 to 16 Guns and the price includes everything except cartridges and hire of guns if required. No Shotgun Certificate required and the sport can be enjoyed by complete beginners or very experienced shots. Loaders and instructors always on hand.

Venues: include Hazleton Manor, Cirencester, Glos., Catton Hall, Burton-on-Trent, Derbyshire, Chavenage House, nr Tetbury, Glos., Farmington, nr Stow on the Wold, Glos., Combe Manor, nr Hungerford, Berks, Bradley House, Maiden Bradley, nr Warminster, Highclere Castle, nr Newbury, Berks, Wherwell House & Priory, nr Andover, Hants., Hampton Estate, nr Farnham, Surrey, Hampden House, Great Missenden, Bucks.
*Owner:* Plummer Dixon Associates
*Contact:* Wendy Plummer
*Staff:* Loaders and instructors always on hand
*No of available days:* Throughout the year
*Gun hire:* By arrangement (not included in price). Cartridges supplied but not included in price
*Lunch:* Breakfast, mid-morning refreshment, lunch in private house and tea all included.
*Price structure:* From £280 per Gun plus VAT
*Accommodation:* All venues offer accommodation. Local pubs and hotels are also available
*Access:* All venues easily accessible by main roads, rail and air. Transport by arrangement
*Other comments:* Well-behaved dogs welcome

# PURBECK SHOOTING SCHOOL

Woolbridge Manor
Wool
Wareham
Dorset
BH20 6HQ

Tel: 01929 405101          Fax: 01929 405101
Mobile: 07976 931341
gb@eclipse.co.uk           www.shooting.co.uk

: Organised in an almost identical fashion to a day's driven game shooting, simulated game offers all the excitement of a day's sport, using clays instead of live game. Guns can dress exactly as for a day's shooting or adopt a more informal approach if they choose. It is an excellent introduction to live shooting for the novice shot or beginner and instructors will ensure that the guests are suitably looked after on the day. Three categories of sport can be arranged - Gold, Silver and Bronze Days. A Gold Day is intended for corporate day shooting or the serious game shooter who wishes to keep his eye in during the closed season. Double guns are welcome. The Silver Day will cater for a group of up to 16 Guns at intermediate level, with shooters sharing duty as loaders. The Bronze Days are intended for the small home shoot syndicate who wish to have a fun day at their own location. Using totally automatic Pro-matic traps, realistic simulated game shooting is arranged in conjunction with various landowners in southern England.

*Venues*: All in Dorset, these include Encombe Estate, Corfe Castle and Morden Estate
*Owner*: Purbeck Shooting School
*Contact*: Graham Brown
*Sporting agent*: N/A
*Gun hire*: Can be arranged
*Lunch*: Lunch is served on site
*Price structure*: From £90 per Gun plus VAT
*Accommodation*: Local inns/hotels available at all locations
*Access*: All estates within easy access of main roads and rail. Dorchester, adjacent to the A35 and A37, is only nine miles away with a main line station
*Other comments*: Well-behaved dogs are welcome

# SHUGBOROUGH SHOOTING SCHOOL

*CANNOCK CHASE, STAFFORDSHIRE*

Oakedge Park
Wolseley Bridge
Stafford
ST17 0XS

Tel: 01889 881391                    Fax: 01889 881391

The Shugborough Shooting School specialises in fun days for parties of eight minimum up to 20. Game Shooting syndicates find the sporting layout and general approach particularly useful and they can shoot as many flushes and sporting birds as they wish. The grounds are in an attractive woodland setting on the edge of Cannock Chase.

*Shooting acreage*: 66 acres
*Owner*: Graham Hudson
*Gun hire*: Guns can be hired
*Cartridges*: Clients can bring their own or purchase them on the ground
*Lunch*: Taken in the Corporate Room on site and can be at client's discretion
*Price structure*: £85 per person to include 250 shots. Does not include cost of cartridges.
*Access*: The Shugborough Shooting School lies on the A513 between Stafford and Rugeley and is 2.5 miles south of Shugborough Hall. From the M5 take Jct. 14 from the north and Jct. 13 from the south

E * 114

# SCOTLAND

# PHEASANTS

# AIRLIE AND BALINTORE SHOOTS

Little Kenny
Lintrathen
By Kirriemuir
Angus
DD8 5JD

Tel: 01575 560292 (answerphone)     Fax: 01575 560235
www.avon&airliesporting.com

Outstanding driven grouse, partridges and pheasants over 6,500 and 4,500 acres, including two famous pheasant drives at Airlie Castle. Sporting programme also includes roe and red deer stalking, falconry, rough shooting and fishing all the year round incorporating three up-market self-catering cottages. There is also salmon fishing on the River Isla. All sport is personally hosted by Paddy Fetherston-Godley and full particulars are available on request.

*Shooting acreage*: 11,000
*Status*: Commercial
*Owner*: Avon & Airlie Sporting
*Contact*: Paddy Fetherston-Godley
*Sporting agent*: N/a
*Headkeeper/staff*: David McNaughton plus two under-keepers.
*Number of available days*: 60 plus.
*Number of drives*: 70 plus.
*Bag expectations*: 50 – 400
*Average cartridge to kill ratio*: varies
*Lunch*: Provided, including drinks
*Price structure*: POA
*Accommodation*: Recommended local hotels, B&Bs and self-catering cottages.
*Access*: A90 from Dundee, then A928. By rail: Dundee Station. By air: Dundee Airport
*Other comments*: Well trained gundogs welcome

# ARDMADDY ESTATE

## *NR OBAN, ARGYLLSHIRE*

2 India Street
Edinburgh
EH3 6EZ

Tel: 0131 476 6500                    Fax: 0131 475 6501
info@sportingestates.com         www.sportingestates.com

The estate offers mixed shooting packages for pheasants, duck, woodcock and occasional snipe. There are a number of flight ponds and a small hill loch as well as several miles of coastline. Roe stalking is also available.

*Shooting acreage*: 3,000
*Status*: Private with let days
*Contact*: George Goldsmith
*Headkeeper/staff*: Charlie Boyd
*Number of available days*: 2-3 shooting weekends
*Number of drives*: 18
*Bag expectations*: Drive 150, walked up 50-60
*Average cartridge to kill ratio*: 4:1
*Lunch*: Taken at Ardmaddy Castle or Caddleton Farmhouse
*Price structure*: From £2,500 for a shooting weekend
*Accommodation*: Caddleton Farmhouse offers comfortable accommodation for up to 12 guests on a self-catering basis, although it is also suitable for smaller parties. The farmhouse and stable cottage can sleep up to 16
*Access*: By road: A82 then A85. By air: Glasgow airport.
*Other comments*: Well trained gundogs welcome

# BREDA ESTATE

## *BY ALFORD, DEESIDE, ABERDEENSHIRE*

Tel: 01651 806375                    Fax: 01651 806547
contact@kingscliff.co.uk             www.kingscliff.co.uk

Breda is a much-loved and unspoilt private estate which rises from the banks of the River Don to stunning heather moorland. It combines deep hidden valleys, beech woodland and avenues, steep banks and pretty meadowland. Sporting opportunities include excellent pheasant, partridge, wild duck, woodcock and grouse shooting, plus good roe stalking. The estate is sensitively farmed and managed by its owner with 'quality rather than quantity' in mind. It includes around 40 acres of game crops. Excluding the grouse shooting, pegs are easily accessible for people with limited mobility.

*Shooting acreage*: 2,500 acres
*Status*: Private with let days
*Owner*: Hamish McLean of Breda
*Contact*: Chris Harry Thomas
*Headkeeper/staff*: Ronnie McLeod
*Number of available days*: 10
*Number of drives*: 12
*Bag expectations*: 120
*Average cartridge to kill ratio*: 5:1
*Lunch*: Featuring carefully selected local produce, is served at the end of the day in Tullochmill Farmhouse. Drinks provided during the shoot.
*Accommodation*: Nearby Marcliffe of Pitfodels Hotel. Breda House currently being renovated to offer accommodation.
*Access*: By road: 45 minutes by A944 from Aberdeen and Aberdeen Airport
*Other comments*: Well trained gundogs welcome. Accommodation, transport and other activities for partners can be arranged by Chris Harry Thomas

# BUCCLEUCH ARMS HOTEL

*SCOTTISH BORDERS*

The Green
St Boswells
Scottish Borders
TD6 0EW

Tel: 01835 822243          Fax: 01835 823965
www.buccleucharmshotel.co.uk

The Buccleuch Arms Hotel, a former 16th century coaching inn sited close to the Tweed, offers driven pheasants, walked-up, rough shooting for pheasants and partridges and flighting for ducks over 2,000 acres in the heart of the Scottish Borders. In addition, guided inland goose shooting is just half an hour's drive away. The hotel is family-run, providing good food and comfortable en suite accommodation. It offers all one would expect from a sporting hotel.

*Shooting acreage*: 2,000 plus
*Status*: Hotel and commercial shooting
*Owner*: Buccleuch Arms Hotel
*Contact*: Bill Dodds, as above
*Sporting agent*: N/a
*Number of available days*: As required during relevant seasons
*Number of drives*: 10
*Bag expectations*: Driven days from 75 birds. All others by arrangement.
*Average cartridge to kill ratio*: Varies
*Lunch*: Taken in the Buccleuch Arms Hotel either midday or shooting through
*Price structure*: Driven from £21 per bird. Other shooting POA
*Accommodation*: DBB from £45 per person
*Access*: A68 from Jedburgh. 40 miles from Edinburgh. 60 miles from Newcastle.
*Other comments*: Well trained dogs very welcome

*CANONBIE, DUMFRIES & GALLOWAY*

Drybrow
Canonbie
Dumfriesshire
DG14 0TB

Tel: 01387 371555

Canonbie West Shoot covers approximately 2,500 acres of undulating countryside consisting of arable, conifer and mixed hardwood plantations, 'flows' and rivers. Pheasants and woodcock are driven from the plantations, while snipe are walked-up and driven from the flows. Mallard and teal are flighted at dusk over well-fed ponds. Woodcock flighting at dusk can be very rewarding. Altogether an informal day's sport is guaranteed.

*Shooting acreage*: 2,500
*Status*: Private with let days:
*Owner*: Buccleuch Estates/Wellglen Shooting Syndicate
*Contact*: Vic Challoner
*Sporting agent*: N/a
*Headkeeper*: Vic Challoner
*Number of available days*: Two to three days a week from October 1 to Feb 1 for game. Wild duck from Sept 1.
*Number of drives*: 6 or more per day
*Bag expectations*: Approximately five birds per Gun to give a 40 bird bag for eight Guns
*Average cartridge to kill ratio*: 4:1 and 6:1
*Lunch*: Packed lunch required for half hour lunch break
*Price structure*: £70 per Gun per day. £16 per bird for pheasants and partridges for bags of 50 upwards. No charge for various.
*Accommodation*: Hotels used by clients are Powfoot Golf Hotel, Powfoot, Annan, Dumfries: Eskdale Hotel, Langholm, Dumfries and Crosskeys Hotel, Canonbie, Dumfries. All cater for sportsmen.
*Access*: By road: A7 from Carlisle. By rail: Carlisle Station. By air: Glasgow Airport
*Other comments*: Well trained gundogs are welcome.

# CORSEWALL ESTATE

*STRANRAER, DUMFRIES & GALLOWAY*

Atkin Grant & Lang
Broomhill Leys
Windmill Road
Markyate
Hertfordshire
AL3 8LP

Tel: 01582 842280                    Fax: 01582 842318
atkingrant.lang@btinternet.com

Atkin Grant & Lang run their own outstanding game shoot in the beautiful Galloway region of Scotland. The 3,500 acre estate has all the features required to present high and challenging birds, with drives varying from steep wooded hills and glens to a lovely remote sandy beach with spectacular loch-side views. Main drives offer driven pheasants and partridges, but less formal walked-up days, for groups of three to six, usually include snipe, woodcock, greylag or pinkfeet geese, ground game and some of the best teal and duck shooting in Scotland. Evening flights available at no extra cost on driven day. Roe stalking available in season.

*Shooting acreage*: 3,500
*Status*: Commercial
*Owner*: Atkin Grant & Lang
*Contact*: Ken Duglan
*Sporting agent*: N/a
*Headkeeper/staff*: Peter Trotman
*Number of available days*: 16
*Number of drives*: 14
*Bag expectations*: 250-300
*Gun/cartridge recommendations*: 1oz of No 6s
*Average cartridge to kill ratio*: 5–1
*Lunch*: Taken in local farmhouse
*Price structure*: Based on £25 per bird
*Accommodation*: Local hotels and B&B available
*Access*: A75 into Stranraer. Prestwick and Glasgow Airports
*Other comments*: Well-behaved gundogs welcome

# COWANS SPORTING

Cowans Sporting
Kirkgunzeon
Dumfries
South West Scotland
DG2 8JY

Telephone: 01387 760284          Fax: 01387 760602
craig@cowanssporting.co.uk       www.cowanssporting.co.uk

Driven and walked-up pheasants, rough shooting, flighted duck over 15,000 acres covering five shoots. The country consists of large woodland, high ground and very hilly in places. The Galloway side, with its steep sides, shows excellent birds. However all the five shoots vary a great deal in their composition and the type and quality of birds shown.

*Shooting acreage*: 15,000
*Status*: Commercial
*Sporting agent*: Craig Denman
*Headkeeper/staff*: N/a
*Number of available days*: 15-20 driven days and several small walked-up and rough days.
*Number of drives*: Numerous
*Bag expectations*: 25-150
*Average cartridge to kill ratio*: 3:1
*Lunch*: On request
*Price structure*: Average £22 per bird, but varies from £15 to £30 per bird
Rough and walked up days £110 per Gun including duck flight
*Accommodation*: Ample good hotels, inns, B&Bs available locally
*Access*: By road: A75 from Carlisle
*Other comments*: Well trained gundogs welcome.

# CRAIGHOWIE SHOOT

*BLACK ISLE, BY INVERNESS*

Lynedoch House
Barossa Place
Perth
PH1 5EP

Tel: 01738 451600                     Fax: 01738 451900
sporting@ckdgalbraith.co.uk           www.sportinglets.co.uk

The Craighowie Shoot offers a thoroughly enjoyable shooting
experience with testing driven partridges from the beginning of
September, and driven pheasants and partridges from October to the
end of the season. The ground is bounded on one side by the Moray
Firth and on the other by Munlochy Bay, a wildfowl sanctuary. The
countryside comprises Caledonian pines and silver birches, with
ground cover consisting of bracken, heather, broom and reeds. Several
ponds on the higher ground hold duck, and woodcock often join the
bag. The pheasant drives have been developed to provide high, curling
birds and, on one drive, pheasants coming from three directions.

*Shooting acreage*: 1,500 acres
*Status*: Private with let days
*Sporting agent*: Rober Rattray of C.K.D.Galbraith
*Headkeeper/staff*: Arthur Wright
*Number of available days*: 20 plus
*Number of drives*: 12 plus
*Bag expectations*: 220-250
*Average cartridge to kill ratio*: 3.5:1
*Lunch*: Guests greeted with coffee and biscuits; drinks and warm snacks
mid-morning precede a hot lunch. Tea provided at end of day's shooting
*Price structure*: POA
*Accommodation*: Either private Town House Lodge in Inverness, accommo-
dating eight couples or Caledon House Hotel or Dalcross Castle
*Access*: Fly or rail to Inverness, then 30 minutes drive on A9
*Other comments*: Well trained gundogs welcome

# CRAIGSTON CASTLE

## TURRIF, ABERDEENSHIRE

Tel: 01651 806375      Fax: 01651 806547
contact@kingscliff.co.uk      www.kingscliff.co.uk

A small, picturesque shoot which envelopes the traditional 16th century turreted home of the Urquhart clan. Bordered by the River Deveron, famous for its sea-trout, the shoot is dissected by charming tributaries crossed by stone and wooden bridges. It features very deep valleys, with both deciduous and conifer woodland and some arable farmland to provide really testing pheasant, partridge, duck and woodcock shooting. Pegs are easily accessible to people with limited mobility.

*Shooting acreage*: 3,000
*Status*: Commercial
*Owner*: The Urquhart family
*Contact*: Chris Harry Thomas
*Headkeeper/staff*: Steve Foreman, assisted by son Thomas. Shoot days hosted by Chris Harry Thomas
*Number of available days*: 8
*Number of drives*: 14
*Bag expectations*: 120-150
*Average cartridge to kill ratio*: 4:1
*Lunch*: Due to Scotland's short winter daylight hours, lunch is served at the end of the day at nearby Kingscliff Sporting Lodge in front of open fire. Game pie and mash a speciality. Drinks provided during shoot.
*Price structure*: £25 per bird plus VAT
*Accommodation*: Nearby Meldrum House Hotel, a small country hotel.
*Access*: By road: 45 minutes by A947 from Aberdeen and Aberdeen Airport
*Other comments*: Well trained gundogs welcome and can be kennelled

# DUNDAS, HOPETOUN & DALMENY

*WITHIN 15 MINUTES DRIVE FROM EDINBURGH*

2 India Street
Edinburgh
EH3 6EZ

Tel: 0131 476 6500                     Fax: 0131 476 6501
info@sportingestates.com          www.sportingestates.com

This is a first time ever offer of driven shooting over three major estates, each of which includes a stately home and is located next to each other. High quality and challenging shooting is a feature of all three estates and the package includes 250 bird back-to-back days on each estate. Rolling hills, dramatic woodlands and steep valleys ensure superb driven pheasant shooting. At Hopetoun and Dalmeny many drives overlook the Forth Estuary with views of the Kingdom of Fife in the distance. At Dundas birds are driven over a freshwater loch, to offer spectacular and unusual drives. This is highly recommended sport and will meet the requirements of the most demanding shots.

*Status*: Private with let days:
*Sporting agent*: George Goldsmith
*Headkeeper/staff*: N/a
*Number of available days*: On application
*Bag expectations*: 250 bird days
*Average cartridge to kill ratio*: Varies
*Lunch*: Varies by location
*Price structure*: POA. Packages include transfers, all meals and drink
*Accommodation*: Dundas Castle, built in 1818. Luxury accommodation
*Access*: Edinburgh Airport – full details available from agent, varies according to location
*Other comments*: Well-behaved dogs welcome

---

*BY ABERFELDY, PERTHSHIRE PH5 2JX*

Shalden Park Steading
Shalden
Alton
Hampshire
GU34 4DS

Tel: 01256 381821          Fax: 01256 381921
ellis.campbell@virgin.net

The shoot is located on the steep and less steep land sloping north to south in the very beautiful Strath Tay four miles downstream from Aberfeldy. The shoot has been developed over the past 20 years by the owner Michael Campbell and his headkeeper Donald Campbell. Although there was little by way of an established shoot 20 years ago, there were some well positioned small woods and some stunning deep dens which provide very exciting and challenging birds at long but killable range. There is also a drive over the River Tay (Himalaya) where three Guns and pickers-up are taken over by boat. Partridges were introduced in 1999 and have been a great success on the marginal in-bye land on the heather edge. These now represent about 40 per cent of the birds put down and all days include both pheasants and partridges.

*Shooting acreage*: 4,000, and shoot over 2,000
*Status*: Private with let days
*Owner*: Michael D.C.C.Campbell t/a Edradynate Ltd
*Contact*: Michael Campbell
*Sporting agent*: N/a
*Headkeeper/staff*: Donald Campbell. Underkeeper Neil Smith
*Number of available days*: 6
*Number of drives*: 20, but some for only part of the season
*Bag expectations*: 250
*Average cartridge to kill ratio*: 4.5:1
*Lunch*: Both lunch and tea taken in Edradynate House. Toddy at 11am in Fishing Hut on the Tay
*Price structure*: POA
*Accommodation*: Kinnaird Hotel, Farleyer House, Aberfeldy and Kenmore House, Dunkeld
*Access*: From Edinburgh Airport M9 to Forth Road Bridge. Exit 1 to A8000. M90 to Perth, Exit 10. A9 to Inverness, 20 miles A827 to Aberfeldy
*Other comments*: Well trained gundogs welcome

# EILEAN DARACH ESTATE

## *LITTLE LOCH BROOM, HIGHLAND*

Brackloch
Eilean Darach Estate
Dundonell
Wester Ross
IV23 2QW

Tel: 01854 633203

The Eilean Darach Estate of 6,500 acres is situated in the heart of the glorious West Coast scenery in the strath of Little Loch Broom. Under new ownership, the shooting is now becoming extremely attractive, particularly for those who enjoy mixed shooting coupled with a reasonable amount of walking and exercise. There is rough shooting for a mixed bag of walked-up pheasants and partridges, duck flighting and for the more energetic ptarmigan shooting on the high ground. In addition, Guns can also enjoy semi-driven sport with both partridges and pheasants. There is also excellent red deer and goat stalking (see entry under stalking).

*Shooting acreage*: 6,500
*Status*: Private with let days
*Owner*: Mr and Mrs Crawford. See above
*Contact*: As above
*Sporting agent*: N/a
*Headkeeper/staff*: Peter Hann
*Number of available days*: 20
*Number of drives*: Semi-driven 6 – 7
*Bag expectations*: Semi-driven 50 plus. Walk-up 10-14 per Gun
*Average cartridge to kill ratio*: Varies enormously
*Lunch*: Lunch taken on the hill
*Price structure*: £100 per person per day rough shooting. Semi-driven £16 per bird
*Accommodation*: Self-catering lodge sleeping 12 comfortably and also a cottage
*Access*: By road: A9 from Inverness, A835 and then A832. By air or rail: Inverness

# GLENSTRIVEN ESTATES (KNOCKDOW)

*BY DUNOON, ARGYLE*

2 India Street
Edinburgh
EH3 6EZ

Tel: 0131 476 6500                    Fax: 0131 476 6501.
info@sportingestates.com              www.sportingestates.com

This private loch-side estate offers double 250 bird driven pheasant days between November and January for eight to 10 Guns. The three beats on the estate provide a variety of ground from steep hillsides and valleys to open birch woods and classic pheasant drives around the mature policy woodlands. The majority of birds are driven towards the loch from steep crags and over deep gullies, producing high quality curling pheasants. This is testing and very sporting shooting as the kills to cartridges ratio shows.

*Shooting acreage*: 2,000
*Status*: Private with let days
*Sporting agent*: George Goldsmith
*Headkeeper/staff*: Ian Smith is headkeeper
*Number of available days*: 3 weekends in November, December and January
*Number of drives*: 16
*Bag expectations*: 250
*Average cartridge to kill*: 5:1
*Lunch*: Held private room in courtyard off the main house
*Accommodation*: The Victorian country house, Glenstriven Lodge, set in the heart of the estate and overlooking the loch, offers comfortable accommodation for up to 16 guests. The house is fully staffed and all meals are included in the rental. Guests can arrive by helicopter, sea-plane or boat, by arrangement only.
*Price structure*: Total rental for three nights accommodation and shooting for up to eight Guns on fully catered basis, incl. beer and spirits (not wine) £21,475 inc. VAT.
*Access*: Fly to Glasgow Airport where parties can be collected. An antique 12-seater bus to ferry or sea-plane to Lodge

# GRANDTULLY ESTATE

*PERTHSHIRE*

Kenmore House
Old Amulree Road
Kenmore
PH15 2QX

Tel: 01827 300624                    Mobile: 07860 617035

High quality driven pheasants and partridges. Grandtully is a magnificent sporting shoot, set in some of the most spectacular scenery in Perthshire. The shooting, over 3,000 acres, consists mainly of high pheasants and partridges with some drives producing spectacularly high birds if required. Duck flighting at the end of a day's driven sport is available if required. This last is free of charge.

*Shooting acreage*: 3,000 plus
*Status*: Private with let days
*Owner*: Barry Mordue.
*Headkeeper*: Mike Broad plus two full-time keepers
*Sporting agent*: N/a
*Number of available days*: 30
*Number of drives*: 22
*Bag expectations*: 100 to 300
*Average cartridge to kill ratio*: 4-6:1
*Lunch*: On shoot
*Price structure*: £20-£23 per bird based on bag expectation
*Accommodation*: Ample hotels and B&Bs within five miles radius of the shoot
*Access*: By road: A9 from Perth to Dunkeld to Dallinguig and signed to Aberfeldy
*Other comments*: Well-behaved gundogs welcome

Lynedoch House
Barossa Place
Perth
PH1 5EP

Tel: 01738 451600.            Fax: 01738 451900
sporting@ckdgalbraith.co.uk            www.sportinglets.co.uk

Enjoying an extensive acreage of moors, woods, farmland, lochs and hills, the Islay Estates can offer memorable sport. A limited number of days may be available for rough shooting for six Guns. Game, according to season, includes woodcock, pheasants, snipe, hares and duck. The Island is, of course, also famous for its distilleries, golf course and abundant bird life (see also entry under stalking).

*Shooting acreage*: 50,000 plus
*Status*: Private with let days
*Sporting agent*: Robert Rattray of C.K.D.Galbraith, as above
*Headkeeper/staff*: Jack Adamson
*Number of available days*: Limited
*Number of drives*: N/a
*Bag expectation*: 30-50 head
*Average cartridge to kill ratio*: According to Guns' skill
*Lunch*: On the hill
*Price structure*: POA
*Accommodation*: Parties of up to 10 can be accommodated in a comfortable self-catering farmhouse overlooking Loch Skerrols. There is also self-catering accommodation in a recently modernised cottage sleeping four. Alternatively guests can be booked into the Bridgend Hotel.
*Access*: Fly from Glasgow, flights out in the morning and back in the evening or take ferry from Loch Tarbert
*Other comments*: Well-behaved gundogs welcome

# KINNAIRD CASTLE

*BRECHIN, ANGUS*

Estate Office
Haughs of Kinnaird
Brechin
Angus
DD9 6UA

Tel: 01674 810240                    Fax: 01674 810364
southesk@aol.com

Centred on a lovely parkland at Kinnaird Castle, this driven pheasant shoot offers traditional sport in a friendly and thoroughly congenial atmosphere. This is largely woodland shooting, offering birds in a delightful setting. Several drives take place from coverts on the banks of the River South Esk. Ideal shooting for corporate days.

*Shooting acreage*: 1,500
*Status*: Private with let days
*Owner*: South Esk Estate
*Contact*: C.A.H.Gow, Factor
*Headkeeper/staff*: Sandy Mackintosh plus one under-keeper
*Number of available days*: Approximately 15
*Number of drives*: Numerous
*Bag expectations*: 150-350
*Lunch*: By arrangement but usually taken in the Castle
*Price structure*: Base price of £22 per bird plus VAT including lunch and transport
*Accommodation*: Offered in the Castle. Luxury standard and price by arrangement
*Access*: Aberdeen Airport or Montrose Station. Good road off the A90
*Other comments*: Well trained gundogs welcome

# KINNAIRD ESTATE

Lynedoch House
Barossa Place
Perth
PH1 5EP

Tel: 01738 451600.                     Fax: 01738 451900
sporting@ckdgalbraith.co.uk            www.sportinglets.co.uk

The Kinnaird Estate is situated amidst spectacular Perthshire countryside. The established driven pheasant shoot offers a variety of days, from informal walked-up outings of 30 plus head to formal driven days of up to 150 birds. In addition, wild duck flighting and walked-up grouse over pointers is also available, while for the stalking enthusiast there is roe stalking to be enjoyed. Clay pigeon shooting is also available.

*Shooting acreage*: 9,000
*Status*: Private with let days
*Sporting agent*: Robert Rattray of C.K.D.Galbraith, as above
*Headkeeper*: David Stewart
*Number of available days*: On application
*Number of drives*: Not known
*Bag expectations*: 100-200
*Average cartridge to kill ratio*: Varies according to skill
*Lunch*: On the Estate
*Price structure*: POA
*Accommodation*: The original Edwardian mansion of the estate, now converted to a luxury hotel and with nine guest bedrooms, each with its own luxuriously appointed bathroom. In addition, there are eight individually styled cottages at secluded locations around the estate.
*Access*: Fly to Edinburgh or Dundee City Airports and then take the A9 from Perth. Kinnaird Estate is 30 minutes north of Perth by Dunkeld.
*Other comments*: Well-behaved gundogs welcome

# KINNORDY ESTATE

*ANGUS GLENS*

Kinnordy Estate
Kirriemuir
Angus
DD8 4RG

Tel: 01575 572665

Kinnordy Estate is set at the foot of the Angus glens at the start of the Grampian Mountains. The 8,500 acre estate is a mixture of woodland, arable with wooded and open hill ground. Kinnordy also has its own loch and nature reserve. A syndicate shoots a third of the available days and a further 20 pheasant and partridge days are sold. The shooting comprises driven and walked-up pheasants, partridges, snipe, woodcock, golden plover, hares and rabbits. Geese and duck can be flighted over seven ponds. In addition there is year-round roe stalking. This is an informal, friendly shoot with some very exciting drives.

*Shooting acreage*: 8,500
*Status*: Commercial and syndicate
*Owner*: Kinnordy Estates
*Contact*: Mr George Elliott as above
*Sporting agent*: N/a
*Headkeeper*: John Holliday, assisted by Jacqui Holliday
*Number of available days*: 20 plus
*Number of drives*: 12 plus
*Bag expectations*: 30 to 250
*Average cartridge to kill ratio*: 4:1
*Lunch*: Picnics or full prepared meals
*Price structure*: £12 plus per bird walked-up. £20 plus per bird driven. Flights £30
*Accommodation*: Two local hotels, B&Bs and a sporting lodge
*Access*: By road: A90 from Dundee, then A928. By rail: Dundee/Perth. By air: Glasgow, Edinburgh or Dundee Airports
*Other comments*: Well-behaved gundogs welcome

# LAMMERMUIR SHOOT

Lammermuir Game Services
'Swallow Eaves'
Westruther
Gordon
Berwickshire
TD3 6WB

Tel: 01578 740258

Driven partridge, pheasants, duck, grouse, snipe and woodcock. Also mixed walked-up days, to include most game species over approximately 10,000 acres. The Lammermuir Shoot encompasses a wide range of sporting opportunities over a variety of ground. The large acreage holds most game species, including quality high pheasants and partridges driven over deep valleys and undulating ground. Driven duck on the rivers provide good sporting birds and evening flighting. There are also walked-up and driven snipe and woodcock opportunities and a variety of mixed rough shooting days. Roe stalking can also be arranged. The Scottish Borders enjoys a spectacular landscape and the sport experienced here is made all the more enjoyable by the delightful surroundings. Days can be tailored to suit individual requirements and are available throughout the season.

*Shooting acreage*: 10,000
*Status*: Commercial
*Contact*: Doug Virtue
*Sporting agent*: N/a
*Headkeeper/staff*: A. Ainslie plus two beat-keepers
*Numbers of days available*: 40 driven. 30 rough and walked-up
*Number of drives*: Driven days 3 –5 drives per day
*Average cartridge to kill ratio*: Driven partridges 6:1. Driven pheasants 4:1
*Lunch*: Pub lunch at The Old Thistle Inn (in Good Food Guide)
*Price structure*: Driven £22 plus VAT per bird. Rough shoot £150 per Gun per day
*Accommodation*: Local hotels and guest houses
*Access*: A68 then A697 or Edinburgh Airport 40 minutes drive
*Other comments*: Well-behaved gundogs welcome

## LANGHOLM, DUMFRIESSHIRE

Wellglen Shooting Syndicate
Holmhead
Langholm
Dumfriesshire
DG13 0ND

Tel: 01929 480709 Julian Cotterell (sporting tenant) or
Tel: 01387 380253 Andy Denton (headkeeper)

This Border Estate (22 miles north of Carlisle) provides some of the finest pheasant and partridge shooting in Scotland. Beautiful hill country with many challenging drives over valleys and rivers produces a large variety of sporting and interesting shooting. It is considered that the partridge drives are among the best in the country. It is mainly shot by a private syndicate, but a limited number of days are available to let. Bags of between 250 and 300 birds for 8 Guns and smaller rough days are available. Some woodcock, snipe and duck are shot on most days. With four full-time keepers, employed over a large acreage, it is a professionally run shoot of the highest quality.

*Shooting acreage*: 20,000 plus
*Status*: Syndicate with let days
*Contact*: Julian Cotterell (sporting tenant) or Andy Denton, as above
*Sporting agent*: N/a
*Headkeeper/staff*: Andy Denton plus three beat-keepers
*Number of available days*: Numerous
*Number of drives*: 40
*Bag expectations*: 250-300
*Average cartridge to kill ratio*: 4:1 if reasonable shots
*Lunch*: Lodge, mobile hot lunch or pub
*Price structure*: £15 to £24 per bird plus VAT
*Accommodation*: Good accommodation available locally, ranging from country house hotels to pubs or Estate cottages available to rent
*Access*: 15 miles off Jct 44 on M6 or Carlisle train station
*Other comments*: Well-behaved gundogs welcome

*LOCH FINE, ARGYLL*

Estate Office
Otter Estate
Kilfinan
Argyll
PA21 2EP

Tel: 01780 821282

Driven pheasants with some duck and also walked-up days. The Otter Estate is a private pheasant shoot with a hotel attached. There is a maximum of 16 days driven shooting available for letting and back-to-back days of shooting can be provided. The shoot also offers several walked-up days and it is possible to combine them with a driven day. The shoot is situated on the shores of Loch Fine with some beautiful Highland scenery and magnificent views across the loch. The birds are mainly driven from steep woodland and various types of cover on banks. There are often duck in the drives with an opportunity to use the loch-side ponds for an evening duck flight. The shoot is based on showing high birds in a sporting manner to provide a thoroughly enjoyable day. A day's shooting can be tailored according to the wishes and experience of the team. Kilfinan Hotel is situated in the centre of the Estate and it is possible to walk from it to several drives. The hotel offers quality accommodation with 11 rooms, a very friendly atmosphere and delicious fare.

*Shooting acreage*: 3,800
*Status*: Private shoot with hotel attached:
*Owner*: Mr Nicholas Wills
*Estate Manager*: Mr David Newton
*Sporting agent*: N/a
*Headkeeper/staff*: Rod Addy, Tel: 01700 821262.
*Number of available days*: 16 driven
*Number of drives*: 14 (back-to-back days can be arranged)
*Bag expectations*: 150-250 on driven days and 70-90 walked-up.
*Average cartridge to kill to ratio*: 5:1. Fibre wads only
*Lunch*: Taken in Kilfinan Hotel
*Price structure*: £22 per driven bird. £14 per bird walked-up. (2002 prices)
*Accommodation*: Kilfinan Hotel. Tel: 01700 821201
*Access*: By road: A82. Fly or rail to Glasgow or Inverness and then 1¾ hours drive
*Other comments*: Well-behaved gundogs welcome

# PARK

Park
Drumoak
Kincardineshire
AB31 5AD

Tel: 01334 839218

Park, known internationally for its wonderful salmon fishing, has a delightful shoot throughout the 2,000 acres of policies and farmland. Traditional covert shooting takes place with picturesque drives over the River Dee. Wild duck flighting can also be arranged. In addition, each season Park holds a shoot for black powder guns. Clay shooting is also provided in the grounds.

*Shooting acreage*: 2,000
*Status*: Private with let days
*Owner*: The Foster family
*Contact*: The shooting is run by Sandy Brown, as above
*Sporting agent*: N/a
*Headkeeper*: Sandy Brown
*Number of available days*: 4 to 6
*Number of drives*: 15 plus
*Bag expectations*: 100 to 120 bird days
*Average cartridge to kill ratio*: 4:1. Fibre wads preferred
*Lunch*: Usually in Park House or bothy
*Price structure*: £22 per bird upwards
*Accommodation*: Guests usually stay at Park House, enjoying its superb comfort, food and famous cellar
*Access*: By road: just off the A93 Aberdeen Airport 12 miles. Aberdeen Station 12 miles
*Other comments*: Well-behaved gundogs welcome

## PITCASTLE, BY GRANDTULLY, PERTHSHIRE

2 India Street
Edinburgh
EH3 6EZ

Tel: 0131 476 6500.          Fax: 0131 476 6501
info@sportingestates.com     www.sportingestates.com

This well-organised shoot specialises in high quality pheasants driven over lovely Perthshire countryside. Deep valleys and hills ensure spectacular shooting for reasonable bags. This shoot has a reputation for being very well run and guests are also assured of generous hospitality.

*Shooting acreage*: 1,100
*Status*: Private with let days
*Sporting agent*: George Goldsmith
*Headkeeper/staff*: David Fraser
*Number of available days*: Limited days from Nov. to January
*Number of drives*: 14
*Bag expectations*: 125 to 200
*Average cartridge to kill ratio*: 4: 1
*Lunch*: Served in a delightful converted bothy with open fire
*Price structure*: Two days shooting, from £17,000 inc. VAT. This includes all accommodation, meals, wine, champagne and spirits.
*Accommodation*: In Pitt Castle. Extremely comfortable accommodation for up to 16. All bedrooms en-suite.
*Access*: A9 and then A827. Rail or air at Edinburgh or rail at Dunkeld
*Other comments*: Well-behaved dogs welcome

# POLTALLOCH

---

*KILMARTIN, ARGYLL PA31 8QQ*

Ardifuir
Kilmartin
Argyll
PA31 8QH

Tel 01546 510271

This is a comparatively small shoot, with 1,000 pheasants put down, and also offers good woodcock, duck, geese and snipe shooting. This is very much traditional walked-up, rough shooting and offers excellent sport. Hind and doe stalking is available from November to February.

*Shooting acreage*: 4,500
*Status*: Private with let days
*Contact*: Andrew Malcolm, as above
*Sporting agent*: N/a
*Headkeeper/staff*: A.M.Thornton.
*Number of available days*: 7
*Bag expectations*: 35-45
*Average cartridge to kill ratio*: 6:1
*Lunch*: On the hill
*Price structure*: £80 - £120 per Gun per day
*Accommodation*: Full board up to 10 guests
*Access*: By road, two hours from Glasgow
*Other comments*: Well-behaved gundogs welcome

# ROTTAL LODGE ESTATE

## *AIRLIE ESTATE, GLEN CLOVA, ANGUS*

Lynedoch House
Barossa Place
Perth
PH1 5EP

Tel: 01738 451600.                 Fax: 01738 451900
sporting@ckdgalbraith.co.uk        www.sportinglets.co.uk

Lying in the heart of Glen Clova, at the southern foothills of the Cairngorm massif, Rottal Lodge Estate offers a variety of walked-up and driven shooting for grouse, pheasants and partridges and mixed low ground walking up. There is also duck flighting. This is a mixed country of lowlands and uplands, rising from a river valley to high tops at 3,000ft and is, in parts, very rugged.

*Shooting acreage:* 22,000
*Status:* Private with let days
*Sporting agent:* Robert Rattray of C.K.D. Galbraith, as above
*Headkeeper/staff:*
*Number of available days:* On application
*Bag expectations:* Varies
*Average cartridge to kill ratio:* Unknown
*Lunch:* See accommodation
*Price structure:* POA
*Accommodation:* Totally refurbished in 1999, the Lodge provides comfortable accommodation for a party of 16 in 11 bedrooms, including six double and two twin rooms with en-suite bathrooms. There is also a secure gunroom.
*Access:* The Estate lies to the west of Kirriemuir, Upper South Esk towards Glen Clova
*Other comments:* Well-behaved gundogs welcome

# TEASSES ESTATE

*NR CUPAR, FIFE*

2 India Street
Edinburgh
EH3 6EZ

Tel: 0131 476 6500
info@sportingestates.com

Fax: 0131 476 6501
www.sportingestates.com

The very accessible Teasses Estate offers high quality 150-300 bird driven pheasant days, set amidst the rolling wooded hillsides. Small days with partridges and duck are also available, as well as mixed walked-up days, and decoyed pigeon shooting. Clay shooting is also available. Very friendly keepers and staff, all within easy access of Edinburgh Airport. Guests can stay in the very comfortable Teasses Lodge if they wish.

*Shooting acreage*: 1,000
*Status*: Private with let days
*Sporting agent*: George Goldsmith
*Headkeeper*: N/a
*Number of available days*: 8
*Number of drives*: N/a
*Bag expectations*: 150-300
*Average cartridge to kill ratio*: 3.5:1
*Lunch*: Lunch is taken in either Teasses Lodge or in a bothy with the beaters
*Accommodation*: Teasses Lodge is set in the centre of the estate overlooking the loch and accommodates four to six. For larger groups local accommodation can be arranged
*Price structure*: From £800 per week.
*Access*: Edinburgh Airport or rail. M90, Jct. 8.
*Other comments*: Well-behaved gundogs welcome

---

The Estate Office
Tulchan Lodge
Advie
Grantown on Spey
PH26 3PW

Tel: 01807 510200          Fax: 01807 510234
chrisexcell@tulchan.com

Owned since 1993 by Leon Litchfield, a native of Derbyshire, Tulchan offers an excellent driven pheasant shoot, made even more exciting by a series of duck flighting ponds. As an added incentive to the sportsman there is also roe stalking of a very high standard in the woodland. Furthermore, Tulchan's once famous grouse moor has been regenerated (see under Grouse section). The Tulchan Estate comprises 26,000 acres, of which the pheasant shoot covers 8,000 acres, with four beats, each of 2,000 acres. The drives take place in gulleys, rides and valleys and one can shoot five consecutive days without touching the same drive twice. Pheasants are reared on the Estate's own game farm, using French stock. The duck flighting on the flight ponds and river is largely for wild birds, augmented by some reared duck.

*Shooting acreage*: 8,000 for driven pheasants
*Status*: Commercial with lodge and cottage accommodation
*Owner*: Tulchan Sporting Estates Ltd
*Contact*: Estate Office as above
*Sporting agent*: N/a
*Headkeeper/staff*: Factor Chris Excell plus headkeeper and four beat-keepers
*Number of available days*: 40
*Number of drives*: 35 plus
*Bag expectations*: 150-400
*Average cartridge to kill ratio*: Varies enormously
*Lunch*: Three-course lunch taken in Lodge by the river
*Accommodation*: The Estate prefers guests to stay within Estate accommodation
*Access*: By road: A9 from Perth, then A95 east. By air: Inverness or Aberdeen Airports and transportation can then be arranged
*Other comments*: Well trained gundogs welcome and kennels are available

# PARTRIDGES

# ASWANLEY ESTATE

*ONE HOUR WEST OF ABERDEEN, BY HUNTLY*

Lynedoch House
Barossa Place
Perth
PH1 5EP

Tel: 01738 451600.
sporting@ckdgalbraith.co.uk

Fax: 01738 451900
www.sportinglets.co.uk

Set in the Upper Deveron Valley in the Parish of Glass, the Aswanley estate comprises a mixture of heather and woodlands down to arable land by the river. Excellent sporting driven partridges are available during September and October, to which can be added walked-up grouse, driven pheasants, rough shooting and sport with rabbits and pigeons. Accompanied roe stalking with the chance of an excellent head is also on offer. A Gold Medal head was taken in 2000. This is a wonderful estate for young sporting families or for shooting teams occupying two or more cottages. There are pigeon woods and rabbit ground where guests can wander unaccompanied. There is also clay pigeon shooting.

*Shooting acreage*: 5,000
*Status*: Private with let days
*Sporting agent*: Robert Rattray of C.K.D.Galbraith, as above
*Headkeeper/staff*: Angus Smith
*Number of available days*: Variable
*Number of drives*: not known
*Bag expectations*: Bags can be tailored to guests' requirements
*Average cartridge to kill ratio*: Varies according to skill and conditions
*Lunch*: See accommodation
*Price structure*: POA
*Accommodation*: Five comfortable houses on the estate offer accommodation for parties of two, four, six, six and seven. Aswanley House, a 17th century fortified house, is available on a fully hosted basis for driven shooting parties.
*Access*: Air or rail to Inverness, then A96 east to Huntly
*Other comments*: Well-behaved gundogs welcome

# BIGHOUSE ESTATE

*NORTH-EAST SUTHERLAND*

Lynedoch House
Barossa Place
Perth
PH1 5EP

Tel: 01738 451600        Fax: 01738 456900
sporting@ckdgalbraith.co.uk     www.sportinglets.co.uk

The Bighouse Estate on the edge of the Flow Country in Sutherland offers a wide range of sporting opportunities, whether one seeks stalking or shooting. Partridge shooting, duck and goose flighting, snipe and woodcock, rough shooting and, if all that is not enough, you can also tackle the rabbits. Furthermore, if numbers improve, there is a possibility of walked-up grouse. These opportunities are combined in mixed sporting weeks in November, December and January and can be tailor-made to suit requests (see also entry under stalking).

*Shooting acreage*: 50,000 acres, including sister company Strath Halladale
*Status*: Private with let days
*Sporting agent*: Robert Rattray of C.K.D.Galbraith, as above
*Number of available days*: Throughout season
*Bag expectations*: Varies
*Average cartridge to kill ratio*: Varies on Guns' skill and weather conditions
*Lunch*: Taken on the hill
*Price structure*: POA
*Accommodation*: Fourteen people can be accommodated in Forsinard Lodge which is on the edge of the RSPB Reserve at Forsinard. There are seven twin bedded rooms, with three en-suite and a further four bathrooms, a lounge with open fire, game room, dining room, sitting room and drying room. There is full central heating
*Access*: From Inverness (rail or air) via A9 north to Helmsdale, then A897 to Forsinard
*Other comments*: Well trained dogs welcome

*DUNKELD, PERTHSHIRE*

Hendry Ramsay & Wilcox
55/57 North Methven Street
Perth
PH1 5PX

Tel: 01738 443344        Fax: 01738 443327
info@scothunt.co.uk.        www.scothunt.co.uk

This excellent shoot can show driven hill red-legged partridges in a style which closely resembles grouse shooting. It is, basically, a 'simulated grouse' shoot with partridges driven over heather. Birds come at all heights and angles to provide very testing and different shooting. In addition, there is also driven pheasant shooting, and a new innovation is walked-up days over pointers, for both pheasants and partridges in October and November.

*Shooting acreage*: 2,000
*Status*: Commercial
*Contact*: Vernon Waters as above
*Headkeeper*: Dennis Hubbard
*Number of available days*: 20
*Number of drives*: 11
*Bag expectations*: 100-500
Average cartridge to kill ratio: 4:1
*Lunch*: Taken on shoot at midday in converted barn
*Price structure*: POA
Accommodation: Excellent local accommodation and can recommend Dunkeld House, Dunkeld, Kinloch House Hotel, Blair Gowrie or Atholl Arms, Dunkeld
*Access*: By road: main A9. By rail: Dunkeld Station. By air: Edinburgh Airport
*Other comments*: Gundogs welcome

# THE DELL ESTATE

2 India Street
Edinburgh
EH3 6EZ

Tel: 0131 476 6500                          Fax: 0131 476 6501
infor@sportingestates.com                   www.sportingestates.com

The Dell estate with its beautiful birch woodlands running down to Loch Ness offers driven partridges shooting with one drive showing exceptionally high birds. Walked-up partridge shooting is also available and pheasant shooting was also offered for the first time last season. In addition, walked-up grouse shooting can be enjoyed in August and September (see also entry under stalking).

*Shooting acreage*: 5,500 acres
*Status*: Private with let days
*Sporting agent*: George Goldsmith
*Headkeeper/staff*: Colin Barclay
*Number of available days*: Limited weekends from November to January
*Number of drives*: Approximately 14
*Bag expectations*: Walked-up grouse from five brace per day. Driven partridges with some pheasants from 100 bird days, and walked-up around 60 head.
*Average cartridge to kill ratio*: Varies
*Lunch*: Lunch can be taken on the hill or in Dell House
*Price structure*: Lodge from £2,500 per week self-catered. Fully catered packages can be arranged.
*Accommodation*: Dell House, a lovely 18th century Georgian residence, can sleep up to 14 in a double en-suite bedroom, a twin en-suite bedroom, four twin bedrooms and two single bedrooms.
*Access*: A9 south from Inverness, then B851 south-west alongside Loch Ness. One hour's drive
*Other comments*: Well-behaved gundogs welcome

# SNIPE/WOODCOCK

# EILEAN IARMAIN ESTATE

Lynedoch House
Barossa Place
Perth
PH1 5EP

Tel: 01738 451600          Fax: 01738 451900
sporting@ckdgalbraith.co.uk          www.sportinglets.co.uk

Consisting of low hills, glens and ravines with woodlands and heather moorland, the Eilean Iarmain Estate lies in the parishes of Sleat and Strath in South Skye. Principal attraction in winter for sportsmen is the woodcock shooting. The estate currently lets up to 16 shooting days for eight Guns, with an average bag of 10 birds and 60 sightings per day. Smaller days of three—five Guns can be arranged. In addition to the woodcock, some pheasants are released, while duck, snipe and partridges can also be added to the bag. There are also a few days of walked-up grouse shooting with a bag expectation of five to 10 brace per day. Red and roe deer stalking is also available with about 10 stags taken each season.

*Shooting acreage*: 23,000
*Status*: Private with let days
*Sporting agent*: Robert Rattray of C.K.D.Galbraith, as above
*Headkeeper*: Michael Mackenzie
*Number of available day*: On application
*Number of drives*: N/a
*Bag expectations*: Varies
*Average cartridge to kill ratio*: Varies according to skill of guns
*Lunch*: Taken on the hill
*Price structure*: POA
*Accommodation*: All shooting visitors stay at the Hotel Eilean Iarmain, a small traditional inn with an excellent reputation for its cuisine and wine. Accommodation comprises four suites, 12 bedrooms and is ideal for shooting parties
*Access*: Take the A87 from Invergarry to Kyle of Lochalsh and then the bridge to Skye, continue on A87 then south on A851 to Eilean Iarmain
*Other comments*: Well trained gundogs welcome

# KINTRADWELL ESTATE

*BRORA, SUTHERLAND*

2 India Street
Edinburgh
EH3 6EZ

Tel: 0131 476 6500                    Fax: 0131 476 6501
info@sportingestates.com         www.sportingestates.com

Walked-up woodcock shooting is enjoyed over a huge acreage of mixed ground using spaniels, setters and pointers and with a maximum of four Guns. In addition, flighting at dusk for woodcock is available. Usually lasting half-an-hour, this can be very exciting and testing shooting. A mixture of woodcock, pheasant, snipe and rabbit shooting can also be arranged. An estate keeper accompanies the team of Guns at all times and dogs are provided. Hind stalking is also available in season.

*Shooting acreage*: 50,000
*Status*: Private with let days
*Sporting agent*: George Goldsmith
*Headkeeper/staff*: Headkeeper is Harold Stuart
*Number of available days*: Depends on weather
*Bag expectations*: Varies
*Average cartridge to kill ratio*: Varies according to skill of Guns
*Lunch*: On the hill
*Accommodation*: Self-catering cottage or B&B. Royal Marine Hotel, Brora is also used extensively
*Price structure*: From £135 per Gun per day
*Access*: A9. Rail or air to Inverness and then A9 north.
*Other comments*: Well-behaved dogs welcome

# UIG & HAMANAVAY ESTATE

*WEST COAST OF LEWIS*

Lynedoch House
Barossa Place
Perth
PH1 5EP

Tel: 01738 451600                    Fax: 01738 456900
sporting@ckdgalbraith.co.uk          www.sportinglets.co.uk

The estate offers excellent woodcock and snipe shooting, while grouse
are also shot over pointers. Guns are welcome from November to
January when good mixed bags can be expected. This is rugged,
mountainous country with glorious scenery, but guests should be
prepared to work for their sport and a reasonable degree of fitness is
an advantage. Bags vary according to the weather, presence of birds
and the ability of the Guns. (See also the entry under stalking.)

*Shooting acreage*: 50,000
*Status*: Private with let shooting
*Sporting agent*: Robert Rattray of C.K.D.Galbraith, as above
*Headkeeper/staff*: Sporting Manager is Simon Hunt
*Number of available days*: On application
*Bag expectations*: See above
*Average cartridge to kill ratio*: Varies
*Lunch*: On the hill
*Price structure*: POA but note that the shooting is let as a package from
Saturday to Saturday
*Accommodation*: There is comfortable accommodation in the estate house at
Hamanavay. Sited at the head of the sea loch, the setting is truly magical
*Access*: By air. Fly to Glasgow and then transfer on to Stornway. Flights now
include Sunday. By ferry from Ullapool six days a week.

# GROUSE

# ALINE ESTATE

*SE COAST OF LEWIS, HEAD OF LOCH EAFORTH*

Lynedoch House
Barossa Place
Perth
PH1 5EP

Tel: 01738 451600
sporting@ckdgalbraith.co.uk

Fax: 01738 451900
www.sportinglets.co.uk

Walked-up shooting for grouse and snipe over pointers is available in September, while driven woodcock are included from November onwards. Duck flighting on the flight ponds is also available. Three-day shooting weekends make an ideal winter break. The Aline Estate comprises wild rock strewn hills, moors and lochs on the south-east coast of Lewis and demands reasonable fitness. Wildlife abounds in the area, including peregrines, sea-eagles, seals, otters and dolphins. (See also entry under stalking.)

*Shooting acreage*: 10,000 acres on the Aline Estate with a further 20,000 acres of stalking and shooting rights on North Harris
*Status*: Private with let days
*Sporting agent*: Robert Rattray of C.K.D.Galbraith, as above
*Headkeeper/staff*: Jim Mcgarrity is headkeeper
*Number of available days*: On application
*Bag expectations*: Varies
*Average cartridge to kill ratio*: varies on skill and conditions
*Lunch*: Usually taken on the hill
*Price structure*: POA. Lettings are from Thursday to Thursday
*Accommodation*: 18th century lodge with magnificent views down Loch Seaforth to Skye. Five double or twin bedrooms, with two more available in cottage. Sleeps up to 10. Cook available.
*Access*: By air to Glasgow, then transfer to Stornway flight. Ferry from Ullapool

# CAWDOR

*MORAY FIRTH*

Cawdor Estate Office
Nairn
IV12 5RE

Tel: 01667 404666
Helen@cawdor.com

Fax: 01667 404787
www.cawdor.com

The Cawdor moor covers 30,000 acres overlooking the Moray Firth in the Highlands of Scotland. It comprises eight separate grouse beats with driving to 55 lines of butts. Game records began in 1939. The Findhorn River cuts a steep-sided valley through the middle of the moor, about seven miles in length, where Drynachen Lodge and the partridge shoot are located. The partridge shoot was started seven years ago and is considered one of the most exciting shoots for high birds and variety in the UK, with shooting over two days. It is also set in stunning scenery on the banks of the Findhorn. Combined partridge and grouse days are possible when available. Drynachan Lodge is a traditional sporting retreat which combines old world elegance with modern comforts and is fully staffed and catered.

*Shooting acreage*: 30,000
*Status*: Commercial with private let days
*Owner*: Cawdor Estates
*Contact*: As above
*Sporting agent*: Roxton Baily Robinson between September 4 and October 4 for partridge shooting
*Headkeeper/staff*: Roddy Forbes
*Number of available days*: Up to 4 per week
*Number of drives*: Grouse: 55. Partridge: 18
*Bag expectations*: Grouse: 60-100 brace. Partridge: 200-500 birds
*Average cartridge /kill ratio*: 3.5:1 both grouse and partridge
*Lunch*: Either in lunch huts or in the Lodge
*Price structure*: Grouse £110 plus VAT per brace. Partridges/pheasants £26 plus VAT per bird
*Accommodation*: Drynachan Lodge has 8 double rooms (3 en-suite), 1 twin, 4 singles and 8 bathrooms
*Access*: Inverness Airport on British Airways from Gatwick or EasyJet from Gatwick or Luton, followed by 25 minutes drive on A96, B9090
*Other comments*: Well trained gundogs welcome

# COIGNAFEARN

*INVERNESS-SHIRE, WEST OF TOMATIN*

Lynedoch House
Barossa Place
Perth
PH1 5EP

Tel: 01738 451600          Fax: 01738 451900
sporting@ckdgalbraith.co.uk          www.sportinglets.co.uk

The magnificent sporting estate of Coignafearn includes the headwaters of the River Findhorn and the sport includes some of the finest driven and walked-up grouse shooting in Scotland. The estate is undergoing a period of rejuvenation and is managed on ecological principles. This is a landscape of remote and dramatic mountains, a country where golden eagles and ospreys are frequently seen. There are otters in the river and wild cats in the glen. The hill is well roaded and there are butts to provide five separate days driven grouse, while grouse can also be walked-up over dogs. Stalking is also available (see under stalking).

*Shooting acreage*: 40,000 acres
*Status*: Private with let days
*Sporting agent*: Robert Rattray of C.K.D.Galbraith, as above
*Headkeeper/staff*: Sandy Day
*Number of available days*: 5
*Bag expectations*: Varies
*Average cartridge to kill ratio*: Depends on Guns' skill
*Lunch*: Taken on the hill
*Price structure*: POA. Lettings are from Sunday to Saturday
*Accommodation*: Coignafearn Old Lodge has been converted from a traditional steading and now features wood-lined rooms, vaulted ceilings and natural stone features. The bedrooms for 10 plus seven children are combined in units of two which open up onto the courtyard. There are four double, three twin and a family room. There is a central bathroom with deep baths.
*Access*: The estate lies west of Tomatin on the A9 from Perth and Pitlochry. Fly or train to Inverness, then 30 minutes south on A9
*Other comments*: Well-behaved gundogs welcome

# GARYNAHINE

*WEST COAST OF LEWIS, SHORE OF EAST LOCH ROAG*

Lynedoch House
Barossa Place
Perth
PH1 5EP

Tel: 01738 451600.               Fax: 01738 451900
sporting@ckdgalbraith.co.uk      www.sportinglets.co.uk

The very comfortable Lodge at Garynahine is surrounded by its own policies and provides the base for some truly wild and sporting shooting. No birds are reared or hatched in this wild and wonderful place. Walked-up grouse and snipe shooting over pointers starts at the beginning of September and continues to the end of November. In addition, there is exceptional driven woodcock shooting available on a very limited basis for parties of 10 Guns between November and January with an expectation of bags up to 50 birds per day. Stalking can be arranged on neighbouring estates given adequate notice.

*Shooting acreage:* Approx 10,000
*Status:* Commercial
*Sporting agent:* Robert Rattray of C.K.D.Galbraith, as above
*Headkeeper:* Malcolm McPhail
*Number of available days:* variable
*Bag expectations:* Varies enormously according to the weather and Guns' skill
*Lunch:* Taken on the hill or at Garynahine Lodge
*Price structure:* POA but note that the shooting is let as a package
*Accommodation:* The Lodge has 10 bedrooms, six bathrooms and forms a great base for a mixed age party
*Access:* By air: Glasgow Airport to Stornway. Garynahine is on West Coast

# GLENFERNATE LODGE

2 India Street
Edinburgh
EH3 6EX

Tel: 0131 476 6500          Fax: 0131 476 6501
info@sportingestates.com    www.sportingestates.com

Walked-up grouse shooting is available on the extensive Glenfernate Estate with an expectation of between 10-20 brace per day. Pitlochry is only 20 minutes away and Gleneagles an hour and 10 minutes. This is a mixed ground, with beautiful countryside. The estate also enjoys a very private and lovely loch, while the Lodge has a reputation for being extremely comfortable (see also the entry under stalking.)

*Shooting acreage*: 17,000 acres
*Status*: Commercial:
*Sporting agent*: George Goldsmith
*Headkeeper/staff*: Headkeeper is Gordon McGregor
*Number of available days*: Throughout season
*Bag expectations*: Walked-up grouse with bags of 10-20 brace
*Average cartridge to kill ratio*: Varies on skill and conditions
*Lunch*: Taken on the hill
*Price structure*: From £3,250 per week self-catered
*Accommodation*: Glenfernate Lodge offers accommodation for parties of up to 15 with five bedrooms with twin beds, two with double beds, one single bedroom, four bathrooms and a nursery. Cook available if required.
*Access*: A9, and then off A924. Edinburgh Airport or rail to Edinburgh or Inverness.
*Other comments*: Well-behaved dogs welcome

# GLENLOCHY SHOOT

*GRANTOWN-ON-SPEY, HIGHLANDS*

Grindsbrook House
69 Oxford Road
Banbury
Oxfordshire
OX16 9AJ

Tel: 01295 277197            Fax: 01295 268651
james@ejchurchill.com

Glenlochy is essentially an excellent driven grouse moor, but the estate also offers rough shooting. A very picturesque Highland moor, it has a reputation for showing some very testing driven grouse shooting with good bags. Guns will be pleased to know that Argocats are available for their use on the moor. The low ground offers some exciting mixed rough shooting. A typical day's bag may consist of pheasants, wild duck, snipe, woodcock and ground game.

*Shooting acreage*: 8,000 acres
*Status*: Private with let days
*Contact*: E.J.Churchill Sporting
*Sporting agent*: James Chapel at E.J.Churchill as above
*Headkeeper/staff*: Three keepers
*Number of available days*: Driven grouse 6-10 days, late low ground rough days 2-3
*Number of drives*: 20
*Bag expectations*: 50 to 100 brace driven grouse.Rough days 40 to 60 head
*Average cartridge to kill ratio*: Varies enormously. Recommend double-guns for larger grouse days
*Lunch*: Lunch is provided on the hill or in a bothy if the weather is inclement
*Price structure*: POA
*Accommodation*: Seafield Lodge in Grantown-on-Spey
*Access*: 40 minutes drive from Inverness A9/A95 to Grantown-on-Spey. Rail or Airport at Inverness
*Other comments*: Well-behaved gundogs welcome

*PERTHSHIRE, NR AMULREE*

Lynedoch House
Barossa Place
Perth
PH1 5EP

Tel: 01738 451600      Fax: 01738 451900
sporting@ckdgalbraith.co.uk      www.sportinglets.co.uk

Lying only 27 miles from Perth, Glenquaich has a reputation for being one of Scotland's most consistent grouse moors and has recently averaged 700 brace a season. There is a great variety of ground ranging from high crags rising to over 2,500ft to the lower, gently undulating areas close to Loch Freuchie. Access to the moors is good. Enquiries for driven days for parties of up to 10 Guns should be made as early as possible. Excellent rough shooting is also available and the bag may include pheasants, partridges, snipe and woodcock. Glenquaich is very accessible from either Edinburgh or Glasgow, making it an ideal location for a short sporting break. (See also entry under stalking.)

*Shooting acreage*: 10,000
*Status*: Private with let days
*Sporting agent*: Robert Rattray of C.K.D.Galbraith, as above
*Headkeeper/staff*: Stan Riches
*Number of available days*: On application
*Number of drives*: Not known
*Bag expectations*: Driven grouse 50-75 brace. Rough shooting 30-50 head. Small driven pheasant/partridge days 60-100
*Average cartridge to kill ratio*: Varies on skill of Guns
*Lunch*: Packed lunch taken on the hill in purpose-built hut
*Price structure*: POA. Croftmill Cottage from £275 per week
*Accommodation*: The fully equipped Croftmill Cottage sleeps up to five (one double, one single and one twin) and there are also excellent local hotels
*Access*: Dundee City Airport, then A90 to Perth, A9 to Dunkeld and then A822 to Amulree.Rail/drive Perth, then A9, A822 to Amulree
*Other comments*: Well-behaved gundogs welcome

# HOPE ESTATE

---

*HOPE ESTATE, SUTHERLAND*

Lynedoch House
Barossa Place
Perth
PH1 5EP

Tel: 01738 451600              Fax: 01738 456900
sporting@ckdgalbraith.co.uk    www.sportinglets.co.uk

One of seven sporting estates established by a former Duke of Sutherland in the 19th century when expanding road and rail links made the north Scottish coast accessible, there are magnificent views along Loch Hope towards Ben Hope in the south, and northwards down the Hope river towards the estuary. Four mixed sporting weeks are offered in September and October, to include three stags. The shooting is varied and includes walked-up grouse, duck flighting and woodcock in season. The latter can provide excellent sport and individual days of mixed sport can be arranged from November to January.

*Shooting acreage*: 22,000 acres and with exclusive arrangements with the neighbouring Eriboll and Melness Estates providing a total of over 50,000 acres
*Status*: Private with let days
*Sporting agent*: Robert Rattray of C.K.D.Galbraith, as above
*Headkeeper/staff*: Ian MacDonald
*Number of available days*: On application
*Bag expectations*: Varies
*Average cartridge to kill ratio*: Varies according to Guns' abilities
*Lunch*: On the hill
*Price structure*: POA. Lettings are from Sunday to Sunday
*Accommodation*: Hope Lodge, a listed building, is remarkable for being clad entirely in slate and can accommodate up to 12 guests in comfort. There are eight bedrooms: two double, two twins (one with en-suite bath), and four singles and two further bathrooms. There is a games room, large drying room and gun room. It is arguably the best sited of the Sutherland sporting lodges.
*Access*: Air or rail to Inverness, then A9, A839 to Lairg and north to Altnaharra
*Other comments*: Well trained gundogs welcome

# KILDERMORIE

Lynedoch House
Barossa Place
Perth
PH1 5EP

Tel: 01738 451600                    Fax: 01738 451900
sporting@ckdgalbraith.co.uk          www.sportinglets.co.uk

The Kildermorie estate lies in the heart of Ross-shire and is renowned for magnificent scenery. Rising from 600ft to 2,750 ft, this attractive sporting estate offers grouse and ptarmigan shooting. Grouse shooting is available over pointers, while ptarmigan shooting is available for those who enjoy exercise! There is also sport with mallard and teal over flight ponds, and also clay shooting (see also entry under stalking)

*Shooting acreage*: 17,500 acres
*Status*: Private with let days
*Sporting agent*: Robert Rattray of C.K.D.Galbraith, as above
*Headkeeper/staff*: Dougie Russell
*Number of available days*: On application
*Bag expectations*: Varies according to weather and season
*Average cartridge to kill ratio*: according to skill of Guns
*Lunch*: Usually taken on the hill
*Price structure*: POA
*Accommodation*: Meall Mor Lodge has beautifully furnished accommodation with 10 double/twin en-suite bedrooms, and a fully equipped kitchen, large dining room, two lounges, drying room and gun room. Dogs are welcome, but not allowed in the Lodge. Kennels are available. Lettings are on a self-catering basis, Sunday to Sunday
*Access*: Air or rail to Inverness and then one hour's drive north on A9 to Alness
*Other comments*: Well-behaved gundogs welcome with kennelling available

# KINLOCH ESTATE

## KINLOCH, SUTHERLAND

Lynedoch House
Barossa Place
Perth
PH1 5EP

Tel: 01738 451600                    Fax: 01738 451900
sporting@ckdgalbraith.co.uk          www.sportinglets.co.uk

The Kinloch Estate, situated on Scotland's north coast and overlooking the magnificent setting of the Kyle of Tongue, was originally one of the Duke of Sutherland's sporting estates. A wide range of sport encompasses excellent informal walked-up grouse, ptarmigan on the high ground, duck, snipe and woodcock (see also entry under stalking)

*Shooting acreage*: 20,000
*Status*: Private with let days
*Sporting agent*: Robert Rattray of C.K.D.Galbraith, as above
*Headkeeper/staff*: Hugh Montgomery
*Number of available days*: On application
*Bag expectations*: Varies
*Average cartridge to kill ratio*: Varies according to skill of Guns and weather conditions
*Lunch*: Taken on the hill
*Price structure*: POA. Lettings from Sunday to Sunday
*Accommodation*: A well-appointed Victorian sporting lodge sleeping up to 16
*Access*: Air or rail to Inverness, then A9, A839 to Lairg, A836 to Altnaharra and north to Kyle of Tongue
*Other comments*: Well trained dogs welcome

# PHONES & ETTERIDGE

Lynedoch House
Barossa Place
Perth
PH1 5EP

Tel:01738 451600.
sporting@ckdgalbraith.co.uk

Fax: 01738 451900.
www.sportinglets.co.uk

Part of the south-western flank of the Cairngorm Mountains, Phones is a magnificent sporting estate offering outstanding driven grouse on one of Scotland's best grouse moors. Also available are both driven pheasants and partridges, driven blue hares and wildfowling. The estate, which rises to over 3,000ft, enjoys spectacular scenery and the sport is outstanding. (See also entry under stalking)

*Shooting acreage*: 29,000
*Status*: Private with let days
*Sporting agent*: Robert Rattray of C.K.D.Galbraith, as above
*Headkeeper/staff*: Michael Glass
*Number of available days*: On application
*Bag expectations*: Grouse 100 plus brace. Pheasants 250-300
*Average cartridge to kill ratio*: varies on skill of Guns
*Lunch*: See accommodation
*Price structure*: POA
*Accommodation*: Phones Lodge can accommodate up to 18 people with a large drawing room, dining room and kitchen. The lodge is let on a self-catering basis although the services of a cook and housekeeper can be provided. Tenants pay for their own food and drink. Etteridge is a smaller lodge on the Phones estate and sleeps a maximum of eight people on a self-catering basis. Lettings are from Sunday to Sunday.
*Access*: One hour's drive north-west of Perth on the A9 to Kingussie. Air to Dundee and then A90 to A9
*Other comments*: Well trained gundogs welcome

# SCALISCRO

*WEST COAST OF LEWIS*

Lynedoch House
Barossa Place
Perth
PH1 5EP

Tel: 01738 451600                    Fax: 01738 451900
sporting@ckdgalbraith.co.uk      www.sportinglets.co.uk

Providing an ideal Hebridean family holiday location for large parties, Scaliscro offers walked-up grouse and snipe shooting over pointers from early September onwards, while some limited stalking is also available from mid-September. Scaliscro has a relaxed and informal atmosphere and is ideal for a family wishing to introduce their children to shooting and fishing in a wild, rugged and unspoilt environment. Apart from the shooting and stalking, there is also clay shooting, sea angling and lobster fishing.

*Shooting acreage*: 2,000
*Status*: private with let days
*Sporting agent*: Robert Rattray of C.K.D.Galbraith, as above
*Headkeeper/staff*: Angus Mackenzie is headkeeper
*Number of available days*: Throughout relevant seasons
*Bag expectations*: Varies on conditions
*Average cartridge to kill ratio*: varies on skill levels and conditions
*Lunch*: Taken on hill
*Price structure*: From £1,200 per week. Lettings are from Saturday to Saturday
*Accommodation*: Scaliscro Lodge overlooks Little Loch Roag and is reached by a private two mile road. The estate has an organic salmon hatchery, mussel farm and hill farm with Highland cattle and Hebridean sheep. Accommodation is available for up to 21 guests plus cook in staff flat. There is also a self-catering cottage sleeping eight.
*Access*: By air to Glasgow, transferring to flight to Stornway. This service now includes Sunday. Or ferry from Ullapool six days a week.

*INVERNESS-SHIRE & MORAY*

2 India Street
Edinburgh
EH3 6EZ

Tel: 0131 476 6500.
info@sportingestates.com

Fax: 0131 476 6501
www.sportingestates.com

The Strathspey estate is situated some 30 miles south of Inverness, stretching from the banks of the River Spey, and varies from farmland to ancient Caledonian pine forests and heather grouse moors. The sport offered is based around two lodges – Kinveachy near Boat of Garten and Inverallan House near Grantown-on-Spey. Driven, walked-up and grouse shot over pointers is offered, as well as mixed walked-up shooting. There is also stalking for red deer and roe bucks. Mixed stalking and shooting packages can also be arranged.

*Shooting acreage*: 56,000
*Status*: Private with let days
*Sporting agent*: George Goldsmith
*Headkeeper/staff*: Frank Law, is the sporting manager
*Number of available days*: Variable, depending on the season.
*Number of drives*: Not known
*Bag expectations*: Some 70 brace of driven grouse, depending on the season. Walked-up grouse five to 20 brace.
*Average cartridge to kill ratio*: Varies according to skill of Guns
*Lunch*: Taken in bothy on the hill or in fishing hut on banks of Spey
*Accommodation*: Kinveachy Lodge can accommodate up to 19 guests in nine double/twin bedrooms and one single room. Five bedrooms have en-suite facilities. There is also a secure gunroom. Inverallan House, set in private grounds by the Spey, sleeps up to 15 guests in six double/twin bedrooms and a family room. Both lodges are fully staffed and the rental includes all meals (Note: the Kinveachy price is inclusive of drinks).
*Price structure*: From £3,500 per week (accommodation only). Sporting costs on application.
*Access*: Just off the A9. Inverness Airport or rail
*Other comments*: Well-behaved gundogs welcome

# TULCHAN

*HIGHLANDS*

The Estate Office
Tulchan Lodge
Advie
Grantown-on-Spey
PH26 3PW

Tel: 01807 751200          Fax: 01807 751234
chrisexcell@tulchan.com

The 26,000 acre Tulchan Shoot once boasted one of the finest grouse
moors in the Kingdom and amongst the Royal guests who shot there
were King Edward VII (as Prince of Wales and King), King George V
and King George VI (as Duke of York). It is recorded that when
shooting at Tulchan as Prince of Wales in 1898 he shot 17½ brace of
grouse in one drive, a personal record for one drive which he never
bettered. Prior to the purchase of Tulchan by the present owner, Leon
Litchfield in 1993, the 18,000 acre grouse moor had been neglected
and run down. However, extensive heather burning and good
keepering have helped increase the grouse stock, enabling driven
grouse shooting to take place on a substantial scale. Today there is a
strong, healthy stock, and prospects look very encouraging.

*Shooting acreage*: 18,000
*Status*: Commercial with lodge and cottage accommodation
*Owner*: Tulchan Sporting Estates Ltd
*Contact*: Estate Office as above
*Sporting agent*: N/a
*Headkeeper/staff*: Led Mallinson
*Number of available days*: Varies
*Number of drives*: 20. Four days consecutive driving could take place
without repeating a drive
*Bag expectations*: 50 –100 brace
*Average cartridge to kill ratio*: Varies greatly
*Lunch*: Lunch taken in lunch huts on the Tulchan side of the moor
*Price structure*: POA
*Accommodation*: Prefer guests to stay on Estate accommodation
*Access*: By road: A9 from Perth, the A95 east. By Air: Inverness or
Aberdeen Airports. Transportation can be arranged
*Other comments*: Well trained gundogs welcome and kennels available

# WILDFOWLING

11 Queensberry Terrace
Cummertrees
Annan
Dumfriesshire
DG12 5QF

Tel 01461 700 480
www.wildtides.co.uk

Wildfowling, rough shooting and mini-drives on various estates, farms and the Solway Firth. This is basically private shooting with let days. The company offers three-day packages from October 1 to February 1 which include morning and evening flights for geese, rough shooting for pheasants and duck flighting.

*Shooting acreage*: 850 of own shoot plus hundreds of acres on neighbouring estates and farms
*Status*: Private with let days
*Contact*: Gavin Hunt as above
*Number of days available*: Throughout season
*Bag expectations*: Varies
*Gun/cartridge advice*: 10-bores are advised for geese, 12-bores all other species
*Average cartridge to kill ratio*: 4:1
*Lunch*: Packed lunch provided
*Price structure*: From £325 per head for a three-day package
*Accommodation*: Own family guest house
*Access*: By road M6 from the south

# STALKING

# ALINE ESTATE

*COAST OF LEWIS, HEAD OF LOCH SEAFORTH*

Lynedoch House
Barossa Place
Perth
PH1 5EP

Tel: 01738 451600
sporting@ckdgalbraith.co.uk

Fax: 01738 451900
www.sportinglets.co.uk

Red deer stalking takes place in September and October, though earlier stags may be found in the forestry. The Aline Estate comprises wild rock strewn hills, moors and lochs and demands reasonable fitness. Wildlife abounds in the area, including peregrines, sea-eagles, otters, seals and dolphins. (See also entry under shooting.)

*Stalking acreage*: 10,000 acres on the Aline Estate with a further 20,000 acres of shooting and stalking rights on North Harris
*Status*: Private with let days
*Sporting agent*: Robert Rattray of C.K.D.Galbraith, as above
*Staff*: Headstalker is Jim Mcgarrity
*Available stalking*: Throughout relevant season
*Rifle recommendations*: .270 or similar. Estate rifles can be arranged
*Price structure*: From £3,500 per week. Lettings are from Thursday to Thursday
*Accommodation*: 18th century lodge with magnificent views down Loch Seaforth to Skye. Five double or twin bedrooms, with two more available in cottage. Sleeps up to 10. Cook available
*Access*: By air to Glasgow, then transfer to Stornway flight. Ferry from Ullapool

# ALLADALE & DEANICH ESTATES

*ARDGAY, SUTHERLAND*

2 India House
Edinburgh
EH3 6EZ

Tel: 0131 476 6500                     Fax: 0131 476 6501
info@sportingestates.com         www.sportingestates.com

The Alladale and Deanich estates encompass remote glens, woods, lochs, mountains and rivers. Superb stalking is offered for two Rifles at Deanich where garrons are used in the traditional way to bring beasts off the hill. Alladale also offers exceptional stalking for one or two Rifles from the end of July. The highest point on the estate is 3,000ft and from the high tops there are outstanding views to both east and west coasts. Hind stalking packages are also available for up to three Rifles from November.

*Stalking acreage*: 25,000
*Status*: Private with let days
*Sporting agent*: George Goldsmith
*Staff*: Headstalker is Marcus Munro
*Available stalking*: Throughout season
*Rifle recommendations*: .270 calibre or similar recommended. Estate can also provide excellent quality rifles
*Accommodation*: Deanich Lodge lies in a remote situation at the head of Alladale and Deanich estates and can sleep nine guests in one double, three twins and one single bedroom. There is a seven mile unmade road to the Lodge and a 4-wheel drive is advisable. Lettings are from Saturday to Saturday.
*Price structure*: From £1,750 to £7,650 per week.
*Access*: A9 and then A836. Inverness Airport and rail.

# AMHUINNSUIDHE CASTLE ESTATE

*BY TARBERT, NORTH HARRIS*

Lynedoch House
Barossa Place
Perth
PH1 5EP

Tel: 01738 451600                    Fax: 01738 451900
sporting@ckdgalbraith.co.uk          www.sportinglets.co.uk

Exciting red deer stalking in an extensive deer forest set in a rugged, mountainous part of North Harris. The deer corries provide challenging stalking, while the overhanging cliff above Glen Ulladale, known as the 'Amphitheatre Buttress', is a renowned feature. Five stags are included in the let each week in September.

*Stalking acreage*: 35,000 acres
*Status*: Private with let days
*Sporting agent*: Robert Rattray of C.K.D.Galbraith, as above
*Staff*: Roddy McLeod is headstalker
*Available stalking*: Throughout season
Rifle recommendation: .270 calibre or similar
*Price structure*: Individuals from £1,295 per week for accommodation, including full board but excluding drinks. Sport extra. POA.
*Accommodation*: Amhuinnsuidhe Castle, built in 1865, in the Scottish Baronial style, provides comfortable accommodation for up to 18 guests in 10 bedrooms. Weekly lets are on a full board basis (excluding wines and spirits) with household staff. Head chef is David Taylor.
*Access*: By air to Stornaway from Glasgow or ferry from Uig on Skye to Tarbert.

# ARDVERIKIE

*INVERNESS-SHIRE, WEST OF DALWHINNIE*

Lynedoch House
Barossa Place
Perth
PH1 5EP

Tel: 01738 451600      Fax: 01738 451900
sporting@ckd.galbraith.co.uk      www.sportinglets.co.uk

Ardverikie, largely to the south of Loch Laggan, is one of Scotland's oldest and best known deer forests. Four stalking beats are available between the last remnants of the Old Caledonian forest and the spectacular West Coast mountains. Until recently the stalking has largely been retained by the family, and the agents are delighted to be able to offer an unrivalled opportunity to stalk on this testing forest. Stag stalking is available from early September until the end of the season, October 20, on two or three beats for a maximum of two Rifles per day. On some beats stags are taken off the hill using garrons. Roe stalking is also available.

*Stalking acreage*: 4,000 acres
*Status*: Private with let days
*Sporting agent*: Robert Rattray of C.K.D.Galbraith, as above
*Staff*: The headstalker is Dougie Langlands
*Available stalking*: Throughout season
*Rifle recommendations*: .270 or similar for red deer. .243 or similar for roe. Estate rifle can be available
*Price structure*: Lodge and stalking for two Rifles (15 stags) from £6,475 per week
*Accommodation*: Inverpattack Lodge can accommodate up to 12 guests on a self-catering basis. The Lodge has recently been refurbished, is spacious and comfortable. There is one double and three twin bedrooms and two bathrooms on the first floor, and one double bedroom and a third bathroom on the ground floor. A recent addition to the house includes a twin room and shower. There are three estate cottages which are ideal for roe stalking parties or additional guests/staff.
*Access*: The A9 from Perth to Dalwhinnie. The Ardverikie Forest is just to the west of Dalwhinnie

# ARGYLL ESTATES

*CLOSE TO INVERARY, ARGYLL*

Lynedoch House
Barossa Place
Perth
PH1 5EP

Tel: 01738 451600                 Fax: 01738 451900
sporting@ckdgalbraith.co.uk       www.sportinglets.co.uk

The famed Argyll estates incorporate some truly outstanding hill and woodland stalking amidst glorious scenery. The estates have a distinguished history of sporting achievements dating back to the 16th century when Mary, Queen of Scots, shot deer in Glen Shira. Both red and roe are available, while for those shooting hinds duck flighting can also be arranged. In addition, delightful estate walks can be enjoyed by non-stalkers or partners. For the more energetic mountain ranges, including Beinn Bhuidhe, are close by.

*Stalking acreage*: 50,000
*Status*: Private with let days
*Sporting agent*: Robert Rattray of C.K.D.Galbraith, as above
*Staff*: Headstalker is Jock Black
*Available stalking*: Throughout season
*Rifle recommendations*: .270 or similar for red deer, .243 or similar for roe. Estate rifles can be arranged.
*Price structure*: POA. Lettings are from Sunday to Sunday
*Accommodation*: The Lodge, a short distance from the Castle, set by a lovely river and complemented by mature gardens and grounds, can sleep eight in comfort. A cook who serves superb, traditional food, can be arranged.
*Access*: Fly to Glasgow and then A82 north via Loch Lomond-side to Inverary.

# ASSYNT ESTATE

*STRONCHRUBIE LODGE, LOCH, SUTHERLAND*

2 India Street
Edinburgh
EH3 6EZ

Tel: 0131 476 6500
info@sportingestates.com

Fax: 0131 476 6501
www.sportingestates.com

Situated on the beautiful north-west coast of Sutherland, the estate includes Ben More Assynt and Conival, both of which are over 3,000 feet. Superb stalking is available for stags and hinds and for up to four Rifles going to the hill per day. Challenging, west coast stalking, breath-taking scenery.

*Stalking acreage*: In excess of 100,000
*Status*: Private with let days:
*Sporting agent*: George Goldsmith
*Staff*: The headstalker is Peter McGregor
*Available stalking*: On application
*Rifle recommendations*: .270 calibre or similar. Estate rifles can be available
*Price structure*: From £650 - £1,100 per week
*Accommodation*: Stronchrubie Lodge sleeps 9 to 10 guests. A typical and comfortable Victorian Lodge
*Access*: A835, north of Ullapool. Air and rail at Inverness

# ATHOLL ESTATES

*BLAIR ATHOLL, PERTHSHIRE*

2 India Street
Edinburgh
EH3 6EZ

Tel: 0131 476 6500
info@sportingestates.com

Fax 0131 476 6501
www.sportingestates.com

The Atholl Estates in the heart of Highland Perthshire are centred round Blair Castle, traditional home of the Dukes of Atholl. There are two lodges, Forest Lodge and Glen Bruar, each providing its own sport. Both Lodges offer red deer stalking. The sport takes places amidst some of Scotland's most magnificent scenery and the guest will experience memorable sport.

*Stalking acreage*: in excess of 100,000
*Status*: Private with let days
*Sporting agent*: George Goldsmith
*Staff*: Kevin Grant at Bruar Lodge, and Graham Cumming at Forest Lodge
*Rifle recommendations*: .270 calibre or similar recommended for red deer. Estate rifles can be available
*Accommodation*: Forest Lodge, situated eight miles along a private road from the village of Blair Atholl, can accommodate 20 guests, while Glen Bruar, located in its own wild and rugged Glen, has comfortable accommodation for up to 16 guests. This Lodge is accessed by an eight mile private road from Calvine, off the A9 and a 4-wheel drive is recommended
*Price structure*: From £3,500 per week self-catering
*Access*: Edinburgh Airport or train to Blair Atholl from Perth. Nearest main road A9

# BALNAGOWN ESTATES

*BY LAIRG, SUTHERLAND*

2 India Street
Edinburgh
EH3 6EZ

Tel: 0131 476 6500.          Fax: 0131 476 6501
info@sportingestates.com     www.sportingestates.com

The Balnagown estates, which include Balnagown, Inveroykel and Duchally, extend from Easter Ross in the east to the highlands of central Sutherland. Red deer stalking is available over very challenging terrain, including the rugged slopes of Ben More Assynt. In addition, roe and sika can be stalked in the woodlands and forests of the lower glens. Guests need to be reasonably fit, certainly for the higher ground stalking.

*Stalking acreage:* 60,000
*Status:* Private with let days:
*Sporting agent:* George Goldsmith
*Staff:* Headstalker is Donald Clark
*Available stalking:* Throughout season
*Rifle recommendations:* .270 calibre or similar for red deer and sika. .243 or similar for roe. Estate rifles can be available
*Accommodation:* Inveroykel Lodge, a Victorian residence, enjoys unrivalled views down Strath Oykel and has been refurbished to a very high standard. The Lodge can sleep 10 plus two. Duchally Lodge is situated at the head of Glencassley with views to Ben More Assynt. There are four twin bedrooms.
*Price structure:* Inveroykel Lodge £3,000 per week. Duchally Lodge £1,200 per week.
*Access:* A9 and then A836. Inverness Airport and rail.

Lynedoch House
Barossa Place
Perth
PH1 5EP

Tel: 01738 451600.              Fax: 01738 451900
sporting@ckdgalbraith.co.uk    www.sportinglets.co.uk

Described as one of the few remaining wildernesses left in Europe,
the Ben Damph estates include a remarkable range of mountains,
woodlands, fresh-water lochs and sea shore. In addition to challenging
red deer stalking, for those who enjoy a mixed bag and who are
reasonably active there is also shooting for ptarmigan, woodcock and
rough shooting. Activities for non-shooting guests or partners include
an array of four noted Munros in the area, all surrounding Loch
Torridon.

*Stalking acreage*: 14,500
*Status*: Private with let days
*Sporting agent*: Robert Rattray of C.K.D.Galbraith, as above
*Available stalking*: See above
*Rifle recommendations*: .270 or similar. Estate rifle can be arranged
*Price structure*: POA. Lettings are from Saturday to Saturday
*Accommodation*: The very impressive Ben Damph Lodge was built in 1992
with 100-year-old Scots pine and larch from the estate, by French Canadian
master craftsman Donald Ouellet using traditional techniques.
Accommodation is provided for up to 16 in two double and two family
rooms.
*Access*: Fly or rail to Inverness, then A835, A832 and A896 to Torridon.

# BIGHOUSE ESTATE

## *NORTH-EAST SUTHERLAND*

Lynedoch House
Barossa Place
Perth
PH1 5EP

Tel: 01738 451600
sporting@ckdgalbraith.co.uk

Fax: 01738 456900
www.sportinglets.co.uk

The Bighouse Estate on the edge of the Flow Country in Sutherland offers a wide range of sporting opportunities, whether one seeks stalking or shooting. Both red and roe deer stalking are available in season with the possibility of 20 plus stags. Mixed sporting weeks in November, December and January can also be tailor-made to suit requests (see entry under shooting).

*Stalking acreage*: 50,000 acres, including sister company Strath Halladale.
*Status*: Private with let days
*Sporting agent*: Robert Rattray of C.K.D.Galbraith, as above
*Available stalking*: Throughout season
*Rifle recommendations*: .270 or similar for red deer. .243 or similar for roe.
Estate rifles can be arranged
*Price structure*: POA
*Accommodation*: Fourteen people can be accommodated in Forsinard Lodge which is on the edge of the RSPB Reserve at Forsinard. There are seven twin bedded rooms, with three en-suite and a further four bathrooms, a lounge with open fire, game room, dining room, sitting room and drying room. There is full central heating.
*Access*: From Inverness (rail or air) north via A9 to Helmsdale, the A897 to Forsinard

# BRAEHOUR AND BACKLASS ESTATE

2 India Street
Edinburgh
EH3 6EZ

Tel: 0131 476 6500                    Fax: 0131 476 6501
info@sportingestates.com              www.sportingestates.com

Stalking for red deer is available on the extensive Braehour and
Backlass Estate for two rifles from late September and, due to the
topography of the country, demands considerable tactical expertise.
This is flow country consisting of rolling moorland, bent grass and
heather.

*Stalking acreage*: 23,000
*Status*: Private with let days
*Sporting agent*: George Goldsmith
*Staff*: The Hon. Patrick Sinclair is both owner and headstalker
*Available stalking*: Throughout season
*Rifle recommendations*: .270 calibre or similar recommended. Estate rifles
can be available
*Price structure*: POA
*Accommodation*: Strathmore Lodge can accommodate up to 14 guests on a
fully catered basis, but smaller parties can be catered for
*Access*: A9 and then B870. Rail at Wick. Airport at Inverness

# COIGNAFEARN

*INVERNESS-SHIRE, WEST OF TOMATIN*

Lynedoch House
Barossa Place
Perth
PH1 5EP

Tel: 01738 451600         Fax: 01738 451900
sporting@ckdgalbraith.co.uk       www.sportinglets.co.uk

The magnificent sporting estate of Coignafearn includes the headwaters of the River Findhorn and the sport includes some of the finest red deer stalking in Scotland. The estate is undergoing a period of rejuvenation and is managed on ecological principles. This is a landscape of remote and dramatic mountains, a country where golden eagles and ospreys are frequently seen. There are otters in the river and wild cats in the glen. Four Rifles can stalk independently, due to the vast acreage, and the estate is equipped with excellent vehicles, experienced stalkers and a brand new deer larder.

*Stalking acreage*: 40,000
*Status*: Private with let days
*Sporting agent*: Robert Rattray of C.K.D.Galbraith, as above
*Staff*: Headstalker is Sandy Day
*Available stalking*: Throughout season
*Rifle recommendations*: .270 or similar. Estate rifles can be arranged
*Price structure*: POA. Lettings are from Sunday to Saturday.
*Accommodation*: Coignafearn Old Lodge has been converted from a traditional steading and now features wood-lined rooms, vaulted ceilings and natural stone features. The bedrooms for 10 plus seven children are combined in units of two which open up onto the courtyard. There are four double, three twin and a family room. There is a central bathroom with deep baths.
*Access*: The estate lies west of Tomatin on the A9 from Perth and Pitlochry. Fly or train to Inverness, then 30 minutes south on A9.

# CONAGLEN ESTATE

*CONAGLEN, ARDGOUR, INVERNESS-SHIRE*

2 India Street
Edinburgh
EH3 6EZ

Tel: 0131 476 6500                     Fax: 0131 476 6501
info@sportingestates.com          www.sportingestates.com

Set in a stunning location on the edge of Loch Linnhe and close to Ben Nevis, the vast estate offers outstanding and challenging stalking for two Rifles amidst breath-taking scenery. This is typical dramatic West Coast country, mountainous and offering exciting stalking for the fit and able.

*Stalking acreage*: 40,000
*Status*: Private with let days:
*Sporting agent*: George Goldsmith
*Staff*: Headstalker Donald Kennedy and staff
*Available stalking*: Throughout season
*Rifle recommendations*: .270 calibre or similar. Estate rifles can be available
*Price structure*: From £3,880 per week including cook and housekeeper. Sport is additional on request
*Accommodation*: Conaglen is a traditional Highland Victorian sporting lodge, recently refurbished to a very high standard and offering comfortable accommodation for up to 14 guests. There are two double bedrooms (en-suite), five twins (en-suite), one single (en-suite), one double and three twin bedrooms.
*Access*: Fly to Glasgow or Inverness, train to Fort William, A82 through Glencoe, then five minutes by Corran ferry across Loch Linnhe.

# CORBIETON HOUSE

## DUMFRIES AND GALLOWAY

Corbieton House
Haugh of Urr
Castle Douglas
DG7 3JJ

Tel: 01556 660506              Fax: 01556 660506
tony-halpin@tesco-net

Corbieton House, privately owned, is set in four acres of wooded gardens and in the heart of the Dumfries and Galloway region. The mixed Estate is set in the rolling hills of Galloway and includes conifer plantations, mature oak woodland and arable, offering ideal conditions for roe deer. Novice stalkers are very welcome and a full-time stalker will assist in all aspects of stalking and deer management. While stalkers are normally accompanied, there are some areas where the experienced stalker can be unaccompanied. Stalkers are all required to fire a group of sighting shots before commencing stalking, to within 10cm at 100 metres range. They must also be in possession of a current Firearms Certificate and third party insurance to the value of at least £1 million.

*Stalking acreage*: 7,000
*Status*: Lodge stalking
*Owner*: Tony Halpin as above
*Sporting agent*: N/a
*Staff*: Two full-time stalkers
*Available stalking*: Roe deer throughout relevant season
*Rifle recommendations*: .223 upwards
*Price structure*: Roebucks £65 per stalk. Roe does £50 per stalk. No extra charge levied on trophy heads which are the property of the stalker. The carcase is the property of the estate, but may be purchased by the stalker.
*Accommodation*: Guests stay at Corbieton House: B&B and evening meal £45 per person. B&B £35 per person.
*Access*: By road: A75 from Dumfries direction, through Crocketford and Springholm, 3 miles past Springholm take B794 to Dalbeattie. One mile of Haugh of Urr village. Corbieton House is one mile from village.

# CORRIEGARTH

*BY FORT AUGUSTUS, INVERNESS-SHIRE*

Lynedoch House
Barossa Place
Perth
POH1 5EP

Tel: 01738 451600        Fax: 01738 451900
sporting@ckdgalbraith.co.uk       www.sportinglets.co.uk

For the stalking enthusiast three species of deer, red, sika and roe are available on the extensive forest on the western edge of the Monadhliath mountain range. Corriegarth is surrounded by several other well-known forests, including Dunmaglass, Coignafearn and Garrogie. The ground rises from 600ft to 2,658ft. This forest offers challenging stalking for red deer on the high ground with stalking available for one Rifle from the end of August into October. Both sika and roe are also available on the lower ground.

*Stalking acreage*: 11,500
*Status*: Private with let days
*Sporting agent*: Robert Rattray of C.K.D.Galbraith, as above
*Staff*: Headstalker Billy Johnston
*Available stalking*: Seasonal
*Rifle recommendations*: .270 or similar for red deer and sika. .243 or similar for roe. Estate rifles can be arranged
*Price structure*: POA. Red deer from £320 per stag
*Accommodation*: Corriegarth Lodge can accommodate up to 16 people in nine bedrooms and includes a drawing room, dining room and billiard room with full sized table. This comfortable Lodge provides the basis for an excellent sporting holiday.
*Access*: By road: South of Inverness off the A9. By rail or air: Inverness

# COULIN

Lynedoch House
Barossa Place
Perth
PH1 5EP

Tel: 01738 451600  Fax: 01738 451900
sporting@ckdgalbraith.co.uk  www.sportinglets.co.uk

The Coulin estate includes particularly fine scenery with Caledonian pine and birch woods, with spectacular views towards Ben Eighe National Nature Reserve and the Torridon Mountains. Excellent stalking starts towards the end of August over a varied terrain which will suit most requirements. There are three stalking beats and, occasionally, two stalking parties are out each day. Beasts are brought off the forest by garron or Argocat.

*Stalking acreage*: 22,000
*Status*: Private with let days
*Sporting agent*: Robert Rattray of C.K.D.Galbraith, as above
*Available stalking*: see above
*Rifle recommendations*: .270 or similar. Estate rifle can be arranged
*Price structure*: Farmhouse from £750 per week. Red deer stalking £320 per stag. Lettings are Sunday to Sunday.
*Accommodation*: The attractive farmhouse, which has been re-built and modernised with full central heating, sleeps eight to 10 in three twin bedrooms, one room with bunk beds and a study with bed settee. There are two bathrooms and a shower room.
*Access*: The house is situated at the east end of Loch Coulin and access is by unmetalled road. Air or rail to Inverness and then one hour's drive to Kinlochewe by A835 and A832

# CRAIGANOUR ESTATE

## *KINLOCH RANNOCH, PERTHSHIRE*

2 India Street
Edinburgh
EH3 6EZ

Tel: 0131 476 6500                    Fax: 01312 476 6501
info@sportingestates.com              www.sportingestates.com

Lying to the north of Loch Rannoch in North Perthshire, the Craiganour estate enjoys an extensive acreage. Very challenging red deer stalking is available and around 100 stags are culled each season. There is stalking for one Rifle in August and there are two stalkers catering for two Rifles during the peak of the rut in October. This is relatively rolling countryside and not too mountainous, making it suitable for stalkers of all ages. It also offers tactical stalking of a high quality in lovely country.

*Stalking acreage*: 21,000
*Status*: Private with let days:
*Sporting agent*: George Goldsmith
*Staff*: Headstalker is Henry Littlejohn who has been with the estate for 50 years
*Available stalking*: Throughout season
*Rifle recommendations*: .270 calibre or similar. Estate rifles can be available
*Accommodation*: Craiganour Lodge is a comfortable Victorian shooting lodge at the southern end of the estate overlooking Loch Rannoch. The accommodation is let on a full catered and staffed basis for up to 14 to 16 guests
*Price structure*: From £5,750 per week fully catered for 10 people
*Access*: A9 and then B8019/B846. Airport Edinburgh, rail at Rannoch Station

# DUNBEATH ESTATE

## CAITHNESS

2 India Street
Edinburgh
EH3 6EZ

Tel: 0131 476 6500                     Fax: 0131 476 6501
info@sportingestates.com          www.sprtingestates.com

The extensive Dunbeath Estate which lies on the north-east coast of
Scotland is some 90 miles north of Inverness. This is typical flow
country consisting of extensive rolling hills, bent grasses and heather
clad moorland. Dunbeath Castle stands on the cliffs high above the sea
and acts as a prominent landmark. There is challenging stalking for up
to three Rifles on both the stag and hind forests, divided between
Glutt Lodge and Balcraggie Lodge, the former taking one Rifle and
the latter two Rifles. Both Lodges caters for grouse shooting over
pointers.

*Stalking acreage*: 30,000
*Status*: Private with let days:
*Sporting agent*: George Goldsmith
*Staff*: Headstalker at Balcragguie is Billy Milne and at Glutt Lodge is
Freddie MacKay
*Available stalking*: Throughout season
*Rifle recommendations*: .270 calibre or similar. Estate rifles can be available
*Lunch*: On the hill
*Price structure*: Glutt Lodge from £2,000 per week self-catered. Balcraggie
Lodge from £2,500 to £5,000 per week self-catered
*Accommodation*: Glutt Lodge is situated on the east side of the estate and
has comfortable accommodation for up to eight guests. Balcraggie Lodge is a
magnificent Victorian shooting lodge commanding an elevated position
above Dunbeath Water with views over the strath to the distant North Sea.
The lodge is extremely well appointed and has been recently updated,
offering comfortable accommodation for 12-15 guests
*Access*: A9 to Dunbeath, 2½ hours north of Inverness. Air and rail at
Inverness
*Other comments*: Grouse from five brace days, with four walked-up days
per week in season

# EILEAN DARACH ESTATE

*AN TEALLACH, WEST COAST*

Brackloch
Eilean Darach Estate
Dundonnell
Wester Ross
IV23 2QW

Tel: 01854 633203          Fax: 01854 633203

The Eilean Darach Estate, sited in magnificent West Coast scenery, can offer excellent red deer and goat stalking in the heart of the An Teallach range. The stalking, for one Rifle, is very challenging and guests need to be reasonably fit to cope with the terrain as the ground rises from sea-level to 3,000ft. There is, in addition, very good rough and semi-driven shooting (see also the entry under shooting.)

*Stalking acreage*: 6,000
*Status*: Private with let days
*Owner*: Mr and Mrs Crawford
*Contact*: Mr and Mrs Crawford as above
*Sporting agent*: N/a
*Staff*: Headstalker Peter Hann
*Available stalking*: Red deer, 3 stags per week over three beats. Goats, three per week. Nannies unlimited.
*Rifle recommendations*: .270 for red deer. .243 for hinds and goats. .222 ideal for latter.
*Price structure*: Stag £275, Hind £100. Billy £210, nanny £100. Refund if beast not taken
*Accommodation*: Self-catering lodge sleeping 12 comfortably and also cottage
*Access*: By road: A9 from Inverness, then A835 and A832. Bt air: Inverness. By rail: Inverness.

# GLEN AFFRIC

*INVERNESS-SHIRE*

Lynedoch House
Place
Perth
PH1 5EP

Tel: 01738 451600
sporting@ckdgalbraith.co.uk

Fax: 01738 451900
www.sportinglets.co.uk

This famous deer forest lies in the heart of the Highlands. The lower slopes of the glen are cloaked by one of the finest remaining areas of Caledonian pine forest, and the area is surrounded by a wilderness of jagged mountains, narrow glens and steep corries. The stalking is particularly exciting and challenging due to the spectacular scenery, while the main glens and corries all hold large numbers of hefted deer. The stalking is for one Rifle during September and October. For those who seek their deer amidst breathtaking scenery Glen Affric has much to offer.

*Stalking acreage*: 10,000
*Status*: Private with let days
*Sporting agent*: Robert Rattray of C.K.D.Galbraith, as above
*Staff*: Headstalker is Ronnie Buchan
*Available stalking*: Seasonal
*Rifle recommendations*: .270 or similar. Estate rifles can be arranged
*Price structure*: POA. Lettings are from Sunday to Sunday.
*Accommodation*: Regarded as one of the finest sporting lodges in Scotland, Affric Lodge provides exceptional accommodation for up to 12 people and is furnished to a very high standard. The Lodge appears to be perched on an islet at the eastern end of Loch Affric and enjoys stunning views to the Five Sisters of Kintail.
*Access*: Rail or air to Inverness, then one hour's drive to the west of Inverness

# GLENFERNATE LODGE

2 India Street
Edinburgh
EH3 6EX

Tel: 0131 476 6500                    Fax: 0131 476 6501
info@sportingestates.com              www.sportingestates.com

The extensive Glenfernate estate can offer some excellent stalking for
two Rifles from the middle of August. Pitlochry is only 20 minutes
away and Gleneagles an hour and 10 minutes. This is a mixed ground,
with beautiful countryside. The estate also enjoys a very private and
lovely loch, while the lodge has a reputation for being extremely
comfortable. (See also the entry under grouse shooting.)

*Stalking acreage*: 17,000
*Status*: Commercial:
*Sporting agent*: George Goldsmith
*Staff*: Headstalker Gordon McGregor
*Available stalking*: Throughout season
*Rifle recommendations*: .270 calibre or similar. Estate rifles can be available
*Price structure*: From £3,250 per week self-catered
*Accommodation*: Glenfernate Lodge offers accommodation for parties of up
to 15 with five bedrooms with twin beds, two with double beds, one single
bedroom, four bathrooms and a nursery. Cook available if required.
*Access*: A9, and then off A924. Edinburgh Airport or rail to Edinburgh or
Inverness.

# GLENQUAICH

*PERTHSHIRE, BY AMULREE*

Lynedoch House
Barossa Place
Perth
PH1 5EP

Tel: 01738 451600.                Fax: 01738 451900
sporting@ckdgalbraith.co.uk      www.sportinglets.co.uk

Gelenquaich, lying only 27 miles from Perth, has an established reputation for both its stalking and shooting. There is a great variety of ground ranging from high crags rising to over 2,500ft to the lower, gently undulating areas close to Loch Freuchie. The red deer stalking is available for parties with either daily or weekly lets. Stalking can also be arranged on neighbouring estates and hind stalking is available from the end of October. Glenquaich is very accessible from either Edinburgh or Glasgow, making it an ideal location for a short sporting break. (See also the entry under shooting.)

*Stalking acreage*: 10,000
*Status*: Private with let days
*Sporting agent*: Robert Rattray of C.K.D.Galbraith, as above
*Staff*: The headstalker is Stan Riches
*Available stalking*: 20 stags in October for 1 or 2 Rifles
*Rifle recommendations*: .270 or similar. Estates rifles can be arranged
*Price structure*: POA. Croftmill Cottage from £275 per week
*Accommodation*: The fully equipped Croftmill Cottage sleeps up to five (one double, one single and one twin) and there are also excellent local hotels
*Access*: Dundee City Airport, then A90 to Perth, A9 to Dunkeld and then A822 to Amulree. Rail/drive to Perth, then A9, A822 to Amulree

# GLENSHERO ESTATE

*LAGGAN, INVERNESSHIRE*

2 India Street
Edinburgh
EH3 6EX

Tel: 0131 476 6500                      Fax: 476 6501
info@sportingestates.com                www.sportingestates.com

One of the finest deer forests in the north of Scotland, the Glenshero
estate is situated to the north of Dalwhinie. Stalking is available for
two Rifles between mid-August and mid-October. In the region of
120 stags are taken off the hill, with an average forest weight of
78.5kg. Efforts have been made to improve grouse numbers and in
recent years the season's bag of walked-up grouse has varied between
200 and 600 brace.

*Stalking acreage*: 65,000
*Status*: Private with let days
*Sporting agent*: George Goldsmith
*Staff*: Headstalker is Bruce Hendry
*Available stalking*: Throughout season
*Rifle recommendations*: .270 calibre or similar recommended. Estate rifles
can be available
*Accommodation*: The recently modernised Sherramore Lodge offers accom-
modation for up to 10 guests. A cook is available and all running costs are
included in the rent. The Lodge is sited close to the estate's eastern march at
880ft above sea level
*Price structure*: From £3,790 per week to £9,000 including full staff
*Access*: Inverness is under one hour's drive away. A9 and then A889. Airport
at Inverness. Rail at Dalwhinnie or Inverness

# HOPE ESTATE

*SUTHERLAND*

Lynedoch House
Barossa Place
Perth
PH1 5EP

Tel: 01738 451600          Fax: 01738 451900.
sporting@ckdgalbraith.co.uk     www.sportinglets.co.uk

One of seven sporting estates established by a former Duke of
Sutherland in the 19th century when expanding road and rail links
made the north Scottish coast accessible, there are magnificent views
along Loch Hope towards Ben Hope in the south, and northwards
down the Hope river towards the estuary. Four mixed sporting weeks
are offered in September and October, to include three stags. (See also
entry under shooting.)

*Stalking acreage*: 22,000 acres and with exclusive arrangements with the
neighbouring Eriboll and Melness Estates providing a total of over 50,000
acres.
*Status*: Private with let days
*Sporting agent*: Robert Rattray of C.K.D.Galbraith, as above
*Headstalker*: Ian Macdonald
*Available stalking*: Throughout season
*Rifle recommendations*: .270 or similar. Estate rifles can be arranged
*Price structure*: POA. Lettings are from Sunday to Sunday.
*Accommodation*: Hope Lodge, a listed building, remarkable for being clad
entirely in slate, can accommodate up to 12 guests in comfort. There are
eight bedrooms: two double, two twins (one with en-suite bath), and four
singles and two further bathrooms. There is a games room, large drying
room and gun room. It is arguably the best sited of the Sutherland sporting
lodges.
*Access*: Air or rail to Inverness, then A9, A839 to Lairg and north to
Altnaharra

Lynedoch House
Barossa Place
Perth
PH1 5EP

Tel: 01738 451600      Fax: 01738 451900
sporting@ckdgalbraith.co.uk      www.sportinglets.co.uk

Enjoying an extensive acreage of moors, woods, farmland, lochs and hills, the Islay Estates can offer memorable sport. Islay's stags and hinds are notably large and, combined with hills which are not unduly steep, provide excellent stalking with stunning views of the sea and surrounding islands. Woodland stalking for roe is also available. The island is, of course, also famous for its distilleries, golf course and abundant bird life.

*Stalking acreage*: 50,000 acres plus
*Status*: Private with let days
*Sporting agent*: Robert Rattray of C.K.D.Galbraith, as above
*Available stalking*: See above
*Rifle recommendations*: .270 or similar for red deer, .243 or similar for roe
*Price structure*: POA
*Accommodation*: Parties of up to 10 can be accommodated in a comfortable self-catering farmhouse overlooking Loch Skerrols. There is also self-catering accommodation in a recently modernised cottage sleeping four. Alternatively guests can be booked into the Bridgend Hotel.
*Access*: Fly from Glasgow, flights out in the morning and back in the evening or take ferry from Loch Tarbert

# KILDERMORIE

*EASTER ROSS*

Lynedoch House
Barossa Place
Perth
PH1 5EP

Tel: 01738 451600                    Fax: 01738 451900
sporting@ckdgalbraith.co.uk          www.sportinglets.co.uk

The Kildermorie estate lies in the heart of Ross-shire and is renowned for magnificent scenery. Rising from 600ft to 2,750 ft, the estate combines stalking with grouse, ptarmigan and duck shooting. Kildermorie is a well-known forest with two beats set in the heart of magnificent scenery and the topography is such that it makes it possible for two Rifles to stalk in almost any wind. Garrons are used to bring home beasts from the hill, with up to 10 stags taken in the peak weeks. The estate boasts one of the finest Victorian deer larders in Scotland. (See also the entry under shooting.)

*Stalking acreage*: 17,500
*Status*: Private with let days
*Sporting agent*: Robert Rattray of C.K.D.Galbraith, as above
*Staff*: Headstalker is Dougie Russell
*Rifle recommendations*: .270 or similar. Estate rifles can be arranged
*Price structure*: POA
*Accommodation*: Beautifully furnished Meall Mor Lodge has 10 double/twin en-suite bedrooms, and a fully equipped kitchen, large dining room, two lounges, drying room and gun room. Dogs are welcome, but not in the Lodge. Kennels are available. Lettings are on a self-catering basis from Sunday to Sunday
*Access*: Air or rail to Inverness and then one hour's drive north on A9 to Alness

# KINGIE ESTATE

## *INVERGARRY, INVERNESS-SHIRE*

2 India Streeet
Edinburgh
EH3 6EZ

Tel: 0131 476 6500                    Fax: 0131 476 6501
info@sportingestates.com              www.sportingestates.com

The Kingie estate is sited on the south side of Loch Quoich and lies 54 miles to the west of Inverness and 40 miles from Fort William. The stalking has largely been retained by the family since the estate was purchased in 1989 and is now offered as some of the most challenging in Scotland. The deer forest is reached by crossing Loch Quoich and is set in spectacular mountain scenery. Stalking takes place from August to early October, mainly for cull stags to ensure a healthy and improving stock. Hind stalking is occasionally available from late October. In view of the terrain it is recommended that guests should be reasonably fit and agile.

*Stalking acreage*: 15,000
*Status*: Private with let days
*Sporting agent*: George Goldsmith
*Staff:* Headstalker is John Cameron
*Available stalking*: Seasonal
*Rifle recommendations*: .270 calibre or similar. Estate rifles can be available
*Accommodation*: Guests stay at Kingie Lodge, built in 1994, with accommodation for up to 14
*Price structure*: From £2,500 per week
*Access*: Glasgow or Inverness Airports. A82 is main road. Rail to Fort William or Inverness

# KINLOCH ESTATE

## KINLOCH, SUTHERLAND

Lynedoch House
Barossa Place
Perth
PH1 5EP

Tel: 01738 451600        Fax: 01738 451900
sporting@ckdgalbraith.co.uk        www.sportinglets.co.uk

The Kinloch Estate, situated on Scotland's north coast and overlooking the magnificent setting of the Kyle of Tongue, was originally one of the Duke of Sutherland's sporting estates. The stalking has good access with 15 miles of new hill road and established pony paths. An average of 35 stags are shot each season with an average weight of nearly 14 stone, while a target of 100 hinds is usually achieved.

*Stalking acreage*: 20,000
*Status*: Private with let days
*Sporting agent*: Robert Rattray of C.K.D.Galbraith, as above
*Staff*: Headstalker is Hugh Montgomery
*Available stalking*: Throughout season
*Rifle recommendations*: .270 or similar. Estate rifles can be arranged
*Price structure*: POA. Lettings from Sunday to Sunday
*Accommodation*: A well-appointed Victorian sporting lodge sleeping up to 16
*Access*: Air or rail to Inverness and then A9, A839 to Lairg, A836 to Altnaharra then north to Kyle of Tongue

# KINLOCHEWE AND LOCHROSQUE

Lynedoch House
Barossa Place
Perth
PH1 5EP

Tel: 01738 451600
sporting@ckdgalbraith.co.uk

Fax: 01738 456900
www.sportinglets.co.uk

Located at the southern end of Loch Maree, the extensive estate of Kinlochewe and Lochrosque includes some of Scotland's most breathtaking scenery. Walked-up grouse shooting is available from the middle of August until early September and from the second week onwards the lodge is let for red deer stalking. Initially this is for five stags a week and, once into October, 10 stags each week. Some of the most challenging stalking grounds in Scotland are to be found here, especially as there are a number of punch-bowl like corries which demand great skill in order to achieve a successful stalk. According to G. Kenneth Whitehead, Lochrosque, Cabuie and Nest of Fannich represent some of the most testing stalking in Scotland.

*Stalking acreage*: 35,000
*Status*: Private with let stalking
*Sporting agent*: Robert Rattray of C.K.D.Galbraith, as above
*Staff*: Headstalker is Ronnie Ross
*Available stalking*: See above
*Rifle recommendations*: .270 or similar. Estate rifles can be arranged
*Price structure*: POA. Lettings are from Sunday to Sunday
*Accommodation*: Kinlochewe Lodge offers top quality accommodation for up to 18 people including staff. This is a traditional Highland lodge with good access to the hill. There is a full-sized billiard table. Well-controlled dogs welcome though not allowed in the lodge, however kennels are available. There is also a cottage available for larger parties.
*Access*: Air or rail to Inverness, then A9, A835 and A832 to Kinlochewe. One hour's drive from Inverness

# MONACHYLE MHOR

## NR TROSSACHS

Monachyle Mhor Hotel
Balquhidder
Lochearnhead
Perthsire
FK19 8PQ

Tel: 01877 384622                Fax: 01877 384305
info@monachylemhor            www.monachylemhor.com

Monachyle Mhor Hotel has some 2,000 acres available for red deer stalking of both stags and hinds, and also its own grouse moor. Apart from breathtaking countryside offering glorious views, stalkers can enjoy a superb day with the headstalker, Mike Luti. Two Rifles can stalk at any one time and a maximum of four Guns to walk up grouse. The countryside is average walking fitness.

*Stalking acreage*: 2,000 acres
*Status*: Commercial:
*Contact*: Tom and Angela Lewis, as above
*Sporting agent*: N/a
*Staff*: Mike Luti is headstalker
*Available stalking*: Throughout season
*Rifle recommendations*: .270 or similar
*Price structure*: £250 plus VAT (stag), £185 plus VAT (hind)
*Accommodation*: Double bed and breakfast in award-winning hotel from £165 for two
*Access*: Glasgow or Edinburgh Airports. By rail to Stirling. By road 11 miles north of Callender on the A84, turn right at Kingshouse, then 6 miles on glen road

# PHONES & ETTERIDGE

*KINGUSSIE, INVERNESS-SHIRE*

Lynedoch House
Barossa Place
Perth
PH1 5EP

Tel: 01738 451600                    Fax: 01738 456900
sporting@ckdgalbraith.co.uk          www.sportinglets.co.uk

Part of the south-western flank of the Cairngorm Mountains, Phones
is a magnificent sporting estate offering outstanding shooting and
good and varied stalking. The estate, which rises to over 3,000ft,
enjoys spectacular scenery. The stalking is for both red and roe. From
the middle of September there is stalking for one Rifle with the
expectation of five stags per week. (See also the entry under
shooting.)

*Stalking acreage*: 29,000
*Status*: Private with let days:
*Sporting agent*: Robert Rattray of C.K.D.Galbraith, as above
*Staff*: Michael Glass is Headstalker
*Available stalking*: See above
*Rifle recommendations*: .270 or similar for red deer, .243 or similar for roe.
Estate rifles can be arranged.
*Price structure*: POA
*Accommodation*: Phones Lodge can accommodate up to 18 people with a
large drawing room, dining room and kitchen. The lodge is let on a self-
catering basis although the services of a cook and housekeeper can be
provided. Tenants pay for their own food and drink. Etteridge is a smaller
lodge on the Phones estate and sleeps a maximum of eight people on a self-
catering basis. Lettings are from Sunday to Sunday. Well trained gundogs
welcome.
*Access*: One hour's drive north-west of Perth on the A9 to Kingussie. Air to
Dundee and then A90 to A9.

# RHIDORROCH

Lynedoch House
Barossa Place
Perth
PH1 5EP

Tel: 01738 451600        Fax: 01738 456900
sporting@ckdgalbraith.co.uk      www.sportinglets.co.uk

Spectacular mountainous and hill scenery, with numerous hill lochs and two salmon rivers, makes Rhidorroch a very special mixed sporting estate. For the stalker both red deer and sika are available and during July, August and September two red stags can be taken per week and then, in October, up to five stags per week. Stalking for sika stags can be arranged given prior notice. For the non-sporting guest or partner the estate offers gentle hill walks, while for the more adventurous there are several Munros, including An Teallach and Stac Pollaidh, within a short distance. The village of Ullapool offers a nine hole golf course as well as other amenities.

*Stalking acreage*: 20,000
*Status*: Private with let days
*Sporting agent*: Robert Rattray of C.K.D.Galbraith, as above
*Available stalking*: Red and sika: two stags per week July to September. Five stags per week in October.
*Rifle recommendations*: .270 or similar. Estate rifle can be arranged.
*Price structure*: Sporting week from £3,200. Lettings are from Saturday to Saturday
*Accommodation*: Rhidorroch House, a traditional lodge set above Loch Achall with unrivalled views to east and west. Accommodation available for up to 14 guests. Features include oak-panelled dining room and full-size billiard table.
*Access*: To Inverness by rail or air. One hour's drive to Ullapool from Inverness on A835.

# ROTTAL LODGE ESTATE

*AIRLIE ESTATE, ANGUS*

Lynedoch House
Barossa Place
Perth
PH1 5EP

Tel: 01738 451600                   Fax: 01738 456900
sporting@ckdgalbraith.co.uk     www.sportinglets.co.uk

Lying in the heart of Glen Clova, at the southern foothills of the
Cairngorm massif, Rottal Lodge Estate offers stalking for red and roe
deer. This is a mixed country of lowlands and uplands, rising from a
river valley to high tops at 3,000ft and is, in parts, very rugged.

*Stalking acreage*: 22,000 acres
*Status*: Private with let days
*Sporting agent*: Robert Rattray of C.K.D.Galbraith, as above
*Available stalking*: On application
*Rifle recommendations*: .270 or similar for red deer, .243 or similar for roe
*Price structure*: POA
*Accommodation*: Totally refurbished in 1999, the Lodge provides
comfortable accommodation for a party of 16 in 11 bedrooms, including six
double and two twin rooms with en-suite bathrooms. There is also a secure
gunroom.
*Access*: The Estate lies to the west of Kirriemuir, Upper South Esk towards
Glen Clova
*Other comments*: N/a

# STRAHANNA

## GALLOWAY

Strahanna Farm
Dalry
Castle Douglas
Kirkcudbrightshire
DG7 3UF

Tel: 01644 460 660           Fax: 01644 460 660
wildlife@strahanna.fsnet.co.uk

Strahanna is situated in the Galloway hills and is blessed with glorious views and scenery to provide a perfect base for stalkers and also walkers. The area consists of a mixture of newly planted land and older forestry, and to assist stalking a considerable number of high seats have been installed. The stalking for roe and red deer is on a one-to-one basis or two stalkers to one guide can be organised.

*Stalking acreage*: 18,000
*Status*: Commercial, lodge stalking
*Owner*: Thure Holm
*Contact*: The owner as above
*Sporting agent*: N/a
*Staff*: Two stalking guides
*Available stalking*: Roebucks and does and red deer in their seasons
*Rifle recommendations*: Minimum calibre .243
*Price structure*: This depends on the season, the number of stalkers and the length of stay. The price is negotiable but as an indication roe buck stalking on a 2:1 basis is £125 per day per person, including stalking and trophies. Doe and hind stalking on a 2:1 basis is £70 per person per day.
*Accommodation*: Private accommodation at Strahanna Farm, complemented by good home cooking. Double B&B £40.
*Access*: Strahanna is 90 minutes from the Scottish Border. Prestwick Airport is 45 minutes, Glasgow Airport 90 minutes.

# THE DELL ESTATE

2 India Street
Edinburgh
EH3 6EZ

Tel: 0131 476 6500                    Fax: 0131 476 6501
infor@sportingestates.com       www.sportingestates.com

The Dell Estate with its beautiful birch woodlands running down to Loch Ness offers challenging stalking for red, roe and sika for two Rifles. (See also the entry under shooting.)

*Stalking acreage*: 5,500
*Status*: Private with let days
*Sporting agent*: George Goldsmith
*Staff*: Colin Barclay is headstalker
*Available stalking*: Prime sika stalking, and also roe stalking, is available on Loch Ness side, with red deer on the open hill
*Rifle recommendations*: .243 for roe, and .270 or similar for sika and red deer. Estate rifles can be available.
*Accommodation*: Dell House, a lovely 18th century Georgian residence, can sleep up to 14 in a double en-suite bedroom, a twin en-suite bedroom, four twin bedrooms and two single bedrooms
*Price structure*: Lodge from £2,500 per week self-catered. Fully catered packages can be arranged. Stalking is from £320 per stag, sika and roe from £200.
*Access*: A9 south from Inverness, then B851 running south-west alongside Loch Ness. One hour's drive

# UIG & HAMANAVAY ESTATE

*WEST COAST OF LEWIS*

Lynedoch House
Barossa Place
Perth
PH1 5EP

Tel: 01738 451600        Fax: 01738 456900
sporting@ckdgalbraith.co.uk        www.sportinglets.co.uk

The Uig & Hamanavay Estate offers stalking for both red stags and hinds and Rifles are welcome in the appropriate seasons. This is rugged, mountainous country, amidst glorious scenery, and stalkers should be prepared to work for their sport. A reasonable degree of fitness is an advantage. The stalking is for 40 stags and 30 hinds.

*Stalking acreage*: 50,000
*Status*: Private with let stalking
*Sporting agent*: Robert Rattray of C.K.D.Galbraith, as above
*Staff*: Sporting Manager is Simon Hunt
*Available stalking*: Throughout season
*Rifle recommendations*: .270 or similar. Estate rifles can be arranged
*Price structure*: POA but note that the shooting is let as a package from Saturday to Saturday
*Accommodation*: The comfortable Estate house at Hamanavay sited at the head of the sea loch, provides a truly magical setting
*Access*: By air. Fly to Glasgow and then transfer on to Stornway. Flights now include Sunday. By ferry from Ullapool six days a week.

# SIMULATED GAME SHOOTING

# BREDA ESTATE (CONOISSEUR CLAYS)

## BY ALFORD, DEESIDE, ABERDEENSHIRE

Tel: 01651 806375
contact@kingscliff.co.uk

Fax: 01651 806547
www. kingscliff.co.uk

Simulated Connoisseur Clays offers a tremendous array of simulated shooting in breathtaking surroundings. Days are run along the lines of a traditional game day, with pegs drawn for drives and a full safety briefing. Breda is a much-loved and unspoilt private estate which rises from the banks of the River Don up to stunning heather moorland. It combines deep hidden valleys, beech woodland and avenues, steep banks and pretty meadowland. Clays are presented from hidden automatic traps, using a radio-controlled computer operated system, which can be modified to suit the shooting team's ability and the drives selected. Both novices and experienced Guns welcome.

*Company*: Kingscliff Sporting Lodge t/a Connoisseur Clays
*Contact*: Chris Harry Thomas
*Staff*: Ronnie McLeod supported by fully trained staff from Kingscliff Sporting Lodge
*Gun hire*: £40 per gun
*Lunch*: A three-course lunch, featuring carefully selected local produce, is served in Tullochmill Farmhouse, with coffee and bacon rolls on arrival and afternoon tea on departure. A half day starting with lunch and shooting in the afternoon only can also be arranged.
*Price structure*: £300 plus VAT per person for the full day. £260 plus VAT for the half day. Fibre wad cartridges, instructors and transport to and from the shoot charged as extras
*Accommodation*: Selection of local hotels. Breda House currently being renovated to offer accommodation
*Access*: By road: 45 minutes by A944 from Aberdeen and Aberdeen Airport
*Other comments*: Days available from April until August during the close season. Suitable for parties of 10-20 people.

# WALES

# PHEASANTS

## BETTWS CEDEWAIN, NR NEWTON AND MONTGOMERY

St George's House
29 St George's Road
Cheltenham
Glos
GL50 3DU

Tel: 01242 514478          Fax 01242 224697
info@coley.co.uk           www.coley.co.uk

Sited in glorious Welsh countryside, the Bettws Shoot offers truly challenging driven pheasants and partridges from woodland and game crops set amidst hills and valleys. This is superb shooting and headkeeper Michael Lewis and his team can be guaranteed to keep Guns on their toes.

*Shooting acreage*: 2,000
*Status*: Commercial
*Sporting agent*: Ian Coley Sporting, as above
*Headkeeper/staff*: Michael Lewis is headkeeper
Number of days available: 30
*Number of drives*: Varies
*Bag expectations*: 300
*Average cartridge to kill ratio*: 4:1
*Lunch*: Lunch is taken in The Willows, Bettws Hall
*Price structure*: £27 per bird plus VAT
*Accommodation*: Bettws Hall
*Access*: Off the A483/A489. Mainline rail at Shrewsbury
*Other Comments*: Well controlled dogs welcome

# BRIGANDS SHOOT

## NR MACHYNLLETH, NORTH-WEST WALES

St George's House
29 St George's Road
Cheltenham
Glos.
GL50 3DU

Tel: 01242 514478        Fax: 01242 224697
info@coley.co.uk        www.coley.co.uk

The Brigands Shoot is set in spectacular scenery on the edge of Snowdonia's National Park in mountainous countryside. This is a newly developed shoot, which will undoubtedly provide very challenging shooting for both pheasants and partridges and, it is claimed, will be the equal of any of the top shoots in the country. The landscape lends itself to showing very high and testing birds.

*Shooting acreage*: 10,000
*Status*: Commercial
*Sporting agent*: Ian Coley Sporting, as above
*Headkeeper/staff*: Brian Jones
Number of days available: 30
*Number of drives*: Numerous
*Average cartridge to kill ratio*: Expected to be 5 or 6:1
*Lunch*: To be announced
*Price structure*: £27 per bird plus VAT
*Accommodation*: Brigands Inn on the shoot.
*Access*: Off A470/A458 some 12 miles north-east of Machynlleth
*Other Comments*: Well-controlled gundogs welcome

# GLANUSK

The Estate Office
Glanusk Park
Crickhowell
Powys, NP8 1LP

Tel: 01873 810414                    Fax: 01873 811385
glanuskestate@internet.com           www.glanusk.com

Set in the beautiful Usk Valley in the Brecon Beacon National Park, with stunning views, this well-known Welsh pheasant shoot (with some partridges) uses the surrounding hills to the full. The drives are very varied on each day, with perhaps park, a woodland ride, game crops and open stands from high coverts included. All are testing and of high quality with birds spread across the whole line, which is normally pegged for nine Guns. Novices not recommended. There are normally three drives in the morning (with 'elevenses') and either one or two in the afternoon. Four-wheel drives are essential and Guns are asked to provide three, only one being provided by the owner.

*Shooting acreage*: 2,500
*Status*: Private syndicate with up to eight let days
*Owner*: William Legge-Bourke DL
*Contact*: The Estate Office as above
*Sporting agent*: N/a
*Headkeeper/staff*: Mark Lewis (staff of two)
Number of days available: Eight (single guns)
*Number of drives*: Total of 12, 4-5 each day
*Bag expectations*: 250-300 in Nov/Dec. – 200 from mid-January
*Average cartridge to kill ratio*: 4.5-8:1 depending on the day and the Guns. (the Tan-y-lan drive averages 10:1)
*Lunch*: There is a full luncheon with wine etc included, taken in the 'Rod Room' of the house, for up to 16 guests. At the end of the day tea is also served here.
*Price structure*: £30 per bird (no VAT) with no 'overage' or 'underage' (unless disaster strikes). The owner attempts to manage a full day for the expected bag.
*Accommodation*: Several good hotels within easy reach including Gliffaes Country House Hotel (one mile), The Bear Hotel, Crickhowell (two miles) and the 5 star Llangoed Hall (16 miles)
*Access*: Three hours from London, 1.5 hours from Birmingham, 1 hour from Cardiff or Bristol. Dual carriageway from M4 and M50 within 6 miles. Airports at Cardiff and Bristol.
*Other comments*: Well trained dogs are very welcome. For non-shooting wives there is good shopping in Crickhowell and Hay on Wye with its books and antiques (35 minutes). Abergavenny and Brecon are also 30 minutes away, but lunch is normally at 1pm.

# LAKE VYRNWY HOTEL

## MONTGOMERYSHIRE, MID WALES

Lake Vyrnwy Estate
Llanwddyn
Montgomeryshire
Mid Wales
SY10 0LY

Tel: 01691 870692                    Fax: 01691 870259
res@lakevyrnwy.com                   www.lakevyrnwy.com

Driven and walked-up pheasants over 24,000 acres. Lake Vyrnwy is probably one of the most scenic parts of the British Isles. The Estate is set in a large basin, the Lake in the bottom surrounded by steep woodland and bracken beds rising to heather moorlands. This typography enables very testing driven birds to be shown. Although a commercial shoot, it is run more in the style of a syndicate and renowned for being a very friendly yet professional organisation. The shoot prides itself on quality not quantity. For those Guns who prefer a less formal day walked-up shooting is also available. Full details available from the hotel.

*Shooting acreage*: 24,000
*Status*: Hotel/Commercial
*Owner*: Lake Vyrnwy Hotel
*Contact*: John Roberts
*Sporting agent*: N/a
*Headkeeper/staff*: Guto Roberts.
*Number of available days*: 24
*Number of drives*: 15 total – 6 per day
*Bag expectations*: 100 –300, depending on the season. Average 200 bird days.
*Gun/cartridge recommendations*: No 5 shot, fibre wads only.
*Average cartridge to kill ratio*: Not known
*Lunch*: Refreshments served in the field from vintage Bedford Army lorry. Shoot lunch provided at the end of the day in the hotel.
*Price structure*: £30 per bird plus VAT. During January the hotel offers a shoot package which includes 1 day's shooting with 2 nights full board for a team of 8 Guns - £550 per person.
*Accommodation*: Lake Vyrnwy Hotel. 3 Star, 2AA Rosette Victorian Sporting Hotel overlooking Lake Vyrnwy
*Access*: One hour from M54. Helicopter from Welshpool Airport. Rail to Welshpool, 21 miles away. Transport by arrangement
*Other comments*: Dogs welcome with heated kennelling provided at the hotel

Milford
The Crescent
Hartford
Cheshire CW8 1QS

Tel: 01606 74736          Fax: 01606 79069
robvine@btinternet.com

The Lymore Shoot is located on the Welsh English border near the Georgian town of Montgomery. The Estate, which is owned by Lord Powys, extends to some 4,000 acres of what can be described as traditional game shooting country. The beautiful, undulating countryside has many wooded areas and, in addition to numerous small ponds and copses, the Estate boasts two large lakes in classic settings. The waters hold duck and teal renowned for their height and speed. The driven pheasant rearing policy, exercised by the headkeeper, is aimed at ensuring he can present high birds to the Guns from the first week in October and throughout the season.

*Shooting acreage*: 4,000
*Status*: Private, with let days
*Contact*: Rob Vine
*Headkeeper/staff*: Martin Diment. Assistant keeper Tim Diment
*Number of days available*: Each season there is a Tuesday walk-up day for 4 Guns and 40 birds; a Thursday driven day for 9 Guns and 100 birds and a Saturday driven day for 9 Guns for 150 birds. During September on Saturdays there are driven duck days for 9 Guns for 180 birds.
*Average cartridge to kill ratio*: For pheasants 3:1, for duck 7:1
*Lunch*: Welcoming tea or coffee is available before shooting. A sit-down lunch is taken in the Gun Room at the headkeeper's cottage and to complete the day tea or coffee and cakes are served after shooting. For an additional £5 to the shooting fee a full fried breakfast can be ordered in advance from the keeper's wife
*Price structure*: Walk-up days: £175 per Gun. 100 bird driven days: £300 per Gun. 150 bird driven days: £450 per Gun. 180 driven duck days: £300 per Gun. All prices include VAT
*Accommodation*: There are a number of very good B&B accommodations in Montgomery or the well appointed Royal Oak Hotel at nearby Welshpool. Contact Rob Vine for further information
*Access*: The Lymore Shoot is located near the towns of Newtown and Welshpool on the English-Welsh border
*Other comments*: Teams of Guns are welcome and should discuss their requirements with Rob Vine. Guns are welcome to take away a complimentary brace of birds. Well trained gundogs welcome

# OLD HALL SHOOT

*LLANDRINDOD WELLS, POWYS*

Old Hall
Dolau
Llandrindod Wells
Powys
LD1 5TL

Tel: 01597 851247

Old Hall Shoot is sited at the junction of several steep-sided valleys. The ground lies between 950 to 1,385ft above sea-level with game crops planted at around the 1,200ft contour. It is hardly surprising that the shoot is renowned for the quality and height of its pheasants. Amongst the many notable drives are the Mill Hill drive which produces spectacular birds, while on the Bracken Bank drive the birds curl back, over and along the line of Guns. From the steep side behind the dams one can expect a mixture of high duck, pheasants and the odd partridge or two, while the Old Hall Wood can produce seriously high birds crossing the valley.

*Shooting acreage*: 260
*Status*: Commercial
*Owner*: Old Hall Partnership
*Contact*: Charmian Middleton or her son Tom Richards as above
*Sporting agent*: N/a
*Headkeeper/staff*: David G.Eaton
*Number of available days*: 12
*Number of drives*: 11
*Bag expectations*: 200 plus, reducing to 100 before Christmas, then 100 to 60 in January
*Average cartridge to kill ratio*: 5:1
*Lunch*: This is taken in Old Hall house. Sloe gin to fortify, and then soup, sherry and roast Welsh Black beef sandwiches. After shooting, a cream tea and spirits if required.
*Price structure*: £24 per bird
*Accommodation*: B&B, or The Bell County Inn, Llanyre, Guidfa House, Crossgates, Radnorshire Arms, Presteigne or Severn Arms, Penybont
*Access*: Old Hall is 3½ miles north of the A44 on the A488. Knighton is 10 miles. By rail the Mid Wales lines runs through Dolau (request halt) to Craven Arms.
*Other comments*: Gundogs welcome, and also obedient non-shooting guests

# THE FOELAS SHOOT

## PENTREFOELAS, SNOWDONIA NATIONAL PARK

Hiraethog
Pentrefoelas
Betys y Coed
Conwy LL24 0LE

Tel: 01690 770156

The Foelas Estate is set in a beautiful upland area of the Snowdonia National Park, near the small village of Pentrefoelas approximately seven miles east of Betwys y Coed and 25 miles west of Llangollen. The shoot has been established for over 30 years and provides excellent sport with top quality birds. There are over 3,500 acres of coverts for driven pheasants and partridges and the many established drives ensure that high quality sporting birds are shown on every shoot day. Each drive is different but all are interesting and produce testing but shootable birds. In addition, the Foelas Shoot offers walked-up days for which there is additional acreage, showing duck, woodcock and snipe, as well as pheasants and partridges.

*Shooting acreage*: Approximately 5,000
*Status*: Private with let days
*Owner*: Partnership – H.C.Thomas and Mrs J.R.Thomas
*Contact*: Cledwyn Thomas on 01690 770156
*Headkeeper*: Kim Adams
Number of days available: 11
*Number of drives*: 19 established drives. (5 or 6 per day)
*Bag expectations*: 150 – 200
*Average cartridge to kill ratio*: 3.5:1
*Lunch*: Lunch is taken in the Shoot Gunroom at the Headkeeper's house, where the Guns meet on arrival. On partridge days shoot through and eat at end of the day. On pheasant days lunch can be either at mid-day or at the day's end. An excellent 3 course meal with wine is included. Coffee/tea on arrival
*Price structure*: Driven pheasants/partridges 150-200 bird days £26 per bird. Maximum 8 Guns with meal included. Extra meals £10 each. All prices include VAT. Walked-up 40-50 bird days for 6-8 Guns at £130 per person, lunch included. Extra meals £10 each. All prices include VAT
*Access*: At Pentrefoelas on A5, seven miles east of Betwys y Coed. Shoot is half a mile from centre of village off B5113
*Accommodation*: Guests usually stay at the 2 Star Foelas Coaching Inn at Pentrefoelas, but there are 4 Star hotels in Betwys y Coed
*Other comments*: Mr Thomas is concerned that all Guns have good sport and an enjoyable day and to ensure this he personally escorts the Guns at all times, and is in constant radio contact with his headkeeper. Well-trained gundogs are welcome.

# THE RHALLT SHOOT

Cefn Cledan
Nebo
Llanon
Cardiganshire
SY23 5LE

Tel: 01974 272634                    Fax: 01974 272634
Mobile: 07970 746084
charles.cefngwyn@btopenworld.com

Offering driven pheasant and partridge, the 2,000 acre Rhallt shoot has a long pedigree for shooting high sporting birds. A favourite of King George VI and Neville Chamberlain, the shoot is immaculately keepered and well run. Guns will thoroughly enjoy themselves even if the birds are a little too testing on some of the drives! The shoot aims for a high level of hospitality and ensuring that Guns will have an excellent shooting day.

*Shooting acreage*: 2,000
*Status*: Syndicate with let days
*Contact*: Charles Grisedale
*Sporting agent*: N/a
*Headkeeper/staff*: Alan Forbes
*Number of available days*: 20
*Number of drives*: 20
*Bag expectations*: 150 plus
*Gun/cartridge recommendations*: No 5 shot recommended
*Average cartridge to kill ratio*: 4.5:1. The Zigzag drive is 8:1!
*Lunch*: Served in comfortable shoot room
*Price structure*: £24 per bird
*Accommodation*: Local hotels and pubs available
*Access*: By road: Approx 3 miles from Welshpool. By rail: Welshpool Station. By air: Manchester Airport or Welshpool Aerodrome
*Other comments*: Well-behaved dogs welcome

# WYNNSTAY PARK

*RUABON, WREXHAM, NORTH WALES*

Brook Lodge
Higher Lane
Dutton
Warrington
Cheshire
WA4 4JQ

Tel: 01925 730912          Mobile: 07703 191641
john.patten@virgin.net

Established for some 25 years, the Wynnstay Park shoot provides some quite outstanding driven pheasants and very testing partridges over 3,500 acres of wooded valleys. This is a traditional shoot with the emphasis on good sport and a thoroughly friendly approach. There is easy access to most pegs and the terrain is suitable for all. Historic Chester is 20 minutes away for non-shooting guests. (See also entry 'Ruabon Moor' under shooting.)

*Shooting acreage*: 3,500
*Status*: Private with let days
*Owner*: John Patten
*Contact*: John Patten
*Sporting agent*: N/a
*Headkeeper*: Darren Hart
*Number of available days*: 15
*Number of drives*: 28 (5-6 per day)
*Bag expectations*: 200-400
*Average cartridge to kill ratio*: 5:1
*Lunch*: Served in a fully equipped shooting lodge at Wynnstay Park
*Price structure*: Pheasants £20 per bird plus VAT or fixed price
*Accommodation*: All types of accommodation are available including some excellent local hotels
*Access*: By road: 1 hour from M6. By rail: Wrexham Station. By air: Manchester and Liverpool Airports within one hour's drive. Transport available by arrangement
*Other comments*: Dogs welcome

# PARTRIDGES

# RUABON MOOR

Brook Lodge
Higher Lane
Dutton
Warrington
Cheshire
WA4 4JQ

Tel 01925 730912                    Mobile: 07703 191641
john.patten@virgin.net

Driven red-legged partridges over 7,000 acres of moorland. Once famous as a grouse moor, Ruabon now produces quite outstanding driven partridge shooting. The birds are driven over gulleys to provide spectacular shooting of the highest standard and at a fraction of grouse shooting. Historic Chester is 20 minutes away for non-shooting guests (see entry for Wynnstay Park for further information: W * 9).

*Shooting acreage*: 7,000
*Status*: Private with let days
*Owner*: John Patten
*Contact*: John Patten
*Sporting agent*: N/a
*Headkeeper*: Darren Hart
*Number of available days*: 15
*Number of drives*: 18 (5-6 per day)
*Bag expectations*: 200-500
*Average cartridge to kill ratio*: 5:1
*Lunch*: Served in fully equipped shooting lodge
*Price structure*: £21 per bird plus VAT
*Accommodation*: All types of accommodation are available including some excellent local hotels
*Access*: By road: 1 hour from M6. By rail: Wrexham Station. By air: Manchester and Liverpool Airports within one hour's drive. Transport available by arrangement
*Other comments*: Dogs welcome

# WOODCOCK/SNIPE

---

## SOUTH-WEST PEMBROKESHIRE

1 Southwell Gardens
London
SW7 4SB

Mobile: 07774 418725

Driven woodcock and snipe over several different estates in beautiful Pembrokeshire, these shoots have received much praise over the years in the sporting press. Michael Dawnay has run this shoot for over 14 years, with a high majority of the guns returning every season in their dedicated pursuit of wild quarry. It should be noted that while every effort is made by the host and his outstanding team of beaters to ensure a good bag, no guarantee can be given due to the wild nature of the birds, and success depends on the weather and the competence of the Guns. A modicum of fitness is required although the older or less fit can expect an easier passage by general agreement of the party.

*Shooting acreage*: 8,000
*Status*: Commercial
*Owner*: Michael Dawnay (shooting rights)
*Contact*: Michael Dawnay
*Sporting agent*: N/a
*Number of available days*: Approximately 20 per season
*Number of drives*: As many as possible
*Bag expectations*: Bags average from mid to high teens
*Gun/cartridge recommendations*: Twelve or 20-bores with 1oz No 7
*Average cartridge to kill ratio*: 5:1
*Lunch*: Usually taken in a local pub
*Price structure*: £200-£225 per Gun per day
*Accommodation*: Several local hotels and pubs are available
*Access*: M4 to Pembrokeshire
*Other comments*: Provided they are benign to other dogs and are Well-behaved, dogs are welcome

# WILDFOWLING

# CEFNGWYN HALL

*CEFN, CELDON NEBOLLANON, CARDIGS. SY23 5LB*

Brook Lodge
Higher Lane
Dutton
Warrington
Cheshire WA4 4JQ

Tel: 01925 730912               Mobile: 07703 191641
john.patten@virgin.net

Inland goose and duck shooting over 1,000 acres. This is outstanding shooting and considered by many to offer some of the finest wildfowl shooting in Europe. A typical September wildfowl count would be 5,000 mallard, 500 teal, 100 wigeon and 300 geese. As the season progresses the wigeon, teal and other species increase with seven species of duck being shot in one day. Rubber boots are essential.

*Shooting acreage*: 1,000
*Status*: Private with let days
*Contact*: Charles Grisedale, as above
*Sporting agent*: N/a
*Headkeeper/staff*: Caerwyn Evans
*Number of available days*: 15
*Number of drives*: N/a
*Bag expectations*: A team of Guns can expect a bag of 200 plus duck for a day's shooting.
*Gun/cartridge recommendations*: As heavy as possible
*Average cartridge to kill ratio*: 4.5:1
*Lunch*: Served in private farmhouse on site
*Price structure*: £16 per bird
*Accommodation*: Local hotels and pubs available
*Access*: By road: 6 miles from Abevaeron. By rail: Aberystwyth Station. By air: Aberporth and Cardiff.
*Other comments*: Well-behaved dogs are welcome

# NORTHERN IRELAND

# BELLE ISLE

*COUNTY FERMANAGH*

Belle Isle Estate
Lisbellaw
Co Fermanagh, BT94 5HG
Northern Ireland

Tel: 028 6638 7231             Fax: 028 6638 7261
accommodation@belleisle-estate.com  www.belleisle-estate.com

Dating back to 1680, Belle Isle Castle sits on an island on Upper Lough Erne and can be accessed by a bridge. The driven snipe shooting takes place on the many bogs surrounding Upper Lough Erne or on bogs which are 20 minutes away. Depending on the water level, the shore of the Lake is shot from 17ft boats with some Guns on land and the sport is extremely challenging. In late autumn, Belle Isle offers all driven woodcock shooting over 450 acres or at Baronscourt, which is one hour's drive away with the majority of Guns standing and some walking. Minimum number of Guns is six and maximum ten – all should be reasonably fit, as there is limited vehicle access to the bogs. The interior of Belle Isle Castle was designed by David Hicks and full details, with photographs, of the accommodation available appear on the website.

*Shooting acreage*: 8,450 over the two Estates of Belle Isle and Baronscourt
*Status*: Private with let days
*Owner*: Duke of Abercorn
*Contact*: Charles Plunket at Belle Isle Estate
*Headkeeper/staff*: One head beater and three to 10 beaters plus dogs on a shooting day
*Number of available days*: 20
*Number of drives*: 8+ drives per day for snipe, 15 for woodcock
*Bag expectations*: Up to 25 snipe in a day and 15 woodcock, depending on Guns' skill and weather
*Average cartridge to kill ratio*: Never counted
*Lunch*: There is a break for lunch, which is served either in the Castle front hall or in the local pub. Tea is also provided at the end of the day
*Price structure*: £105 per Gun per day, including VAT
*Accommodation*: Full board and lodging in Belle Isle Castle. Price £100 per day, including VAT. Drinks, cartridges or tips are excluded. Cartridges can be purchased at cost price. Belle Isle has an extensive wine cellar.
*Access*: By air: to Belfast. By ferry: Larne and Belfast Port. Approximately 1½ hours drive from Belfast, guests make their own way. Full directions are available on the website. Car hire is available from the airport.
*Other comments*: A Northern Ireland Firearm Licence is required, so guests should not come via Dublin otherwise a Republic of Ireland licence will also be required. Licence application form can be downloaded from the website.

# COLEBROOKE PARK

## *BROOKEBOROUGH, CO FERMANAGH*

Colebrooke Park
Brookeborough
Co Fermanagh
BT94 4DW
Northern Ireland

Tel: 028 8953 1402
alan@colebrooke.info                    www.colebrooke.info

Driven snipe shooting over 2,000 acres. Colebrooke Park provides unusual driven snipe shooting off the 'red bogs' of Fermanagh and Tyrone. Birds fly high and low, fast and slow are often tricky to shoot for those used to reared bird shooting! If it is frosty then woodcock are driven, though Guns must remember that their presence cannot be guaranteed. Guns move from bog to bog by car and there is room for more than one drive on some bogs.

*Shooting acreage*: 2000
*Status*: Private with let days
*Owner*: Viscount Brookeborough
*Contact*: Viscount Brookeborough
*Sporting agent*: N/a
*Headkeeper/staff*: Not supplied
*Number of days available*: There are 8 to 10 two-day shoots. Season is from the middle of October to the end of January
*Bag expectations*: the bag varies according to size of the bogs
*Gun/cartridge recommendations*: No 7 shot fibre wads
*Average cartridge to kill ratio*: Very good 6:1, average 10:1, not so hot 20:1, worst 30:1 plus!
*Lunch*: Normally in the house
*Price structure*: Set price for eight Guns
*Accommodation*: The package includes three nights full board and two days' shooting which normally means arriving on Thursday evening to depart Sunday. Guests stay at Colebrooke Park, where there are 10 en-suite bedrooms and two more with dedicated bathrooms. The food is delicious and the heating works!
*Access*: By air to Belfast, then 1¼ hours to Colebrooke Park.
*Other comments*: Ladies are most welcome and often enjoy going with the beaters, as on such open ground they can see the sport and are aware of the individual Gun's performance!

# GLENARM CASTLE

*BALLYMANA, CO ANTRIM*

2 Castle Lane
Glenarm
Ballymana
Co Antrim
BT44 0BQ
Northern Ireland

Tel: 028 28 841203          Fax: 028 28 841203
info@glenarmcastle.com      www.glenarmcastle.com

This is an exclusive private pheasant shoot, with some partridges, run by Lord Dunluce. Glenarm Castle is situated on a 1,300 acre estate, set in a glen which lends itself to showing particularly challenging, but shootable, birds. It is readily accessible, having the advantage of being under an hour's drive from Belfast's two airports, and only 20 minutes from the ferry.

*Shooting acreage*: 1,300
*Status*: Private with let days
*Owner*: Antrim Estates Company
*Contact*: Adrian Morrow, Estate Manager, as above.
*Sporting agent*: N/a
*Headkeeper/staff*: Robert Luff
*Number of available days*: 4
*Number of drives*: 14
*Bag expectations*: 250 – 350
*Average cartridge to kill ratio*: 4:1
*Lunch*: Taken in the Castle dining room at 1pm, and including drinks
*Price structure*: £25.50 per bird
*Accommodation*: This is available in Glenarm Castle. Full details on request
*Access*: 45 minutes drive from Belfast City and Belfast International Airports, on M2, then A26. Some 20 minutes drive from Larne P & O Ferry on A36.
*Other comments*: Well-trained gundogs welcome

# SHANES CASTLE

Shanes Castle
Antrim
Co Antrim
BT41 4NE
Northern Ireland

Tel: 028 94428216  Fax: 028 94468457
shanescastle@nireland.com

Shanes Castle is situated in the north-east corner of Lough Neagh (the largest lake in these islands). The River Maine runs through the Estate into Lough Neagh and the river valley provides some of the best pheasant drives on the Estate. The rest of the property is fairly flat, although it is well wooded with a 50/50 mixture of agricultural land and forestry. Pheasants have been reared here since the Second World War, with red-legged partridges introduced about 15 years ago.

*Shooting acreage*: 150
*Status*: Private with let days
*Owner*: The Hon. Shane O'Neill
*Contact*: The Hon. Shane O'Neill, Shanes Castle Estates Co Ltd
*Sporting agent*: N/a
*Headkeeper/staff*: William Storer and assistant keeper
Number of days available: On application
*Number of drives*: 20
*Bag expectations*: 150 to 200
*Average cartridge to kill ratio*: 3.5:1
*Lunch*: Guns shoot through and lunch is then taken in the House
*Price structure*: Varies on whether walked-up or driven. £15 - £21 per bird
*Accommodation*: Dunadry Inn Hotel and Hilton Hotel, Templepatrick
*Access*: By air: Belfast, then M2 to Antrim.

# ETIQUETTE

## GETTING IT RIGHT

Of all branches of the shooting, while the driven field is perhaps the one most littered with potential trip-wires for the unwary novice, whatever the type of shooting or stalking pursued, whether driven grouse or decoyed pigeons, flighted geese or stalked roe, every aspect of the sport is subordinate to safety. Any shooting man or woman who exhibits the slightest tendency to ignore the basic and essential rules of gun or rifle safety should be politely, but firmly, requested to leave the field and return home.

Safety is the reason why, in today's shooting field, it is expected that guns will be broken to expose empty chambers whenever there is no anticipation of a shot. There was a time, perhaps 50 or more years ago when shooting men carried their guns closed at all times, but today such behaviour is frowned on. In fact, it is the exception, on a driven shoot, to see a closed shotgun other than in a slip between drives.

For the beginner, I suggest that a course of instruction at a reputable clay shooting ground is absolutely essential. There, the rules of gun safety and handling will be hammered home and many instructors will demonstrate the lethal nature of a shotgun at both near, and distant, range. The novice must understand that he or she is dealing with a weapon which, at close quarters, can be far more devastating in its effect than a rifle.

Let's take a typical day's driven shooting to emphasis the points of etiquette which are an accepted and understood part of the day. Normally Guns will have been instructed to assemble at 9am to 9.15am. This means they should allow sufficient time to turn up on time. Nothing is more annoying than the man who makes a practice of arriving late at a shoot. He will make himself thoroughly unpopular with his fellow Guns, the keeper and host. If you are unfamiliar with the shoot, ask for detailed instructions and allow sufficient time to get lost.

If it is an unfamiliar shoot, don't automatically assume that your gundog will be welcome. Some shoots prefer the Guns to rely on the team of pickers-up, others are perfectly content for guests to bring their own animals provided they are well behaved and trained, but the moment one sees a Gun pegging his dog to the ground or, far worse and more dangerous, attaching it to himself, you can anticipate the worst.

Always make sure you have sufficient cartridges for the day. It is an insult to your host and the number and quality of his birds to have to borrow cartridges. A safe rule-of-thumb is to have with you as many cartridges as the expected bag. One won't need them, but at least they are a reassurance factor. Make sure, too, that you carry a capacious cartridge bag as you may not return to your vehicle until lunch, or the end of the day if you shoot through.

As far as guns are concerned, the side-by-side has always been the traditional and accepted gun for the driven day, but in recent years over-and-unders, once frowned upon, have come almost to dominate the scene. One need hardly add that any other type of gun, such as a semi-auto or pump-action, would ensure that the owner was swiftly sent packing.

The driven shooting field is still a bastion of tradition, nowhere more so than in the field of dress. There was indeed a time when the tweed knickerbocker suit reigned supreme and there is no question but a neatly cut tweed suit still carries a certain cachet. However, modern man-made water and cold weather repellent fibres now dominate the field for outer clothing at least, often worn with Plus-2s, and, provided they are smart and unobtrusive, are perfectly acceptable. Tweed caps are the normal wear, though personally I prefer a trilby.

As far as the day's sport is concerned, make sure you have a gunslip in which to carry your gun between drives and to protect it from knocks when travelling on a shoot vehicle. Having drawn for your peg, your host will explain the system of moving up at each drive, a system which tends to vary from shoot to shoot and which can cause total confusion unless one pays attention. Many shoots now hand out a card to each Gun which gives the names of the drives and the peg numbers. The host or shoot captain will also explain the rules concerning ground game (normally forbidden) and whether, for instance, woodcock are to be shot. Some shoots also indulge in a sacrosanct albino pheasant or two, whose demise will incur a substantial fine. Be aware!

At your peg, quickly assess your arc of fire. Check to see if you have pickers-up behind you or stops to one side or in front and note the position of your neighbouring Guns. The cardinal sins are three: shooting low in front or behind; shooting across or through the line of Guns on either side and shooting, or poaching, a next door Gun's birds. To shoot through the line is unbelievably crass, for not only is the Gun next to you in danger, but also the remainder of the line. Ignore low birds, don't even raise a gun to them. Knock down 'sitters' in a cloud of feathers and you will soon acquire a reputation for being a thoroughly unsporting and greedy shot.

When is a bird shootable? This varies from shoot to shoot. The birds acceptable on a flat ground shoot where it may be difficult to show high birds, would be scorned on a steep-banked, deep valley shoot where it is so much easier to produce stratospheric birds. Avoid also the thoroughly dangerous and unpleasant habit of cradling your gun in your arms so that it is pointing at your neighbour. If you find yourself the target for a 'cradler' politely, but firmly, point out that you can see he is using No 6 shot!

Many shoots today prefer to take all the drives through, pausing after the second or third drive for refreshments, and then, when the day's sport is over, enjoying a shoot lunch. There are a number of advantages, not least that birds can get to roost early on short winter days, and the beaters do not have to turn out again after lunch. Which ever system is preferred, at the end of the day the Guns are customarily handed a brace of birds by the keeper, a ritual which requires that a financial acknowledgement of the day's sport changes hands. How much to tip? There was a time, until recently, when £10 per hundred birds in the bag was the accepted rate. Now, however, £15 or even £20 may be considered acceptable. If in any doubt, discreetly ask the host or a fellow Gun.

Politeness costs nothing. Always make a point of thanking the beaters and the pickers-up for their efforts. Too often Guns slink away without any acknowledgement to the team who have made their day's sport possible. Finally, it is a matter of common courtesy to send a note of thanks to one's host, whether a private or commercial day. A simple gesture, yet one often neglected.

As far as the increasingly popular walked-up or rough days are concerned, safety is a matter of principal concern. It is essential to know exactly where everyone is, beaters, pickers-up and gundogs, before firing a shot. By the nature of the sport birds may be low and going away, so a total awareness of one's surrounding is needed before the trigger is pulled. Beware, too, any fence climbing or ditch jumping where guns are concerned. At all times make sure your gun is empty and, if handing it to someone, demonstrate the vacant chambers.

Apart from the all-important safety factor, there is one other essential element which applies in particular to driven shooting. It is quality not quantity which should be the chief criterion of a day's sport, combined with an understanding that the birds are not simply clay pigeons with wings. One is privileged to enjoy sport in the heart of the countryside and should understand and try to appreciate something of the nature of the wildlife surrounding one and the natural rhythms of the shooting year. Above all, remember that you shooting wild creatures. Make certain you know how to do this efficiently and with the minimum distress to the birds and animals concerned. It is your responsibility.

# IMPORTATION OF FIRE ARMS

*Visitors' Permits:* Visitors to the UK may obtain firearm and shotgun permits for up to 12 months. It is, however, common to limit the validity to the length of the visit. The general rules and conditions which apply to the grant of a firearm or shotgun certificate also apply to obtaining a permit, with the following exceptions.

*European Firearms Pass:* Residents of EU countries must be in possession of a European Firearms Pass which has to be forwarded with the application for a permit. There is no general exception in Great Britain for prior notification of the temporary import of guns for hunting and target shooting.

*Application:* Application for a permit must be made to the police by a person resident in the area on behalf of the visitor. Group applications are cheaper and may be made for up to 20 visitors provided they are all shooting on the same premises during the same period. Additional individual or group permits may be issued for groups of more than 20 people. Applications should be made as far in advance of the planned visit as possible but, in the case of last minute invitations to shoot, the police will make every effort to process the application in time. Applications should be accompanied by the original, or a copy of, any certificates held by the visitor in his or her own country and evidence of an invitation to shoot in the UK. Such evidence will normally satisfy the "good reason" requirement for the issue of a permit.

*Firearm permit:* This permits the possession (but not purchase) of firearm(s) and the acquisition or purchase of ammunition. The firearm(s) must be listed as with a firearm certificate and the quantities of ammunition to be purchased, acquired and held must be specified. Territorial and other conditions similar to those for a firearm certificate are placed on firearm permits. If the visitor needs to use expanding ammunition this must be included on the permit.

*Shotgun permit:* This permits the possession, purchase and acquisition of shotguns and ammunition. Shotguns must be listed as with a shotgun certificate. No territorial restriction is placed on a shotgun permit but the standard conditions for shotgun certificates will be applied. Unlike a shotgun certificate, an applicant for a visitor's shotgun permit must show good reason for possessing, purchasing or acquiring each shotgun to which the permit relates. If a shotgun is purchased the visitor is required to notify the police. EU residents who wish to purchase a shotgun and export it must first obtain an export licence to remove the gun from Great Britain and will not be able to purchase the shotgun until they have done so. Licences are obtained from the Export Licensing Branch of the Department of Trade and Industry. A visitor who wishes to purchase but not use a shotgun in the UK will be required to follow the export procedure explained below. Care should be taken with multi-shot shotguns which, in Great Britain, require a firearms permit. The significance of this may not be appreciated by the visitor when notifying the sponsor of the guns to be listed on the permit. This may lead to seizure of the gun(s) by HM Customs & Excise at the point of entry.

*Refusal of permits:* There is no right of appeal against the refusal to issue a permit but the sponsor should be notified of the reason. The police are required to make such a notification in good time to avoid unnecessary travel costs.

*Validity:* Permits are normally valid for 12 months but are often only issued for the duration of the visit. They may be retained on leaving the country and used again if the conditions imposed so allow. Permits are never renewed and once expired must be replaced by a fresh application. Permits must be produced to the Customs & Excise authorities when guns are brought into the UK and again when the visitor returns to his or her own country.

*Variations:* An oral or written application may be made to the police by the sponsor if the visitor's circumstances change in such a way that the original conditions are no longer appropriate.

*Guns for export:* No firearm or shotgun certificate is needed to purchase a firearm or shotgun for export provided it is bought from a registered firearms dealer and the purchaser has not been in the UK for more than 30 days in the preceding 12 months and the firearm or shotgun is to be exported without first coming into the purchaser's direct possession. Foreign visitors should produce their passport as evidence of exemption from the requirement to hold a certificate.

*Northern Ireland:* The law relating to firearms and shotguns is much stricter in Northern Ireland than in Great Britain. Before taking any such weapon to Northern Ireland a Certificate of Approval must be obtained from the Northern Ireland Police Service, Firearms Licensing, Lisnasharragh, Montgomery Road, Belfast BT6 9LD. Tel 028 9065 0222. The certificate is free and must be applied for at least one month before arrival in Northern Ireland.

# SHOOTING SEASONS

Species designated as game under the Game Act 1831.

| | |
|---|---|
| Grouse | August 12 to December 10 |
| Ptarmigan | August 12 to December 10 |
| Blackgame | August 20 to December 10 |
| Pheasant | October 1 to February 1 |
| Partridge | September 1 to February 1 |

A Game Licence is required to take or kill any of the above game. A Game Licence is also required to shoot deer other than on enclosed land. Game Licences can be obtained from Money Order Post Offices for the following periods:

Annual, expiring July 31 £6.00
August 1 to October 31 £4.00
Any period of 14 days £2.00

Birds in Schedule 2 of the Wildlife and Countryside Act 1981 which may be killed or taken outside the close season and which may be sold dead from September 1 to February 28.

| | |
|---|---|
| Woodcock | |
| England and Wales | October 1 to January 31. |
| Woodcock* | |
| Scotland | September 1 to January 31. |
| Common snipe * | August 12 to January 31 |
| Golden Plover | September 1 to January 31. |
| | |
| Mallard | All above the high water |
| Pintail | mark of ordinary spring |
| | tides September 1 to January 31. |
| Teal | All below the high water mark of |
| Wigeon | ordinary spring tides September 1 |
| Tufted | to February 20. |
| Pochard | |
| | |
| Coot | September 1 to January 31 |
| Moorhen | September 1 to January 31 |

*Require a game licence although not game within the meaning of the Act.*

Birds in Schedule 2 of the Wildlife and Countryside Act 1981 which may be killed or taken outside the close season but which may not be sold dead:

| | |
|---|---|
| Canada goose | All above the high water mark of |
| Greylag goose | ordinary spring tide September 12 |
| Pinkfooted goose | to January 31. All below the high |
| Whitefronted goose | water mark (not in Scotland) of |
| Gadwall | ordinary spring tide September 1 |
| Goldeneye | to February 20. |

Birds for which there is no close season and which may be killed or taken by authorised persons at all times under open general licence. Only woodpigeon may be sold dead:

Crow, magpie, jackdaw, jay, rook, woodpigeon, collared dove, great black-backed gull, lesser black-backed gull, herring gull, feral pigeon, starling, house sparrow.

Note: There is no close season for rabbits or hares, but the latter may not be offered for sale from March 1 to July 31. It is also illegal to shoot game on Sundays, Christmas Day or at night. No game may be sold more than 10 days after the end of its open season.

DEER OPEN SEASONS

| | |
|---|---|
| Red and sika stags | *England and Wales*<br>August 1 to April 30.<br>*Scotland*<br>July 1 to October 20. |
| Red and sika hinds | *England and Wales*<br>November 1 to February 28/29.<br>*Scotland*<br>October 21 to February 15. |
| Fallow buck | *England, Wales, Scotland*<br>August 1 to April 30. |
| Fallow doe | *England and Wales*<br>November 1 to February 28/29.<br>*Scotland*<br>October 21 to February 15. |
| Roe buck | *England and Wales*<br>April 1 to October 30.<br>*Scotland*<br>April 1 to October 20. |
| Roe doe | *England and Wales*<br>November 1 to February 28/29.<br>*Scotland*<br>October 21 to March 31. |
| Muntjac | No statutory close season. |
| Chinese Water-deer | No statutory close season. |

# GAME RECIPES

## CLARISSA DICKSON WRIGHT

### ANDALUCIAN PIGEONS

The Spanish eat a lot of pigeons and I always think theirs is a very good way of doing them. I have halved the oil, toasted the bread and added capers, as I always think they add colour and a bit of bite.

4 young pigeons drawn and trussed / 8 anchovy fillets / 1 tablespoon of capers / 6 fl. oz. olive oil / 8 small onions / half pint of dry white wine / 2 garlic cloves / 1 sprig of parsley / salt / 4 triangles of good bread

Rub the pigeons with salt and stuff them with the anchovies. Heat half the oil in a pan. Add the pigeons and cook over a low heat for 15 minutes, turning them until they are lightly browned all over. Now fry the onions separately in the rest of the oil for about 5 minutes until they are golden, then add them to the pigeons with the wine, garlic and parsley. Simmer for 45 minutes until the sauce is reduced by half and the pigeons are tender. Remove the parsley and garlic and skim off any surface fat. Arrange the pigeons on a serving dish, strain the sauce, pour over the birds, surround them with onion and sprinkle with capers. Serve with toasted sourdough bread.

## PHEASANTS WITH SAUERKRAUT

This Alsatian recipe is a very good way of using up old birds and is also useful for supper parties because you can do all the simmering early and then just put it in the oven before dinner. I happily use two pheasants to this amount of sauerkraut.

2 pheasants trussed, drawn and barded / 1 oz of goose fat / 1 large onion, finely chopped / 2 lb. sauerkraut rinsed and squeezed / 8 fl. oz wine / 8 fl. oz Madeira / 8 fl. oz of stock / 5 oz of streaky bacon cut into strips / salt / pepper

Melt half the goose fat in a pan and lightly brown the pheasants all over, remove, add the onions and lightly brown, add the sauerkraut, wine, stock and a pinch of salt and pepper. Return the pheasants and simmer gently, covered, for one hour. Transfer to a greased casserole, add bacon, cover and cook at 190C/375F/gas mark 5 for 30-40 minutes. Season and serve.

## PARTRIDGE & CHIPS

*William Evans' Staff Recipe*: Although roasting may not merit a recipe, the results vary to a startling degree. The recommended method is to put some seasoned butter inside the bird and cook breast down. Streaky bacon can be laid on top as a heat shield and removed after 25 minutes, the bird observed and allowed to brown for five minutes. The oven should be hot (gas mark 7). If some water is placed in the roasting tin this will capture some of the game essence for a base for gravy.

Bread sauce: This sauce is not made well in the UK. We recommend infusing the flavoured milk immediately with breadcrumbs. The flavouring can come from an exfoliated onion with cloves and a bay leaf. Given that modern milk is homogenised it is necessary to add cream at the beginning of the process, not at the end, otherwise the sauce will break down. At the end some unsalted butter should be added, to enrich the sauce, as well as a pinch of nutmeg (mace can also be used).

Game chips: Once mastered this process is very easy and 'hand made' crisps will appear a poor palliative. Use a mandolin to slice a firm potato as thinly as you can manage. Leave the slices to soak in water for at least ¾ hour. In a large frying pan heat some vegetable oil flavoured with olive oil (say 90:10) to gas mark 5 only. The first batch of chips will take 12-14 minutes to cook, thereafter the process reduces to 7-8 minutes.

### WILD DUCK WITH APLLE STUFFING

2 Ducks / 1/8 of a pint of double cream / ½ pint of dry cider / 2 tablespoons of brandy / 2 tablespoons of water

Stuffing: 4 oz of fresh white breadcrumbs / 1 lb of cooking apples / 30 oz of butter / 1 desert spoon of brown sugar / pinch of cinnamon / pepper / salt

*William Evans' Staff Recipe*: Dry the ducks and rub with salt, then peel, core and chop apples into small squares. Fry breadcrumbs in butter until slightly brown, add apples and cover cooking gently for 10 minutes until soft. Stir and add seasoning and cinnamon. Now stuff ducks and close end, then place in roasting dish with water. Roast for 15 minutes per pound. Fifteen minutes before the end, pour cider over ducks and bast several times. When cooked, place ducks on carving dish: with foil cover shiny side inwards, then place dish on hob and simmer until gravy reduced to half quantity. Remove stuffing and cut ducks in half. Add cream and brandy to reduced gravy (strain if wanted) and serve.

A * 14

# WINES AND GAME

## SIMON BERRY

Wine has played an important part in English society for over three hundred years, not least as the ultimate accoutrement for enjoying one's food, the company of one's friends and, of course, in oiling the wheels of entertaining and social events. The camaraderie of shooting, and certainly of eating the spoils afterwards, has always been a natural to fine wine. There is no question that the ideal drink while in sporting pursuit is Berry's King's Ginger Liqueur. This warming, brandy-based liqueur, developed specially by Berry's for King Edward VII, is a long-standing favourite amongst the shooting fraternity, not least the Prince of Wales. A hip flask of this drink is at its best on a bitterly cold day.

Berry's and shooting are inextricably linked, both through the enthusiasm of its customers and staff for this pursuit and through its proximity to William Evans, on St James's Street. As a result Berry's has become well-versed in matching its wines to the various types of game. It has a tradition of taking into account the preferences of others—Sherlock Holmes was famously documented for always drinking Montrachet with French partridge—and has investigated their suitability before advising their customers. (Berry's regrettably declines to recommend Holmes' combination as a perfect match.)

Many years ago a long-standing customer contacted Berry's to complain that our port no longer contained the same amount of sediment that it used to, and that this was severely affecting the enjoyment of the couple's regular grouse dinners. Resisting the temptation to suggest that maybe the port was opened when it was too young, we enquired how their enjoyment was affected. The customer explained that she and her husband's enjoyment was increased immeasurably by smearing the toast on which the grouse was roasted with the port's residue. We found the couple to be absolutely right.

For many getting hold of game, whether you are shooting it or buying it from your butcher, is the easy bit. Finding the right wine to bring out the best in both the food and wine, is the more tricky part. There are, however, very few rights and wrongs in wine; its enjoyment is such a subjective experience that there can never be a definitively correct code of practice. Nevertheless, there are certain guidelines that we have found to be reliably correct, and we have tried to suggest possibilities for that most elusive of experiences, the perfect wine/food combination, in relation to the delicious arena of game in all of its guises.

The accepted 'classic' combinations of wine and food-matching have largely come about from the traditional regional gastronomy of countries such as France, Italy and Spain. The UK has always been a keen importer of tastes and flavours, no more so than today, and it is no surprise to see that wines from continental Europe are regarded as the traditional partners for British game. Today, however, with wines on offer from the four corners of the globe, there are many more options to consider. Therefore for the purposes of this short guide, I will suggest three options to be paired with each type of game: the traditional or classic choice (1), something classic but with a budget in mind (2), and a non-European alternative (3).

In many cases, it is often not the meat that is the most important factor in deciding which wine to choose as a partner, but more the accompanying sauce. Popular accompaniments for game include berries, truffles, mustard, garlic and a variety of herbs and spices. In many cases these will have more flavour than the meat itself. Plus, of course, the time the game has been hung for is important. A good rule of thumb is that the more mature the game, the more mature the wine should be, and vice-versa. If you plan to eat a tender young grouse (that is, say, only six months old) the same day it has been shot, you might choose a young vibrant red Burgundy. The method of cooking will also play a role—meat that has been barbecued or spit-roasted will have a stronger flavour than something steamed or grilled. For the sake of simplicity, the wines suggested below were chosen with simple oven-roasting in mind.

### PARTRIDGE
This is the lightest of the game birds and can be swamped by big red wines with high tannins. Lighter reds from grapes like Pinot Noir are therefore a natural choice but be careful to avoid wines that are too bright and fruity. Something with a slightly earthy character is good:
(1) Vosne-Romanée, Les Brûlées, 1er Cru, Domaine Réné Engel, Burgundy
(2) Berry's' Reserve Red Burgundy, Charles Viénot
(3) King Estate Pinot Noir, Oregon

### PHEASANT
Pheasant has a stronger, richer flavour than partridge but is still relatively lean and therefore works best with wines with finesse rather than pure power. Pheasant casserole is a popular dish and with that you can start to choose something a little heartier—look to wines such as St. Joseph from the northern Rhône. With roast pheasant, try:
(1) Echézeaux, Domaine Jean Grivot, Burgundy
(2) Côtes de Nuits Villages, Nicolas Potel, Burgundy
(3) Alana Estate Pinot Noir, Martinborough, New Zealand

## WOODPIGEON

This boasts a stronger, earthier flavour, however, an overdose of tannins in your wine of choice would still be inadvisable as the flesh is relatively delicate. Roast woodpigeon combines well with Riojas and Clarets. A popular dish is woodpigeon salad but beware of vinegar-based dressings that wreak havoc with most wines:

(1)Ch. Pichon-Longueville, Comtesse de Lalande, 2ème Cru Classé, Pauillac, Bordeaux

(2) Viña Ardanza Reserva, La Rioja Alta, Spain

(3) Weinert Merlot, Mendoza, Argentina

## GROUSE

A darker, intense meat with a strong, rich flavour. Look to bolder flavours from grapes such as Cabernet Sauvignon, Cabernet Franc or Syrah:

(1) Ch. Léoville-Barton, 2ème Cru Classé, St. Julien, Bordeaux

(2) Ch. Jonqueyres, Bordeaux Supérieur

(3) Montes Alpha Syrah, Colchagua Valley, Chile

## WOODCOCK

Like grouse, woodcock has a strong, rich flavour and therefore needs a wine of similar character to complement it:

(1) Côte-Rôtie, La Landonne, Etienne Guigal, Rhône

(2) Crozes-Hermitage, La Matinière, Domaine Ferraton, Rhône

(3) Jackal's River Pinotage, Beaumont, Stellenbosch, South Africa

## WILD DUCK

This is rich and succulent with a high fat content and far more flavour than its farm-reared cousins. Wild duck needs a wine of considerable dimensions but also a degree of sweetness, as you would find in a good ripe vintage, to support it. Wines made from Cabernets Sauvignon and Franc are again a strong favourite but Australian Shiraz and the reds of the Northern Rhône also match well.

(1) Ch. Lafite-Rothschild, 1er Cru Classé, Pauillac, Bordeaux

(2) Berry's' Australian Shiraz, Mitchelton, Victoria

(3) Escudo Rojo, Maipo Valley, Chile

## WILD BOAR

Wild boar yields a sturdy meat that can be tough, so a robust wine with some rustic character is ideal. Wild boar is not as fatty as the domestic porker but you should still try to find wines with ripe tannins and a degree of softness to match this element. Grapes such as Mourvèdre, Syrah or Nebbiolo are perfect: Barolo Ginestra, Paolo Conterno, Piedmont, Italy

(1) Gigondas, Ch. de Trignon, Rhône
(2) Charles Melton Nine Popes Grenache/Shiraz/Mourvèdre,
(3) Barossa Valley, Australia

### WILD RABBIT

Lighter in colour but with plenty of flavour and a low fat content, wild rabbit is a meat that does not suit overly intense wines, so we recommend choosing something relatively soft and young:

(1) Clos de Tart, Mommessin, Burgundy
(2) Dolcetto d'Alba, Controvento, Bava, Piedmont
(3) Bouchard Finlayson Galpin Peak Pinot Noir, Walker Bay, South Africa

### HARE

Hare offers the opportunity to bring out a really sturdy and powerful wine, as its succulent and bold-flavoured meat is made for fuller reds. The traditional Jugged Hare needs something very powerful such as Amarone (try the Amarone Classico, Monte Danieli, Corte Rugolin):

(1) Sassicaia, Tenuta San Guido, Tuscany
(2) Vacqueyras, Domaine le Courolou, Rhône
(3) Yarra Yering Underhill Shiraz, Victoria, Australia

### VENISON

Robust, dark and strongly-flavoured with a tendency to chewiness, venison demands a powerful red wine with good ripe tannins and real muscle. Top quality Pinot Noirs, such as a Musigny or Chambertin are fantastic but a favourite combination is mature southern Rhône:

(1) Ch. de Beaucastel, Châteauneuf-du-Pape, Rhône
(2) Côtes du Rhône Villages, Cairanne, Domaine de l'Ameillaud
(3) Weinert Malbec, Mendoza, Argentina

Hopefully the above guide is useful, although one should keep in mind that constant experimentation is always the best way of discovering what wine most suits your taste. Louis Pasteur said 'a meal without wine is like a day without sunshine'—we have far too many of the latter.

*Simon Berry* is Deputy Chairman of Berry Bros & Rudd. Tracing its origins to 1698, Berry's still trades from the same site, 3 St. James's St, London SW1. Further information on wine may be found on Berry's award-winning website, www.bbr.com.

# INDEX OF SHOOTS

Dunbeath Estate, (S-74)
Garynahine, (S-42)
Glenfernate Lodge, (S-43, 77)
Glenlochy Shoot, (S-44)
Glenquaich, (S-45, 78)
Glenshero Estate, (S-79)
Hope Estate, (S-46, 80)
Kildermorie, (S-47, 82)
Kinloch Estate, (S-48, 84)
Kinlochewe & Lochrosque, (S-85)
Lammermuir Shoot, (S-19)
Phones & Etteridge, (S49, S-87)
Rottal Lodge Estate, (S-25)
Scaliscro, (S-50)
Strathspey Estate, (S-51)
Tulchan, (S-27, S-52)

PARTRIDGES

*England*
Almer Shoot (E-1)
Baydon (E-2)
Beckerings Park Shoot (E-4)
Belvoir Castle (E-3)
Boreham Hall Shoot (E-67)
Brimpsfield Park Estate (E-5)
Buscot Park Shoot (E-7)
Calthorpe Shoot (E-8)
Checkley Wood Shoot (E-9)
Chippenham Park Estate (E-68)
Eagle Hall Shoot (E-69)
Exwick Barton Shoot (E-19)
Eynsham Park Shoot (E-20)
Faccombe (E-21)
Fifield Shoot (E-22)
Friesland Shoot (E-23)
Gurston Down (E-25)
Heydon Hall Estate (E-26)
Hunston Shoot (E-70)
Kempton Shoot (E-28)
Linkenholt Manor Estate (E-29)
Longwitton Shoot (E-71)
Manor Farm Shoot (E-32)
Melcombe Shoot (E-33)
Mells Park (E-34)
New Hainton Shoot (E-35)
North Ormsby & Acthorpe (E-72)
Pawton Manor (E-73)
Plum Park (E-38)
Racecouse Shoot Goodwood (E-40)
Salperton Park Estate (E-74)
Scholtz & Co Ltd (E-43)
Sherborne Castle Honeycombe

Shoot (E-45)
Snilesworth Shoot (E-86)
Southill Estate (E-46)
Spernal Park Shoot (E-47)
Stanway Shoot (E-48)
Stoke Edith Shoot (E-50)
Summerdown Farm (E-75)
Swan's Hall Shoot (E-51)
Teffont Magna Shoot (E-76)
The Burgate Shoot (E-53)
The Dalton Estate (E-77)
The Fawley Court Shoot (E-55)
The Glemham Hall Estate Shoot (E-56)
The Steventon Estate (E-59)
The Tarrant Shoot (E-60)
Wasing Park Shoot (E-62)
Weston Park - The Bradford Estates (E-64)
Widdington Farm Shoot (E-78)

*Scotland*
Airlie & Balintore Shoots (S-1)
Aswanley Estate (S-29)
Bighouse Estate (S-30, 66)
Breda Estate (S-3)
Cardney Estate (S-31)
Cawdor (S-40)
Corsewall Estate (S-6)
Craighowie Shoot (S-8)
Craigston Castle (S-9)
Edradynate Shoot (S-11)
Eilean Darach Estate (S-12, 75)
Eilean Iarmain Estate (S-35)
Glenquaich (S-47, 78)
Grandtully Estate (S-14)
Kinnordy Estate (S-18)
Lammermuir Shoot (S-19)
Langholm (S-20)
Phones & Etteridge (S-87)
Rottal Lodge Estate (S-25)
Teasses Estate (S-26)
The Dell Estate (S-32)

*Wales*
Bettws Shoot (W-1)
Brigands Shoot (W-2)
Glanusk (W-3)
Lake Vyrnwy Hotel (W-4)
Old Hall Shoot (W-6)
The Foelas Shoot (W-7)
The Rhallt Shoot (W-8)
Ruabon Moor (W-11)

*Ireland*
Shanes Castle (I-4)

PHEASANTS

*England*
Almer Shoot (E-1)
Baydon (E-2)
Beckerings Park Shoot (E-4)
Belvoir Castle (E-3)
Boreham Hall Shoot (E-67)
Brickhouse Shoot (E-4)
Brimpsfield Park Estate (E-5)
Buscot Park Shoot (E-7)
Calthorpe Shoot (E-8)
Checkley Wood Shoot (E-9)
Chideock Manor (E-10)
Combe Sydenham Shoot (E-11)
Coniston Hall Estate (E-12)
Cornbury Park Shoot (E-13)
Delbury Shoot (E-14)
Docton Shoot (E-15)
Edgcott (E-17)
Elveden (E-16, 102)
Exebridge Shoot (E-18)
Exwick Barton Shoot (E-19)
Eynsham Park Shoot (E-20)
Faccombe (E-21)
Fifield Shoot (E-22)
Friesland Shoot (E-23)
Great Barton Shoot (E-24)
Gurston Down (E-25)
Heydon Hall Estate (E-26)
Hunston Shoot (E-70)
Kempton Shoot (E-28)
Linkenholt Manor Estate (E-29)
Longwitton Shoot (E-71)
Loyton Shoot (E-30)
Lyneham Shoot (E-31)
Manor Farm Shoot (E-32)
Melcombe Shoot (E-33)
Mells Park (E-34)
New Hainton Shoot (E-35)
North Ormsby & Acthorpe (E-72)
Oakford (E-36)
Parnham Estate (E-37)
Plum Park (E-38)
Powderham (E-39)
Racecouse Shoot Goodwood (E-40)
Ravenswick Shoot (E-41)
Salperton Park Estate (E-74)
Sandon Shoot (E-42)
Scholtz & Co Ltd (E-43)
Sherborne Castle Home Shoot (E-44)
Sherborne Castle Honeycombe Shoot (E-45)

Snilesworth Shoot (E-86)
Southill Estate (E-46)
Spernal Park Shoot (E-47)
Stanway Shoot (E-48)
Stocks Down Farm Shoot
Stoke Edith Shoot (E-50)
Summerdown Farm (E-75)
Swan's Hall Shoot (E-51)
Teffont Magna Shoot (E-76)
The Arundell Arms Hotel (E-81)
The Burgate Shoot (E-53)
The Farley Hall Shoot (E-54)
The Fawley Court Shoot (E-55)
The Glemham Hall Estate Shoot (E-56)
The Hoar Edge Shoot (E-57)
The Ripley Castle Shoot (E-58)
The Steventon Estate (E-59)
The Tarrant Shoot (E-60)
Ugbrooke (E-61)
Wasing Park Shoot (E-62)
Watercombe Shoot (E-63)
Weston Park - The Bradford Estates (E-64)
Withington Manor Shoot (E-65)

**Scotland**
Airlie & Balintore Shoots (S-1)
Ardmaddy Estate (S-2)
Aswanley Estate (S-29)
Breda Estate (S-3)
Buccleuch Arms Hotel (S-4)
Canonbie West (S-5)
Corsewall Estate (S-6)
Cowans Sporting (S-7)
Craighowie Shoot (S-8)
Craigston Castle (S-9)
Dundas, Hopetoun & Dalmeny (S-10)
Edradynate Shoot (S-11)
Eilean Darach Estate (S-12, S-75)
Eilean Iarmain Estate (S-35)
Glenlochy Shoot (S-44)
Glenquaich (S-45, 78)
Glenstriven Estate (Knockdow) (S-13)
Grandtully Estate (S-14)
Islay Estate (S-15)
Kinnaird Castle (S-16)
Kinnaird Estate (S-17)
Kinnordy Estate (S-18)
Kintradwell Estate (S-36)
Lammermuir Shoot (S-19)
Langholm (S-20)
Otter Estate (S-21)
Park (S-22)

Phones & Etteridge (S-87)
Pittcastle (S-23)
Poltalloch (S-24)
Rottal Lodge Estate (S-25)
Teasses Estate (S-26)
Tulchan (S-27)

**Wales**
Bettws Shoot (W-1)
Brigands Shoot (W-2)
Glanusk (W-3)
Lake Vyrnwy Hotel (W-4)
Lymore Shoot (W-5)
Old Hall Shoot (W-6)
The Foelas Shoot (W-7)
The Rhallt Shoot (W-8)
Wynnstay Park (W-9)

**Ireland**
Glenarm Castle (I-3)
Shanes Castle (I-4)

PIGEON

**England**
Philip Beasley Sporting Agency, (E-95)
Pigeon Shooting, (E-96)
Pro Sports, (E-92)

**Scotland**
Aswanley Estate, (S-31)
Teasses Estate, (S-26)

PTARMIGAN

**Scotland**
Ben Damph, (S-67)
Eilean Darach Estate, (S-12, 75)
Kildermorie, (S-47, 82)
Kinloch Estate, (S-48, 84)

SIMULATED SHOOTING

**England**
BBSH Lt. (E-109)
Ian Coley Sporting, (E-110)
Plummer Dixon Associates, (E-112)
Purbeck Shooting School, (E-113)
Shugborough Shooting School, (E-114)
The Kennett Shoot, (E-111)

**Scotland**
Breda Estate (S-95)

STALKING

**England**
Deer Management, (E-99)
Devon Game Services, (E-100)
Egdon Stalking, (E-101)
Elveden, (E-16, E-102)
Greenlee House, (E-103)
North Wiltshire Deer Services, (E-104)
The Field Craft Country Management (E-109)
Scholtz & Co Ltd, (E-43)
The Ultimate Highseat Company, (E-106)
The Viscount Cowdray's Estate (E-107)

**Scotland**
Airlie & Balintore Shoots, (S-1)
Aline Estate, (S-39, 57)
Alladale & Deanich Estate, (S-58)
Amhuinnsuidhe Castle Estate, (S-59)
Ardmaddy Estate, (S-2)
Ardverikie, (S-60)
Argyll Estates, (S-61)
Assynt Estate, (S-62)
Aswanley Estate, (S-29)
Atholl Estates, (S-63)
Balnagown Estates, (S-64)
Ben Damph, (S-65)
Bighouse Estate, (S-30, 66)
Braehour & Backlass Estate, (S-67)
Breda Estate, (S-3)
Coignafearn, (S-41, 68)
Conaglen Estate, (S-69)
Corbieton House, (S-70)
Corriegarth, (S-71)
Corsewall Estate, (S-6)
Coulin, (S-72)
Craiganour Estate, (S-73)
Dunbeath Estate, (S-74)
Eilean Darach Estate, (S-12, 75)
Eilean Iarmain Estate, (S-37)
Garynahine, (S-44)
Glen Afric, (S-76)
Glenfernate Lodge, (S-43, 77)
Glenquaich, (S-45, 78)
Glenshero Estate, (S-79)
Hope Estate, (S-46, 80)
Islay Estate, (S-16, 81)
Kildermorie, (S-47, 82)
Kingie Esate, (S-83)
Kinloch Estate, (S-48, 84)

Kinlochewe & Lochrosque, (S-85)
Kinnordy Estate, (S-18)
Kintradwell Estate, (S-36)
Monachyle Mhor, (S-86)
Phones & Etteridge, (S-51, S-87)
Poltalloch, (S-25)
Rhidorroch, (S-88)
Rottal Lodge Estate, (S-26, S-89)
Scaliscro, (S-50)
Strahanna, (S-90)
Strathspey Estate, (S-53)
The Dell Estate, (S-91)
Uig & Hamanavay, (S-37, 92)

## WALKED-UP/ ROUGH SHOOTING

### England
Elveden, (E-16, 102)
Exwick Barton Shoot, (E-19)
Great Barton Shoot, (E-24)
Holkham, (E-91)
Loyton Shoot, (E-30)
Melcombe Shoot, (E-33)
Oakford, (E-36)
Sandon Shoot, (E-42)
Snilesworth, (E-86)
The Fawley Court Shoot, (E-55)
The Hoar Edge Shoot, (E-57)
Wasing Park Shoot, (E-62)

### Scotland
Airlie & Balintore Shoots, (S-1)
Aline Estate, (S-39, 57)
Ardmaddy Estate, (S-2)
Aswanley Estate, (S-29)
Atholl Estates, (S-63)
Ben Damph, (S-65)
Bighouse Estate, (S-30, 66)
Buccleuch Arms Hotel, (S-4)
Canonbie West, (S-5)
Cardney Estate, (S-31)
Coignafearn, (S-43, 68)
Corsewall Estate, (S-6)
Cowans Sporting, (S-7)
Dunbeath Estate, (S-74)
Eilean Darach Estate, (S-12, 75)
Eilean Iarmain Estate, (S-35)
Garynahine, (S-44)
Glenfernate Lodge, (S-45, 77)
Glenlochy Shoot, (S-44)
Glenquaich, (S-47, 78)
Glenshero Estate, (S-79)
Hope Estate, (S-46, 80)
Islay Estate (S-15, S-81)

Kildermorie, (S-47, 82)
Kinloch Estate, (S-48, 84)
Kinlochewe & Lochrosque, (S-85)
Kinnaird Castle, (S-16)
Kinnaird Estate, (S-17)
Kinnordy Estate, (S-18)
Kintradwell Estate, (S-36)
Lammermuir Shoot, (S-19)
Otter Estate, (S-21)
Poltalloch, (S-24)
Rottal Lodge Estate, (S-25)
Scaliscro, (S-50)
Strathspey Estate, (S-51)
Teasses Estate, (S-26)
The Dell Estate, (S-91)
Wild Tides, (S-55)

### Wales
Lake Vyrnwy Hotel, (W-4)
The Foelas Shoot, (W-7)

### Ireland
Shanes Castle, (I-4)

## WILDFOWLING

### England
Chesil Bank Duck Shoot, (E-89)
Grange Farm, (E-90)
Holkham, (E-91)
Pro Sports, (E-92)

### Scotland
Phones & Etteridge, (S-87)
Wild Tides, (S-55)

### Wales
Cefngwyn Hall, (W-15)

## WOODCOCK/SNIPE

### England
Docton Shoot, (E-15)
Grange Farm, (E-90)
Manor Farm Shoot, (E-32)
Melcombe Shoot, (E-33)
The Arundell Arms Hotel, (E-81)
The Fawley Court Shoot, (E-55)
The Hoar Edge Shoot, (E-57)
Wasing Park Shoot, (E-62)

### Scotland
Aline Estate, (S-41, 59)
Ardmaddy Estate, (S-2)
Ben Damph, (S-67)

Bighouse Estate, (S-30, S-66)
Breda Estate, (S-3)
Canonbie West, (S-5)
Corsewall Estate, (S-6)
Craigston Castle, (S-9)
Edradynate Shoot, (S-11)
Eilean Darach Estate, (S-12, S-75)
Eilean Iarmain Estate, (S-35)
Garynahine, (S-42)
Glenlochy Shoot, (S-44)
Glenquaich, (S-45, S-78)
Hope Estate, (S-46, S-80)
Islay Estate, (S-15, S-81)
Kinloch Estate, (S-48, S-84)
Kinnordy Estate, (S-18)
Kintradwell Estate, (S-36)
Lammermuir Shoot, (S-19)
Langholm, (S-20)
Poltalloch, (S-24)
Scaliscro, (S-50)
Uig & Hamanavay, (S-37, S-92)

### Wales
The Foelas Shoot, (W-7)
Dawnay, (W-13)

### Ireland
Belle Island (I-1)
Colebrooke Park (I-2)

# Useful Addresses

**ENGLAND**

*BUCKINGHAMSHIRE*

Hartwell House, Oxford Road, Nr Aylesbury, Buckinghamshire, HP17 8NL. Tel: (01296) 747444

*CAMBRIDGESHIRE*

The Old Bridge Hotel, 1 High Street, Huntingdon, Cambridgeshire; PE29 3TQ. Tel: (01480) 424300

CHANNEL ISLANDS

La Grand Mare, Vazon Bay, CasTel, Guernsey, Channel Islands, GY5 7LL. Tel: (0 1481) 253544

*CHESHIRE*

Crabwall Manor Hotel, Parkgate Road, Mollington, Chester, Cheshire, CHI 6NE. Tel: (01244) 851666

*COUNTY DURHAM*

Fox Hounds, Cotherstone, Barnard Castle, County Durham, DL12 9P. Tel: (01833) 650241

The Manor House Inn, Caterway Heads, Shotley Bridge, Consett, County Durham, DH8 9LX. Tel: (01207) 255268

The Morritt Arms Hotel, Greta Bridge, Barnard Castle, County Durham, DL12 9SE. Tel: (01833) 627232

The Old Well Inn, 21 The Bank, Barnard Castle, County Durham, DL12 8PH. Tel: (01833) 690130

The Rose and Crown Hotel, Romaldkirk-Barnard Castle, Co Durham, DL12 9EB. Tel: (01833) 650213

*CORNWALL*

Halfway House, St Jidgey, Wadebridge, Cornwall, PL27 7RE. Tel: (01208) 812524

Rose-in-Vale Country House Hotel, Mithian, Cornwall, TR5 OQD. Tel: (01872) 552202

St Martin's On The Isle, St Martin's, Isles of Scilly, TR25 OQW. Tel: (01720) 422092

The BudockVean Hotel, Helford River, Mawnan Smith, Falmouth, Cornwall, TR11 5LG. Tel: (01326) 250288

The Cornish Arms at Pendoggett, Port Issac, PL30 3HH. Tel: (01208) 880263

The Jubilee Inn, Pelynt, Near Looe, Cornwall, PL13 2JZ. Tel: (01503) 220312

The Old Success Inn, Sennen Cove, Cornwall, TR19 7DG. Tel: (01736) 871232

Tredethy House, Helland Bridge, Bodmin, Cornwall, PL30 4QS. Tel: (01208) 841262

*CUMBRIA*

Crosby Lodge, High Crosby, Crosby-on-Eden, Carlisle, Cumbria, CA6 4QZ. Tel: (01228) 573618

Dale Head Hall Lakeside Hotel, Lake Thirlmere, Keswick, Cumbria, CA12 4TN. Tel: (01768) 772478

Greenhead Hotel, Greenhead, Brampton, Cumbria, CA8 7HB. Tel: (01697) 74741 I

Kirkstile Inn, Loweswater, Cockermouth, Cumbria, CA13 ORU. Tel: (01900) 85219

A * 24

Lindeth Howe Country House Hotel, Longtail Hill, Bowness on Windermere, Cumbria, LA23 3JF. Tel: (01539) 445759

Lowbyer Manor Country House Hotel, Alston, North Pennines, Cumbria, CA9 3JX. Tel: (01434) 381230

Nanny Brow Country House Hotel, Near Ambleside, Cumbria, LA22 9NF. Tel: (01539) 432036

Tarn End House Hotel, Talkin Tarn, Brampton, Cumbria, CA8 1LS. Tel: (01697) 72340

Temple Sowerby House Hotel, Temple Sowerby, Penrith, Cumbria, CA10 1RZ. Tel (01768) 361578

The Blacksmiths Arms, Talkin Village, Brampton, Cumbria, CA8 1LE. Tel: (01697) 73452

The Miller Howe Hotel, Windermere, Cumbria, LA23 1FY. Tel: (01539) 442536

Trout Hotel, Crown Street, Cockermouth, Cumbria, CA13 OEJ. Tel: (01900) 823591

DERBYSHIRE

Cavendish Hotel, Baslow, Derbyshire, DE45 ISP. Tel: (01246) 582311

Riber Hall, Matlock, Derbyshire, DE4 5JU. Tel: (01629) 582795

The Lathkil Hotel, Over Haddon, Bakewell, Derbyshire, DE45 IJE. Tel: (01629) 812501

The Wind In The Willows Hotel, Derbyshire Level, Glossop, Derbyshire, SK13 9PT. Tel: (01457) 868001

DEVON

Arundell Arms, Lifton, Devon, PL16 0AA. Tel: (01566) 784 66, Fax: (01566) 78494

Combe House At Gittisham, Honiton, Near Exeter, Devon, EX14 3AD. Tel: (01404) 540400

Half Moon Inn, Sheepwash, Near Hatherleigh, Devon, EX12 5NE. Tel: (01409) 231376

Highbullen Hotel, Chittlehamholt, Umberleigh, Devon, EX37 9HD. Tel: (01769) 540561

Holne Chase Hotel, Ashburton, Devon, TQ13 7NS. Tel: 01364 631471, Fax. 01364 631453

Lydford House Hotel, Lydford, Devon, EX20 4AU. Tel: (01822) 820347

Mill End Hotel, Sandy Park, Chagford, Devon, TQ13 8JN. Tel: (01647) 432282

Prince Hall Hotel, Near Two Bridges, Dartmoor, Devon, PL20 6SA. Tel: (01822) 890403

The Arundell Arms, Lifton, Devon, PLI6 OAA. Tel: (01566) 784666

The Manor House Hotel: And Golf Club, Moretonhampstead, Near Exeter, Devon, TQ13 8RE. Tel: (0 1647) 440355

The Nobody Inn, Doddiscombsleigh, Near Exeter, Devon, EX6 7PS. Tel: (01647) 252394

The Rising Sun Hotel, Harbourside, Lynmouth, North Devon, EX35 6EQ. Tel: (01598) 753223

The Staghunters Hotel, Brendon, Lynton, North Devon, EX35 6PS. Tel: (01598) 741222

Plumber Manor, Sturminster Newton, Dorset, DTIO 2AF. Tel: (01258) 472507

The Anvil Hotel, Pimperne, Blandford, Dorset, DTI1 8UQ. Tel: (01258) 453431

The Half Moon, Sherborne, Dorset, DT9 31N. Tel: (01935) 812017

GLOUCESTERSHIRE

Bibury Court Hotel, Bibury, Near Cirencester, Gloucestershire, GL7 5NT. Tel: (01285) 740337

Calcot Manor Hotel, Near Tetbury, Gloucestershire, GLS 8YJ. Tel: (01666) 890391

Corse Lawn House Hotel, Corse Lawn, Gloucester, Gloucestershire, GL19 4LZ. Tel: (01452) 780771

Fosse Manor Hotel, Stow-on-the-Wold, Cheltenham, Gloucestershire, GL54 IUX. Tel: (0145 I) 830354

Hatton Court Hotel, Upton Hill, Upton, St, Leonards, Gloucestershire, GL4 8DE. Tel: (01452) 617412

The Frogmill Inn, Andoversford, Cheltenham, Gloucestershire, GL54 4HT. Tel: (01242) 820547

The Greenway Hotel, Shurdington, Cheltenham, Gloucestershire, GL51 5UG. Tel: (01242) 862352

The Malt House, Broad Campden, near Chipping Campden, Gloucestershire, GL55 6UU. Tel: (01386) 840295

The Prestbury House Hotel, Restaurant, Prestbury, Gloucestershire, GL52 3DN. Tel: (01242) 529533

Three Ways House, Mickleton, Chipping Campden, Gloucestershire, GL55 6SB. Tel: (01386) 438429

The Wild Duck Inn, Drakes Island, Ewen, Cirencester, Gloucestershire, GL7 6BY. Tel: (01285) 770310

## HAMPSHIRE

Ashburn Hotel, Restaurant, Station Road, Fordingbridge, Hampshire, SP6 1JP. Tel: (01425) 652060

Esseborne Manor Hotel, Hurstbourne Tarrant, Andover, Hampshire, SPII OER. Tel: (01264) 736444

Lainston House Hotel, Sparsholt, Winchester, Hampshire, SO21 2LT. Tel: 01962 863588, Fax: 01962 776672

The Chewton Glen Hotel, Christchurch Road, New Milton, Hampshire, BH25 6QS. Tel: (01425) 275341

The Master Builder's House Hotel, Buckler's Hard, Beaulieu, Hampshire, S042 7XB. Tel: (01590) 616253

Upland Park Hotel, Garrison Hill, Droxford, Southampton, Hampshire, S032 3QL. Tel: (01489) 878507

Wykeham Arms, 75 Kingsgate Street, Winchester, Hampshire, S023 9PE. Tel: (01962) 853834

## HEREFORDSHIRE

Kilverts Hotel, The Bulking, Hay-on-Wye, Herefordshire, HR3 5AG. Tel: (01497) 821042

The Ancient Camp Inn, Ruckhall, Near Eaton Bishop, Herefordshire, HR2 9QX. Tel: (01981) 250449

The Red Lion Hotel, Bredwardine, Hereford, Herefordshire, HR3 6BU. Tel: (01981) 500303

The Talbot, Ledbury Herefordshire, HR8 20X. Tel: (01531) 632963

## ISLE OF WIGHT

The George Hotel, Yarmouth, Isle of Wight, P041 OPE. Tel: (01983) 760331

## LANCASHIRE

Inn at Whitewell, Clitheroe, Lancashire, BB7 3AT. Tel: (01200) 448222, Fax. (01200) 448298

## LEICESTERSHIRE

Stapleford Park, Near Melton Mowbray, Leicestershire, LEI4 2E. Tel: (01572) 787522

The Old White Hart Inn, 51 Main Street, Lyddington, Rutland, Leicestershire, LEI5 9LR. Tel: (01572) 821703

Lady Anne's Hotel, St Martin's, Stamford, Lincolnshire, PE9 2LJ. Tel: (01780) 481184

The Brownlow Arms Country Hotel, Restaurant, Hough-on-the-Hill, Lincolnshire, NG32 2AZ. Tel: (01400) 250234

The George Hotel, 71 St Martins, Stamford, Lincolnshire, PE9 2LB. Tel: (01780) 750750

The Red House Inn, Knipton, Grantham, Lincolnshire, NG32 IRH. Tel: (01476) 870352

## NORFOLK

Congham Hall Country House Hotel, Grimston, King's Lynn, Norfolk, PE32 1AH. Tel: (01485) 600250

Strattons, 4 Ash Close, Swaffham, Norfolk, PE37 7NH. Tel: (01760) 723845

The Rose and Crown, Snettisham, Norfolk, PE31 7LX. Tel: (01485) 541382

## NORTHAMPTONSHIRE

Tudor Gate Hotel, Finedon, Northants, NN9 5JN. Tel: (01933) 680408

## NORTHERN IRELAND

Belle Isle Estate, Lisbellaw, County Fermanagh, Northern Ireland, BT94 5HF. Tel: (028) 6638 7231, Fax: (028) 6638 7261

Colebrooke Park, Brookeborough, County Fermanagh, Northern Ireland, BT94 4DW. Tel: (028) 8953 1402, Fax: (028) 8953 1686

Glenarm Castle, Antrim Estates Company, Glenarm, Ballymena, County Antrim, Northern Ireland, BT44 0BQ. Tel: (028) 2884 1203, Fax: (028) 2884 1305

## NORTHUMBERLAND

Otterburn Tower, Otterburn, Northumberland, NE19 1NS. Tel: (01830) 520620, Fax: (01830) 521504

The Collingwood Arms Hotel, Cornhill-on-Tweed, Northumberland, TD12 4UH. Tel: (01890) 882424

The Travellers Rest, Slaley, Hexham, Northumberland, NE46 1TT. Tel: (01434) 673231

Tillmouth Park Country House Hotel, Cornhill-on-Tweed, Berwick upon Tweed, Northumberland, TD12 4UU. Tel: (01890) 882255

## OXFORDSHIRE

The Inn For All Seasons, The Barringtons, Burford, Oxfordshire, OX18 4TN. Tel: (01451) 844324

King's Head Inn, Restaurant, Bledington, Near Kingham, Oxfordshire, OX7 6XQ. Tel: (01608) 658365

The Beetle and Wedge Hotel, Moulsford, Wallingford, Oxfordshire, OX10 9JF. Tel: (01491) 651381

The Lamb Inn, Sheep Street, Burford, Oxfordshire, OX18 4LR. Tel: (01993) 823155

The Stonor Arms Hotel, Stonor, Near Henley-on-Thames, Oxfordshire, RG9 6HE. Tel: (01491) 638866

## SHROPSHIRE

Longmynd Hotel, Cunnery Road, Church Stretton, Shropshire, SY6 6AG. Tel: (01694) 722244

## SOMERSET

Carnarvon Arms Hotel, Dulverton, Somerset, TA22 9AE. Tel: (01398) 323302

Charlton House, Shepton Mallet, Near Bath, Somerset, BA4 4PR. Tel: (01749) 342008

Royal Oak Inn, Winsford, Somerset, TA24 7JE. Tel: (01643) 851455, Fax. (01643) 851009

Tarr Steps Hotel, Hawkridge, Near Dulverton, Somerset, TA22 9PY. Tel: (01643) 851293

The Anchor Hotel, Ship Inn, Porlock Weir, Minehead, Somerset, TA24 8PB. Tel: (01643) 862753

The Crown Hotel, Exmoor National Park, Exford, Somerset, TA24 7PP. Tel: (01643) 831554

The Exmoor White Horse Inn, Near Hendrie, Exford, Minehead, Somerset, TA24 7PY. Tel: (01643) 831229

The Hood Arms, Kilve, Near Bridgwater, Somerset, TA5 1EA. Tel: (01278) 741210

The Royal Oak Inn, Withypool, Exmoor, Somerset, TA24 7QP. Tel: (01643) 831506

The Wheelwrights Arms, Monkton Combe, Near Bath, BA2 7HD. Tel: (01225) 722287

## SURREY

Gatton Manor Hotel, Golf and Country Club, Standon Lane, Ockley, Near Dorking, Surrey, RH5 5PQ. Tel: (01306) 627555

## SUSSEX

Amberley Castle, Amberley, Near Arundel, West Sussex, BN18 9ND. Tel: (01798) 831992

South Lodge Hotel, Brighton Road, Lower Beeding, Horsham, West Sussex, RH13 6Pß. Tel: (0 1403) 891711

The Spread Eagle Hotel, Health Spa, South Street, Midhurst, West Sussex, GU29 9NH. Tel: (01730) 81691 1

## TYNE & WEAR

Redesdale Arms Hotel, Rochester, Otterburn, Neweastle-upon-Tyne, Tyne & Wear, NE19 1TA. Tel: (0 1830) 520668

## WILTSHIRE

Antrobus Arms Hotel, 15 Church Street, Amesbury, Salisbury, Wiltshire, SP4 7EU. Tel: (01980) 623163

Bishopstrow Hotel, Warminster, Wiltshire, BA12 9HH. Tel: (01985) 212312

Longs Arms, Steeple-Ashton, Trowbridge, Wiltshire, BA14 6EU. Tel: (01380) 870245

Lucknam Park Hotel, Colerne, Near Bath, Wiltshire, SN14 8AZ. Tel: (01225) 742777

The Old Rectory Hotel, Crudwell, Wiltshire, SN16 9EP. Tel: (01666) 577194

## WORCESTERSHIRE

Buckland Manor, Near Broadway, Worcestershire, WR12 7LY. Tel: (01386) 852626

Hadley Bowling Green Inn, Hadley Heath, Near Droitwich, Worcestershire, WR9 0AR. Tel: (01905) 620294

Talbot Inn, Knightwick, Worcester, WR6 5PH. Tel: 01886 821235, Fax. 01886 821060

The Chequers Inn, Fladbury, Pershore, Worcestershire, WR10 2PZ. Tel: (01386) 860276

The Lygon Arms, Broadway, Worcestershire, WR12 7DU. Tel: (01386) 852255

The Mill At Harvington, Anchor Lane, Harvington, Evesham, Worcestershire, WR11 5NR. Tel: (01386) 870688

*YORKSHIRE*

Coniston Hall Hotel, Coniston Cold, Skipton, North Yorkshire, BD23 4EB. Tel: (01756) 748080, Fax: (01756) 749487

Nags Head Country Inn, Pickhill, Thirsk, Yorkshire, Y07 4JG. Tel: (01845) 567391

Sportsman's Arms Hotel, Wath in Nidderdale, Harrogate, North Yorkshire, HG3 5PP. Tel: (01423) 711306, Fax. (01423) 712524

The Blue Lion Inn, East Witton, North Yorkshire, DL8 4SN. Tel: (01969) 624273

The Boars Head Hotel, Ripley, Near Harrogate, North Yorkshire, HG3 3AY. Tel: (01423) 771888

The Falcon Inn, Arncliffe, Skipton, North Yorkshire, BD23 5QE. Tel: (01756) 770205

The Grange Hotel, 1 Clifton, York, YO30 6AA. Tel: (01904) 644744

The Hawnby Hotel, Hawnby, York, YO62 5QS. Tel: (01439) 798202

Castle Oaks House Hotel, Castleconnell, Co Limerick, Ireland. Tel: 00 353 61377666

Clonanav Fly Fishing Centre and School, NireValley, Ballymacarby, Clonmel, Co Waterford, Ireland. Tel: 00 353 52 36141

Delphi Lodge, Leenane, Co Galway, Ireland. Tel: 00 353 9542222

Dromoland Castle, Newmarket-on-Fergus, Co Clare, Ireland. Tel: 00 353 61368 144

Fermoyle Lodge, Co Tello, Co Galway, Ireland. Tel: 00 353 91786 111

Humewood Castle, Kiltegan, Co Wicklow, Ireland. Tel: 00 353 508732 15

Lough Inagh Lodge Hotel, Recess, Connemara, Co Galway, Ireland. Tel: 00 353 9534706

Mount Juliet, Conrad, Thomastown, Co Kilkenny, Ireland. Tel: 00 353 5673000

Newport House, Newport, Co Mayo, Ireland. Tel: 00 353 9841222

Pontoon Bridge Hotel, Pontoon, Foxford, Co Mayo, Ireland. Tel: 00 353 9456120

The Glencar House Hotel, Glencar, Co Kerry, Ireland. Tel: 00 353 669760 102

The Kildare Hotel and Country Club, Straffan, Co Kildare, Ireland. Tel: 00 353 16017200

# IRELAND

# SCOTLAND

Ashford Castle, Cong, Co Mayo, Ireland. Tel: 00 353 9246003

Ballynahinch Castle Hotel, Recess, Co Galway, Ireland. Tel: 00 353 9531006

Ballyvolane House, Castlelyons, Co Cork, Ireland. Tel: 00 353 2536349

Blackwater Lodge, Upper Ballyduff, Co Waterford, Ireland. Tel: 00 353 5860235

Camillaun/Corrib County Angling Centre, Eighterard, Oughterard, Co Galway, Ireland. Tel: 00 353 91552678

Careywille, Fermoy, Co Cork, Ireland. Tel: 00 353 2531712

Achness Hotel, Rosehall, By Lairg, Sutherland, IV27 4BD. Tel: (01549) 441239, fax: (01549) 441324

Ailean Chraggan Hotel, Weem, By Aberfeldy, Perthshire, PH15 2LD. Tel: (01887) 820346

Altnaharra Hotel, Altnaharra, Lairg, Sutherland, IV27 4UE. Tel/Fax. (01549) 411222

Ardanaiseig Hotel, Kilchrenan by Taynuilt, Argyll, PA35 IHE. Tel: (01866) 833333

Atholl Arms Hotel, Blair Atholl, Perthshire, PH18 5SG. Tel: (01796) 481550, Fax. (01796) 481550

Balbirnie House Hotel, Markinch, By Glenrothes, Fife, KY7 6NE. Tel: (01592) 610066

Blairmore House, Glass, Aberdeenshire, AB5 4XH. Tel: (01466) 700200

Buccleuch Arms Hotel, St Boswells, Scottish Borders, TD6 0EW. Tel: (01835) 822243, Fax: (01835) 823965

Burts Hotel, Market Square, Melrose, TD6 9PL. Tel: (01896) 822285

Clachan Inn, 10 Main Street, St John's Town of Dalry, Castle Douglas, DG7 3UW. Tel: (01644) 430241, Fax. (01644) 430631

Corrour House Hotel, Rothiemurchus, By Aviemore, Inverness, shire, PH22 IQH. Tel: (01479) 810220

Drumnacree House, St Ninians Road, Alyth, Perthshire, PH11 8AP. Tel/Fax. (01828) 632194

Dunain Park Hotel, Dunain, Inverness, IV3 8JN. Tel: (01463) 230512

Dunans Castle, Glendaruel, Argyll, PA22 3AD. Tel: (01369) 820380

Dundas Castle, Contact George Goldsmith, 2, India Street, Edinburgh EH3 6EZ. Tel: (0131) 476 6500, Fax: (0131) 476 6501

Farleyer House Hotel, Aberfeldy, Perthshire, PH15 2JE. Tel: (01887) 820332

Four Seasons Hotel, St Fillans, Perthshire, PH6 2NF. Tel: (01764) 685333

Friars Carse Country Hotel, Auldgirth, Dumfries, DG2 0SA. Tel: (01387) 740388, Fax. (01387) 740550

Glenapp Castle, Ballantrae, Ayrshire, KA26 ONZ. Tel: (01465) 831212

Kinloch House Hotel, By Blairgowrie, Perthshire, PH10 6SG. Tel: (01250) 884237

Knockomie Hotel, Grantown Road, Forres, Moray, IV36 2SG. Tel: (01309) 673146

Loch Lomond Golf Club, Rossdhu House, Luss, Dunbartonshire, G83 8NT, Tel: (01436) 655555

Lochboisdale Hotel, Lochboisdale, Isle of South Uist, Western Islands, HS8 5TH, Tel: (01878) 700332, Fax. (01878) 700367

Lochmaddy Hotel, Isle of North Uist, Western Isles, HS6 5AA, Tel: (01876) 500331

Milton Park Hotel, Dalry, Castle Douglas,

Kirkcudbrightshire, DG7 3SR. Tel: (01644) 430286

Monachyle Hall Mhor, Balquhidder, Lochearnhead, Perthshire, FK19 8PQ. Tel: 01877 384622, Fax: 01877 384305

Ossian Hotel, The Brae, Kincraig, Kingussie, Inverness, shire, PH21 I QD. Tel: (01540) 651242

Park House, John Foster, The Office, Craigie Farm, Leuchars, St Andrews, Fife, KY16 0DT. Tel: 01334 839218, Fax: 01334 839 503

Pittodrie House Hotel, Chapel of Garioch, Inverurie, Aberdeenshire, AB51 5HS. Tel: (01467) 681444

Priory Hotel, The Square, Beauly, Inverness, shire, IV4 7BX. Tel: (01463) 782309

Royal Marine Hotel, Golf Road, Brora, Sutherland, KW9 6QS. Tel: (01408) 621 252, Fax: (01408) 621 181

Saplinbrae House Hotel, Old Deer, Mintlaw, Peterhead, Aberdeenshire, AB42 4LP. Tel: (01771) 6235 15

Seafeld Lodge Hotel, Woodside Avenue, Grantown-on-Spey, Morayshire, PH26 3JN. Tel: (01479) 872152

Taychreggan Hotel, Kilchrenan, Taynuilt, Argyll PA35 IHQ. Tel: (01866) 833211

The Brown Trout Hotel, Watten, Wick, Caithness, KW1 5YN. Tel: (01955) 621354

The Carnegie Club, Skibo Castle, Clashmore, Dornoch, Sutherland, IV25 3RQ. Tel: (01862) 894600

The Castle Hotel, Huntly, Aberdeenshire, AB54 4SH. Tel: (01466) 792696

The Craigellachie Hotel, Speyside, Banffshire AB38 9SR. Tel: (01340) 881204

The Creggans Inn, Strachur, Argyll, PA27 8BX. Tel: (01369) 860279

The Dowans Hotel, Aberlour, Banffshire, AB38 9LS. Tel: (01340) 871488

The Eskdale Hotel, Market Place, Langholm, Dumfriesshire, DG13 OJH. Tel: (01387) 380357

The Gleneagles Hotel, Auchterarder, Perthshire PH3 IN. Tel: (01764) 662231

The Killiecrankie Hotel, By Pitlochry,

Perthshire, PHI6 5LG. Tel: (01796) 473220
The Newton Hotel, Inverness Road, Nairn, Highland, IV12 4RX. Tel: (01667) 453144
The Roxburghe Hotel, Helton, by Helso, Roxburghshire, TD5 8JZ. Tel: 01573 450331, Fax. 01573 450611
The Royal Golf Hotel, Dornock, Sutherland, IV25 3LG. Tel: (01862) 810283
Tomdoun Hotel, Invergarry Invernessshire, PH35 4HS. Tel: (01809) 511218
Tormaukin Hotel, Glendevon, By Dollar, Perthshire, FK14 7JY. Tel: (01259) 781252
Traquair Arms Hotel, Traquair Road, Inner-leithen, Borders, EH44 6PD. Tel: (01896) 830229
Turnberry Hotel, Turnberry, Ayrshire, KA26 9LT. Tel: (01655) 331000

The Griffin Inn, Llyswen, Brecon, Powys, LD3 OUR. Tel: (01874) 754241
Tufton Arms Hotel, Market Square, Appleby-in-Westmorland, Cumbria, CA16 6XA. Tel: 01768 351593, Fax. 01768 352761
Warpool Court Hotel, St David's, Pem-brokeshire, SA62 6BN. Tel: (01437) 720300

## WALES

Caer Beris Manor, Builth Wells, Powys, LD2 3NP. Tel: 01982 552601, Fax. 01982 552586

Gliffas Country House Hotel, Crickhowell, Powys, NP8 1RH. Tel: 01874 730371, Fax: 01874 730463

Lake Vrnwy Hotel, Llanwyddyn, Mont-gomeryshire, SY10 0LY. Tel: 01691 870692, Fax. 01691 870259

Llangoed Hall, Llyswen, Brecon, Powys, LD3 0YP. Tel/Fax: 01874 754525

Mllebrook House Hotel, Mllebrook, Stanage, Knighton, Powys, LD7 ILT. Tel: (01547) 528632

Palé Hall, Pale Estate, Llandderfel, Bala, Gwynedd, LL23 7PS. Tel: (01678) 530285

The Bear Hotel, Crickhowell, Powys, NP8 IB. Tel: (01873) 810408

The Bryn Morfydd Hotel, Llanrhaeadr, Near Denbigh, Denbighshire, LL16 4NP. Tel: (01745) 890280

## OTHER ADDRESSES

*William Evans (Gun and Riflemakers) Ltd*
67 St James's Street, London SW1A 1PH
Tel: 020 7493 0415
Fax: 020 7499 1912
Email: sales@williamevans.com
Website: www.williamevans.com
Tube: Green Park

*Campaign for Shooting*
The Old Town Hall
367 Kennington Road, London, SE11 4PT
Tel: 020 7840 9235
Fax: 020 7793 7264
Email: cfs@countryside-alliance.org

*Deer Commission for Scotland*
Knowsley,
82 Fairfield Rd, Inverness IV3 5LH
Tel: 01463 231751
Fax: 01463 712931

*English Nature*
Northminster House
Peterborough PE1 1UA
Tel: 01733 455000
Fax: 01242 584270
Website: www.english-nature.org.uk

*Forestry Commission*
231 Corstorphine Rd
Edinburgh EH12 7AT
Tel: 0131 334 0303
Fax: 0131 334 3047

*Countryside Alliance*
367 Kennington Rd
London SE11 4PT
Tel: 0207 840 9200
Fax: 0207 793 8484
Email: info@countryside-alliance.org
Website: www.countryside-alliance.org

*Scottish Countryside Alliance*
The Royal Highland Showground
Eastgate, Ingliston
Edinburgh EH28 8NF
Tel: 0131 335 0200
Fax: 0131 335 0201
info@scottishcountrysidealliance.org

*British Association for Shooting &*
*Conservation*
Marford Mill, Rossett
Wrexham, Clwyd LL12 0HL
Tel: 01244 573000
Fax: 01244 573001
Email: enq@basc.org.uk
Website: www.basc.org.uk

*British Deer Society*
Burgate Manor
Fordingbridge, Hampshire SP6 1EF
Tel: 01425 655434
Fax: 01425 655433
Email: hq@bds.org.uk
Website: www.bds.or.uk

*British Falconers Club*
J.R.Fairclough, Home Farm, Hints
Tamworth, Staffordshire B78 3DWTel/
Fax: 01543 481737
Email: admin@britishfalconersclub.co.uk
Website: www.britishfalconersclub.co.uk

*British Hawking Association*
P. Beecroft
7 Arneside Close
Tywford, Berks RG10 9BS
Tel: 0118 934 1572
Website: www.bhassoc.org

*National Birds of Prey Centre*
Jemima Parry Jones MBE, Director
Newent, Gloucestershire GL18 1JJ
Tel: 01531 820286
Fax: 01531 821389
Website: www.nbpc.co.uk

*British Shooting Sports Council*
PO Box 11
Bexhill-on-Sea, East Sussex TN40 1ZZ
Tel/Fax: 01424 217031
Website: www.bssc.org.uk

*Gun Trade Association*
PO Box 43
Tewkesbury, Gloucestershire GL20 5ZE
Tel: 01684 291868
Fax: 01684 291864
Website: www.guntrade.association.com

National Rifle Association
Bisley Camp
Brookwood
Woking, Surrey GU24 0PB
Website: www.nra.org.uk

The Union of Country Sports Workers
PO Box 129
Banbury OX17 2HX
Tel: 01327 811066
Email: office@ucsw.org

Game Conservancy
Burgate Manor,
Fordingbridge, Hampshire SP6 1EF
Tel: 01425 652381
Fax: 01425 655848

Kennel Club
1-5 Clarges Street
Piccadilly, London W1H 0EN
Tel: 0207 493 6651
Fax: 0207 518 1014
Website: www.the-kennel-club.org.uk

Country Land and Business Association
16 Belgrave Square, London SW1X 8 PQ
Tel: 0207 235 0511
Fax: 0207 235 4696
Email: mail@cla.org.uk
Website: www.cla.org.uk

Campaign for the Protection of Rural
England
Warwick House
25 Buckingham Palace Road
London SW1W 0PP
Tel 0207 976 6433
Fax 0207 976 6373

Clay Pigeon Shooting Association
P.O. Box 750
Woking, Surrey GU24 0YU
Tel: 01483 485400
Fax: 01483 485410
Email: info@cpsa.co.uk
Website: www.cpsa.co.uk

Shooting Times & Country Magazine
King's Reach Tower
Stamford Street, London SE1 9LS
Tel: 0207 261 6180
Fax: 0207 261 7179

The Field Magazine
King's Reach Tower
Stamford Street, London SE1 9LS
Tel: 0207 261 5069
Fax: 0207 261 5127

Sporting Gun Magazine
King's Reach Tower
Stamford Street, London SE1 9LS
Tel: 0207 261 5069

National Gamekeepers Organisation
Ann Robinson-Ruddock,
National Secretary
PO Box 107, Bishop
Auckland DL13 5YUTel/
Fax: 01388 665899
Email: ann.robinsonruddock@talk21.com

CLA Game Fair
PO Box 6452
Basingstoke, Hampshire RG25 2KQ
Tel: 01256 389767
Fax: 01256 389200
Website: www.gamefair.co.uk

Federation of Field Sports Associations of
the EU (FACE)
Rue F Pelletier Str 82
B-1040, Brussels
Belgium
Tel: 00322 7326 900
Fax: 00322 7327 072